Life on the THIN BLUE LINE
TALES OF THE NYPD EXECUTIVE CHIEF SURGEON

Gregory Fried, M.D.

Executive Chief Surgeon,
New York Police Department (Retired)

Copyright © 2017 Gregory Fried, M.D.

All rights reserved. No part of this book may be used or reproduced by any means, graphic, electronic, or mechanical, including photocopying, recording, taping or by any information storage retrieval system without the written permission of the author except in the case of brief quotations embodied in critical articles and reviews.

Archway Publishing books may be ordered through booksellers or by contacting:

Archway Publishing
1663 Liberty Drive
Bloomington, IN 47403
www.archwaypublishing.com
1 (888) 242-5904

Because of the dynamic nature of the Internet, any web addresses or links contained in this book may have changed since publication and may no longer be valid. The views expressed in this work are solely those of the author and do not necessarily reflect the views of the publisher, and the publisher hereby disclaims any responsibility for them.

Any people depicted in stock imagery provided by Thinkstock are models, and such images are being used for illustrative purposes only. Certain stock imagery © Thinkstock.

ISBN: 978-1-4808-4627-2 (sc)
ISBN: 978-1-4808-4628-9 (hc)
ISBN: 978-1-4808-4629-6 (e)

Library of Congress Control Number: 2017910081

Print information available on the last page.

Archway Publishing rev. date: 08/24/2017

To my wife Anne, my best friend, my nurse, my partner, who has endured my multiple glimpses of death with steadfast love, care and support.

Contents

INTRODUCTION ix

Chapter 1   NYPD OFFICER STEPHEN MCDONALD, A SPECIAL KIND OF HERO 1

Chapter 2   IN THE BEGINNING 21

Chapter 3   CLASS OF `64 40

Chapter 4   CORNELL UNIVERSITY, FAR ABOVE CAYUGA'S WATERS 50

Chapter 5   MEDICAL SCHOOL 68

Chapter 6   RESIDENCY IN SURGERY 85

Chapter 7   HEPATITIS: I NEARLY DIE 106

Chapter 8   A NEW SURGEON 120

Chapter 9   POLICE SURGEON 147

Chapter 10   BETH ISRAEL 164

Chapter 11   TALES FROM THE NYPD 178

Chapter 12   THE PC: (IT'S GOOD TO BE KING) 188

Chapter 13   ABSENT! 210

Chapter 14   FIVE COPS, ONE NIGHT AND AN EVENING IN HELL 220

Chapter 15	TALES FROM THE OPERATING ROOM	233
Chapter 16	WE JUST DISAGREE	252
Chapter 17	THE DOCTOR BUSINESS	261
Chapter 18	SEPTEMBER 11, 2001	275
Chapter 19	AFTER 9/11	293
Chapter 20	EPILOGUE	307

INTRODUCTION

This is not your ordinary biography of a doctor. Most books by physicians are about breakthroughs that conquered diseases or about new techniques that revolutionize the medical profession. I, however, have a different story to tell.

Born in 1946, I am of that unique generation known as baby-boomers. We lived and experienced the vast changes in America that came to characterize the 60's and beyond. I was in college when the Vietnam War was intensifying and in medical school when the country was being torn apart by Nixon and anti-war protests.

I became a surgeon, training and then working in Manhattan during the 1970's at Bellevue Hospital, seeing endless trauma cases fuelled by the crack epidemic. One of those patients nearly killed me.

In 1980, I became a New York City Police Department Surgeon and continued to practice general surgery. I treated thousands of injured cops experiencing first-hand what it was really like when a cop was killed in the line of duty.

I trained hundreds of surgical residents while I watched surgical practice and medicine change radically over the course of a short number of years. I took care of AIDS patients in my office before the illness even had a name. I was on Times Square when 1999 became 2000. I was in the hospitals when New York City Mayors

Koch, Dinkins, and Giuliani responded to comfort families of cops attacked and killed. I was on the steps of St. Patrick's Cathedral as the surgeon for the Secret Service when Pope John Paul II said Mass there.

I was a first responder in 1993 when the World Trade Center was attacked for the first time and was a first responder on September 11, 2001. I was buried under rubble when South Tower collapsed and nearly died that day. The injuries I sustained led to multiple problems years later, again nearly killing me. So I know what it's like on the other side of the bed.

One of the reasons I wrote this book was at the urging of two special surgical intensive-care nurses who took care of me during my most recent hospitalization. They are two wonderful young ladies who resuscitated, transfused and kept close watch on me. They were so thorough and conscientious that Anne, my wife and my supervising nurse, felt comfortable enough to leave me in their care so she could go home and not have to spend day and night in the hospital. When I had recovered sufficiently, I began recounting some of my exploits to them. They suggested I write them down. So that's what I've done.

Many people have helped me and encouraged me throughout my career or perhaps I should say the many evolutions my career has undergone over the years.

I have changed some names to protect people's privacy or identity. The stories, however, are true.

CHAPTER 1

NYPD OFFICER STEPHEN MCDONALD, A SPECIAL KIND OF HERO

Everyone knows stories of heroic people who experience terrible tragedies or illnesses and have then gone on to overcome their disabilities and lead exemplary, meaningful lives. Whether it's Franklin Roosevelt or Stephen Hawking or a character we've seen in movies like *The Untouchables*, these people leave the observer inspired and motivated from a safe distance. As a police surgeon, I had the rare honor and privilege to become part of the life of a true inspirational hero, Stephen McDonald. Shot on an ordinary day in July 1986, he was rendered quadriplegic, unable even to breathe without a respirator and unable to move from his neck down. His story continues to inspire and is an example of what the term "hero" really means.

My own initiation into the world of police trauma and responsibilies for police lives did not begin with Stephen McDonald. It happened months before I met him on a warm afternoon in May. I had been working as a police surgeon for five years, and things had been pretty routine.

One of the requirements of the Police Surgeon was to be available for 24 hours for serious injuries sustained by police officers. This duty was rotated during the month among 30 police surgeons.

The call schedule was part of the extra two and a half hours the arbitrators had determined that the police surgeons would work. It just so happened that one of my earliest days on call changed everything for me.

It was mid-afternoon, May 28, 1986. Two officers had been shot in Brooklyn and I was contacted to respond. One officer was taken to King's County Hospital while the other, more seriously injured one, had been taken to St. Mary's Hospital in Bedford Stuyvesant, Brooklyn, a neighborhood known at the time for crime and violence. St. Mary's Hospital could never adequately handle a trauma patient, but it was the closest place to where the assault had occurred so the cop ended up there. It was a dump.

I was in Manhattan working in my private office, at the time I was contacted, and the trip was easy. I had never been at that hospital before nor was I aware of my obligations as a police surgeon. I clearly couldn't be expected to perform surgery on the officer as I was unaware of his injuries and did not have privileges at the hospital. Nor was I necessarily comfortable being placed in a situation to make critical decisions before evaluating the patient.

I arrived and introduced myself. A pale, thin man wearing a tan trench coat was strutting around, running back and forth, and giving orders. I'd heard about him but had never met him before. He approached me and introduced himself. He carried a reputation of a kind of nebulous, ever present personality who was both helpful and interfering. I'll refer to him as Trenchcoat because he was often wearing a tan Colombo-like trenchcoat. "I work for Mayor Koch." Noticing a detective shield pinned to his waist, I listened to what he had to tell me. "We're getting a helicopter to transport the officer to Bellevue. They're landing at a ball field close by here in Brooklyn. We'll be moving him soon."

A bit intimidated by someone from the Mayor's office, I still realized that as a physician I had a role in the evaluation and decision-making regarding the officer. I walked into the Emergency Department, which was in the usual state of pandemonium that occurred whenever a cop was shot and brought to a hospital. Bevies of officers standing around in the way created a situation that required experience and discipline. At that time, in those days, no one was in charge. So Trenchcoat took over.

The hospital physicians told me that the officer had four gunshot wounds: neck, jaw, and two in the back. I met the attending physician who was in charge of the officer's care, who angrily told me that the Mayor's Office and Trenchcoat had arranged for the transfer to Bellevue without consulting him. He was concerned, as was I, and I asked him to show me the patient, the X-rays, and give me the history. As this was happening, the officer was being wheeled into the street, in preparation to be transferred to a waiting ambulance, with which to be taken to the nearby field where the helicopter was landing.

Well, it became apparent that someone medical had to be in charge. So I demanded that everything stop until I evaluated the patient. He was bandaged, face swollen, and awake but not terribly alert. He had nasal oxygen. After a quick assessment, I realized that there was no control of his airway and with all the transporting involved, there was a significant possibility that he might suffocate. I demanded that he be brought back into the ED and calmly intubated. First aggressively resisting, then reluctantly complying, Trenchcoat acquiesced. The officer was intubated. I rode with him in the ambulance, entrusting my car keys to a Sergeant who would drive my car to Bellevue because I had every intention of going with the injured officer in the helicopter. This was a police helicopter with no medical equipment. Someone had to watch the officer's breathing tube, IVs and vital signs.

Flying over the East River from Brooklyn to Manhattan, we landed at the 34th Street heliport, a block from Bellevue. They had to unload the officer from the helicopter onto an ambulance and then into the Emergency Department. Alerted that the dramatic transport of an injured officer was in progress, especially during daytime, the press was out in full force. Nothing works better for the front page of a newspaper than the photo of a shot cop on a gurney being wheeled from all sides by other cops and a doctor into a hospital. He was stabilized, taken to surgery, and eventually went home.

Reviewing in my mind what had happened, I became upset and angry at the way things were handled. I made an appointment to see Richard Kohler, Chief of Personnel. The next day I paid one of my first visits to Police Headquarters. As I entered the Chief's office, he greeted me with several handshakes telling me what a great job I had done. I wasn't there for "Atta boys." I didn't need the accolades.

I had a lot to say. Who was this Trenchcoat and why had he made a decision to transport the officer? Why didn't he consult with the physicians at St. Mary's? Did he realize they were unhappy and felt the transfer would be dangerous? Did he contact the receiving doctors at Bellevue and tell them what to expect? Did he know that moving a patient with a fresh gunshot wound of the neck and an unsecured airway was risking the patient's life? Unimpressed with his connection to the Mayor's office, I asked if he had medical training.

I had trained at Bellevue, but I really didn't see anything so special about Bellevue that required that the officer had to be transferred there. In my opinion, the multiple transports, the helicopter, the ambulances, and the dramatic appearance at Bellevue with press waiting to get crucial pictures of the event was simply grandstanding.

Chief Koehler listened and became convinced that I probably knew what I was talking about. He agreed. He'd take care of it. He did. Summoning Trenchcoat to his office, Koehler actually set Trenchcoat straight or at least tried to. Never one to doubt himself, Trenchcoat had long ago convinced himself he always knew best, because no one had ever directly confronted him or called his actions to task. He was told that in the future he was to ask an appropriate medical person if what he was doing made sense and was appropriate. That lasted for at least a few weeks, but within a few months my position and responsibilities changed.

When the discussion with Trenchcoat ended, Chief Koehler asked me to stay behind. He needed to know my background because he apparently was impressed that I would actually bring something that mattered to his attention. He was glad someone spoke up and apparently put a halt to Trenchcoat running amok.

It wasn't long before Trenchcoat resumed making medical decisions again. On a hot Saturday afternoon on July 12, 1986, a young police officer was responding to investigate bicycle thieves in Central Park. Somewhere near 110th Street, Officer Stephen McDonald approached a young Shavod Jones. He flashed a police shield and began to get closer to the suspect. Jones pulled a gun and fired four shots, hitting Stephen in the arm, face, and neck. Jones fled and Stephen, who had been separated from his backup partner, Sergeant King, fell. Having heard shots fired, the Sergeant responded in his radio car seeing McDonald lying shot on the ground. "10-13, officer down!"

Somehow they got him from Central Park in mid-Manhattan to Metropolitan Hospital. Trenchcoat responded to Metropolitan

Hospital and convinced those in charge that the only safe place for Stephen was Bellevue. I was neither consulted nor contacted at the time and actually don't know who, if anyone other than Trenchcoat allowed the transfer. Soon he and I would interact again.

Trenchcoat was quite a character. It's no wonder people believed that he was working out of the Mayor's office. He owned a large black Continental, which he had brought to every radio shop in the city and had every radio of every uniformed service installed. He had a fire department radio, a police radio, a city special operations radio, and a scanner that could receive communications from other services including Westchester and Nassau County. To sit in his car was to experience constant noise and communications about anything and everything all at the same time.

The antennas from all these devices were mounted on the trunk of the car, so anyone seeing him emerge from this car in his tan trench coat had to believe he was very important. In truth he was a detective who had managed to get himself a special assignment position on Mayor Koch's detail. He basically worked for himself and did what he wanted and went where he felt it was appropriate. He worked all night and responded to police, fire, Emergency Medical Service (EMS) calls and roamed the nights showing up alone and giving orders and dropping names.

At that time, I did not respond to Bellevue, not even being aware of the Stephen McDonald incident. At the time, Trenchcoat created a protected environment surrounding Stephen, allowing only those physicians and visitors to enter his darkened room who he felt would contribute anything to the situation. This situation would change drastically soon enough.

Clarence Robinson, M.D. had been Supervising Chief Surgeon. He had retired, deciding that he wanted to spend his remaining years in a less stressful situation. Dr. T. had been appointed to his position, a full-time commitment, although most were dubious about his skills. Robinson had wanted me to take the job, but I was not ready to give up surgery. More about this in later chapters.

Chief Kohler had called upon me multiple times since our first meeting to offer advice outside of my regular duties. He told me he thought I should be officially promoted to Deputy Chief Surgeon. He had been tagged by Mayor Koch to become Corrections Commissioner, but would like to know that I would be empowered and back up Dr. T. Dr. T. had no experience with trauma patients and would provide generic statements rather than make definitive decisions. That's pretty much what internists do. Kohler really wanted to know that I would be a take-charge person responding to hospitals after shootings and serious injuries because I had extensive trauma experience and was also as assertive as one would want in a hands-on physician.

On that same day, Mayor Koch swore in Richard Koehler as Corrections Commissioner. I was in Police Commissioner Ben Ward's office being sworn in as Deputy Chief Surgeon. I would be notified by the Sick Desk located within Health Services Division of the NYPD or notified by Operations, the central information center of the NYPD situated at 1 Police Plaza headquarters, about serious injuries to officers, shootings and other critical incidents. I was in the loop of higher-ranking officers who were notified of these events.

Now promoted, I was relieved of the burden of a two and a half hour daily schedule devoted to putting officers back to work. I became what is known in the department as a "boss." I could self-deploy, that is, respond to situations where I thought it necessary without punching a clock. My hours would increase significantly but that didn't matter to me. Being part of the Civil Service, I was supposed to record my overtime, but I seldom got around to it. My work was fulfilling, exciting and unique. I could actually make a difference in the medical care that officers would receive. I trained at Bellevue and knew many of the physicians there.

I got a new police shield with one star added to it, a raise, and gave the NYPD an unwritten agreement that I would do whatever was necessary. I also got a siren, a police radio, and a flashing light installed in my jeep. Now I could monitor whatever was going on around the city and listen to the continuous blabber coming "over the air." The police radio shop did a clean and neat job on the installation, but when it came time to return the jeep, the Police Department obviously reclaimed their equipment.

The jeep was leased and when it came time to return it to the dealership, there was some unexpected and undesirable damage, caused by the installation holes and other small alterations. The damage was going to cost me hundreds of dollars until I discovered that the leased car inspector had been a former cop and had heard about my responding to hospital and making a difference. Then I guess the damage kind of went away. Things got "taken care of" because he had been "on the job" and I was very much "on the job." (That's cop talk for working for the police department.)

With the experience with the leased car, I decided it was preferable to buy a car and deal with the siren and lights in my own car. This time I avoided the drilling on my bumpers and simply put a console under the dashboard with a speaker under the hood. The flashing light was plugged into the cigarette lighter and put on the hood. All this sounds good but flashing lights and a siren in a car on a crowded highway in New York City simply causes the cars around you to stop. You can't go speeding across an intersection in Manhattan because cars can't tell where the sounds are coming from. Cars do move out of your way, and it's very exciting to have these accouterments for first few weeks. The novelty, however, wears thin especially when you're only using them to go to hospitals where cops have been seriously injured or shot.

I was promoted no more than two days when I was called from Bellevue by my "old friend" Trenchcoat. It was in regard to Stephen McDonald, the young officer who had been shot in July while on patrol in Central Park. I knew about the incident, how he had been evacuated by radio car, taken at first to Metropolitan Hospital then transferred to Bellevue (by Trenchcoat I was sure). Apparently the department and the physicians at the hospitals had lost interest in his care. In truth, Trenchcoat had alienated most of the hospital staff, I discovered later, by interfering in numerous ways. Trenchcoat asked if I would mind coming by to take a look at him.

So I went to Bellevue to see Stephen. Trenchcoat was clearly way over his head. In the weeks after Stephen was shot, the police who generally attend a seriously injured officer had hovered around his room. Trenchcoat had set up a situation where Stephen was apart from everyone and most of the staff at Bellevue had avoided contact with either of them. He lay partially undressed in a darkened room being turned and bathed and fed through a feeding tube in his lower abdomen. He was occasionally sat up, but because of surgery and the gunshot wound of his neck, his head would deviate to the right.

I started from scratch. I introduced myself, told everyone who I was. Trenchcoat was right there and actually listening. The history was overwhelming. Stephen had been shot three times, once in the face, arm and neck. One shot had penetrated the spinal cord at C-2 that I could see on the X-rays. This is usually fatal as it is above the location of the phrenic nerves that allow the diaphragm to move and allow people to inhale. Obviously Stephen had somehow been able to breathe, if only partially, because he had suffered no cognitive brain damage. But at that time, he was definitely the most severely injured officer I had ever seen. The only part of his body that he could move was his face.

Joe Ransahoff, M.D., an attending I had known from my residency days, had been the chief of neurosurgery at that time. He was a WWII U.S. Marine Corps veteran, a tough SOB, who had seen Stephen and felt no surgery on his cord would be in the least bit helpful. He told Trenchcoat and the family that Stephen would be "better off dead." He signed off on the case and walked away. After admission, Stephen developed an abscess in his neck, which might have proved fatal and which apparently no surgeon would touch, but it had drained spontaneously and his condition improved.

I met Stephen's wife, Patti Ann. She was pregnant, innocent and had enormous strength in her Catholic faith that things would get better. She didn't think Stephen would be better off dead. I met Monsignor John Kowsky, a noble, kind-hearted but strong priest who had served as a military chaplain during Vietnam. He attended Stephen daily and would give him communion. He would usually say Mass in the room. I met the Bellevue neuro, trauma and surgery residents who were marginally involved with Stephen's care but had backed off because of their perception of the hopelessness of the situation and the constant hovering of the police and also Trenchcoat.

What to do next? Stephen was a quadriplegic who couldn't even breathe on his own. I called some of my friends who were specialists in rehab medicine for advice. I did a lot of reading. First, get him out of the darkened room and back into the world. Put him in rehab. Move him around. Offering these suggestions that

Stephen be integrated into the Bellevue patient population caused all kinds of pushback, both from Trenchcoat and Patti Ann. So I told it directly to Stephen who at first was fearful but explaining to him that this was the best and at the time only alternative. He agreed. I was there on the first day he went to rehab as he sat with other seriously injured patients looking at himself in a mirror.

He couldn't breathe on his own without a respirator. He had an emergency tracheostomy performed on admission that was revised and cleaned up. The respirator worked well. He couldn't speak but could only communicate by pursing his lips and making popping noises. Then he would mouth some words. He had spotty feeling in parts of his body indicating that the spinal cord wasn't totally transected, but was disrupted to a major degree so that he couldn't move.

Stephen became a focus for all of New York City as a critically injured cop who was struggling to survive. Mayor Koch, a truly warm and caring person, had always visited police officers who were seriously injured. He had seen Stephen from Day One and continued to follow his situation. He would visit unannounced, although we always knew when he was coming. Because of the frequency and regularity of police officers being shot in the 1980's, Mayor Koch and I developed a personal relationship. He knew me as the doctor who was always around when cops got seriously injured. I am quite proud to have known him.

Cardinal O'Connor, who was the Cardinal for the New York Archdiocese, heard about this wonderful, young and faithful family and became a frequent visitor. I'm pretty sure that Mayor Koch called him and told him about Stephen. He was a warm, cheerful person who would gather his optimism in the hall before confronting the reality of Stephen's injury and then go into his room to greet him. I would see Stephen at Bellevue as part of my daily rounds before I went home.

Stephen haunted me. Each day I would visit and then drive home and consider what had happened to him and what the possible outlook would be. In another time, he surely would have died. This was a different time and to date he hadn't died. He hadn't gotten septic and hadn't gotten pneumonia. Endless complications could have befallen him but to date they hadn't. Technology, a good respirator, and devoted nurses had kept him going. And he wanted to live. Many people were pulling for him. He was much more than just a hero. He was an extraordinary kind of hero. I learned much about rehabilitation medicine and much about what could be and needed to be done.

Patti Ann had problems with me. I always lacked any religious faith and she was at the polar opposite believing that perhaps somehow God had chosen Stephen for some kind of mission or message. I couldn't openly disagree or even argue but she knew I didn't believe. Sorry I can't lie. Let us proclaim the mystery of no faith.

So I tried to avoid conflict. This took considerable effort. I really didn't want to offend Patti Ann McDonald, but I guess I'm not a good actor and couldn't pretend to be a believer or a Catholic. I also knew this was a very special and unique situation, so I did what I thought I had to do. Meanwhile Trenchcoat backed off for the time being. Although he was a daily visitor, he continued roaming the nights and haunting the streets of the city.

Life went on outside of the room and the floor at Bellevue. This was the late 80s and it was a bad time for police officers. My new role, a surgeon who would actually respond to police officers who were shot or seriously injured, expanded quickly. I also continued my private practice in surgery. Now that I was an active surgical attending, I settled into the routine of surgical practice. So while I balanced the life of a first responder, a police surgeon, showing up at hospitals and spending nights and weekends responding to police injuries, I continued to perform surgery on patients both electively and emergently.

Steven's recovery and reintegration into life was painstakingly slow but showed a determination and motivation that was far beyond the term heroic. There is an internal spark within him that most people could never muster. I would look at him, a quadriplegic with no motion below his upper neck except for occasional muscle spasms and wonder if Ransahoff's statement of "better off dead" was right. Stephen's vitality and personal fortitude taught me that it is totally inappropriate to make snap judgments about medical situations or the person involved.

Stephen had spent almost six months in Bellevue. During those months, Cardinal O'Connor, Monsignor Kowsky, and many other clergy as well as city and public officials had visited countless times. The Monsignor said Mass each time in Stephen's room. Whenever I happened to be in the room, I would stay for the Mass, but wouldn't receive Communion. Monsignor Kowsky never made an issue of it. Those who are Jewish and especially those of us who are non-believers cannot partake of it according to Catholic doctrine and I always remained respectful of their religion.

Christmas was coming. Stephen was invited to attend Midnight Mass at St. Patrick's Cathedral. I decided to take the family on a short vacation to Kutcher's in the Catskills, but assured everyone at Bellevue that I would be a phone call away. Everything was set for the trip to St. Patrick's. The ambulance would be at the receiving dock at Bellevue. Stephen would be transported and brought into the side door of the Cathedral to sit by the altar. I had my doubts about the wisdom of the move. He had never been outside since the previous July. The Cathedral would be filled to capacity but it was drafty and vast.

It snowed in the Catskills. The weather was cold, nasty and a snow-rain mix was falling. I got the call from Trenchcoat at Bellevue. I would be asked to make the call as to whether he should go. Cancel the plans. Next year, if all goes well, he'll be out in civilization and well enough to attend. I was certainly not going to risk Stephen's life for the sake of a public appearance. Disappointment resounded but I stood my ground. This year, he'd have to watch it on television. He stayed at Bellevue. The Cardinal, in his Christmas Homily, made direct reference to his friend who was at Bellevue. Stephen didn't get pneumonia. He didn't get sick.

In January 1987, Conor McDonald was born. Word on the street was that there was going to be a television hookup between Mercy Hospital in Rockville Centre, Long Island and Stephen's room at Bellevue. At the time, this was more than technology could really handle. So all that was done was to place a fax machine at both locations and occasional fuzzy black-and-white photographs would be sent to Stephen to see his new son.

The morning Conor was born, I thought about what gift I could give Stephen. I had always been one for gadgets and technology so I had bought an early Sony VHS camera. Lugging my camera, I went to Mercy Hospital in Rockville Centre Long Island and recorded the newborn Conor in the nursery. Patty was exhausted and wouldn't want to appear immediately after giving birth. I certainly couldn't blame her but Conor was cleaned up and didn't object to appearing. So first I went to Mercy, took the video and then went back to Manhattan and went to Stephen's room.

"I brought you a little present, new daddy," I said as I smiled and popped the tape into his VHS player. Delighted, he watched 10 minutes of video of his newborn son. The press would eventually see the tape played on the monitor and assume that indeed this was the television hookup that had been reported. I guess that sounded better to the press than me simply being the cameraman.

February 3 is St. Blaise Day. Legend has it that St. Blaise, supposedly a physician before becoming a bishop (I guess that would be considered a promotion) saved the life of a young boy who had gotten a fish bone stuck in his throat and nearly suffocated. Monsignor Kowsky had visited Stephen's room and used two candlesticks crossing his throat to administer the traditional blessing of the throat. Stephen, until now had been unable to speak because the balloon cuff on his tracheostomy tube had been inflated, occluding the ability for him to deliver air past his vocal cords.

Perfect timing, I thought. Approaching Stephen, newly blessed, I figured it was as good a time as any to act. I explained to him that if I deflated the cuff and increased the tidal volume, the amount of air in each breath, some air could come past the cords and he should be able to speak. He was unsure but he also had confidence in me. I assured him that I wouldn't let him suffocate and I wouldn't kill him. So down came the cuff and out croaked a "hello". Immediately we called Patti Ann by phone to whom he croaked, "I love you." We had accomplished much, allowing Stephen to return to the world a little, now being able to communicate with more than pursed lips and smacking sounds.

A few minutes after Stephen called Patty Ann, in walked Cardinal O'Connor. Grabbing the opportunity to warn him so he wouldn't get a major shock, I advised him that he was in for a surprise. "Hello," croaked Stephen, now delighted with his newly discovered method to communicate. "It's a miracle" was the immediate response of the Cardinal. Less enthusiastic about miracles, I pointed out that it was really a deflated endotracheal cuff and an increased air volume from the respirator. I guess, however, the Cardinal was correct, too. Stephen's survival and progress was truly miraculous. His determination and the support of those around him and the devotion of Patti Ann were fostering the miracle.

Over the next few months I became further occupied with other things as the decision regarding Stephen's long-term care would rest with him and his family. Ransohoff suggested Goldwater Hospital, which was a chronic-care facility, but not really a rehab facility. Ransahoff was persona non grata after his "better off dead" comment. The Rusk Institute was noted for rehabilitation but treated mostly stroke patients. Several other facilities were mentioned but one place that was outstanding with a great track record in caring for neurologically impaired patients as severe as Stephen was Craig Hospital in Englewood, Colorado.

I had no basis to offer any opinion and really didn't want to travel to Colorado to assess the capabilities of Craig. Patti Ann had surveyed the situation and was satisfied. Trenchcoat was quite excited and urged Craig as the place. Before anyone knew it, Trenchcoat had gotten a Medevac transport to send Stephen to Craig. One small detail, however, had been overlooked. No one had gotten authorization from the payer, namely the City of New York for transport or treatment at Craig.

Dr. TR, the other Deputy Chief Surgeon, was pretty much in charge of all authorizations. He had not been involved with Stephen's care and treatment nor had he visited him at Bellevue, although he was an attending physician at NYU, directly down the block from where Stephen was at Bellevue. When Stephen arrived at Craig in Colorado with Patti Ann, they were informed that there was no record as to who was responsible for payment and that Craig needed to know who would be paying the bills. Dr. TR was contacted, since he was on record as being in charge of medical bill paying and authorizations. He denied any knowledge of anything remotely connected to Stephen.

So Trenchcoat, who had accompanied them to Colorado, always knew whom to call, because he knew how closely I had been involved with Stephen all those months at Bellevue. Explaining to me the lack of commitment, authorization or financial responsibility for Craig from any official in New York City, I contacted their billing office and obtained all the necessary information and personally signed off on all the authorizations. Clearly, Trenchcoat's usual approach of dropping names and pushing things hit a dead end in Colorado where they actually didn't care if he worked for the Mayor's office or not.

I had no doubt in my mind that this was an appropriate facility. After checking with the physicians at Bellevue, I had no problem authorizing the responsibility for the financials. Trenchcoat flew back by the private jet chartered to deliver Stephen to Colorado.

The bill for the transport to Colorado, although quite costly, could be easily justified. The trip for Trenchcoat returning to New York was a bit more difficult and generated a cost of many thousands of dollars. He got the bill and brought it to the Mayor's office, who sent it to the police department who forwarded it to Dr. TR. He simply refused to pay. Naturally, it ended up in my lap, as did quite a few of things that concerned both Stephen and Trenchcoat. Stephen's costs were usually pretty easy to justify. Trenchcoat's took a bit more imagination. No one had authorized Trenchcoat's flight to Colorado and no one had taken responsibility to pay for him.

Really struggling to find a way to satisfy a large transport bill generated by bringing Trenchcoat back to New York, I was satisfied that Trenchcoat was performing an unselfish and heroic act by accompanying Stephen and Patti Ann. I didn't need him to be punished for his good deed. So I finally took the bill, hat in hand to the President of the PBA, the union that represented the rank and file police officers. I explained how important to Stephen and Patti Ann Trenchcoat's presence was and how he managed to make the trip secure. The president of the union was quite comfortable with assuming the responsibility and pleased to help.

Craig Hospital brought Stephen much further along in his return to a functional life. He was taught to operate a wheelchair controlled by straws which he would "sip and puff" by his mouth. He had a custom wheelchair fashioned to his needs, received therapy, splinting of his paralyzed limbs, and general instructions based on his life as a respirator-dependent quadriplegic.

The PBA had set up a fund in Stephen's name with the hope of eventually finding him a permanent home after he was discharged from Craig. Meanwhile, back in New York, Trenchcoat used his personal connections to tap into a major New York City brokerage house for a big-time contribution. One of the important missions in the charter of the brokerage house was major acts of charity. Two of the partners at the firm donated sufficient amounts of money to accompany the finances in the McDonald fund to purchase a house for Stephen and Patti Ann. It was a small Cape Cod in Malverne, New York and needed major alterations.

Police officers and fire fighters often have secondary skills as contractors, carpenters and construction workers. A volunteer army of the uniformed services from all over the Metropolitan region performed an intense labor of love and reconstructed the house into a home for Stephen, Patti Ann and Conor. The house contained automatic doors, an elevator that could bring Stephen to his upstairs bedroom, large shower facilities, industrial low pile carpeting and anything else that might be needed to accommodate someone wheelchair bound.

A large van for transport was provided by the police department, which was altered to allow him to fit while in his wheelchair. The alterations and the customizing of the wheelchair were done in Colorado. Several union members went to Colorado to drive the van back to New York to be available when Stephen returned home.

I saw the design of the house and could offer little advice since I could perform surgery on people but didn't know much about blue prints. Once again, Trenchcoat had moved ahead without input. He decided that the house should not have a boiler or heating elements with open flames, thinking that Stephen might be on oxygen. The house became a total electric home, heated with individual electric heating units. So the first few winter months generated bills of over $3,000. You can guess where the bills ended up. Because the house was already renovated, it would be necessary to accommodate this situation.

In a joint conference with the Budget Office at City Hall, the Police Department, and Long Island Lighting Company, it was decided that the McDonalds would be responsible for the amount of electricity that a house of that size would average per month. The remainder would be considered part of the line-of-duty obligation of the police department and be paid by the city accordingly.

After Craig, Stephen returned to his new home. We talked frequently and privately. He understood my cynical attitude toward things, and once requested that if he got worse, I shouldn't rush to resuscitate him. I simply asked how I would know that he had gotten worse and also said that I didn't think it was my place to take lives. I'm not a believer in "mercy killing" since I think most people know how to kill themselves. I pointed out that although cynical, what would I feel like the day after I helped him die, if they came up with a cure for spinal cord paralysis. I reminded him that pneumonia was fatal until antibiotics came along, that HIV was fatal until it wasn't, and that no one really knew what tomorrow had in store.

Stephen continued to inspire and was truly the living miracle that Cardinal O'Connor referred to in his amazement at hearing him speak. He forgave the person who shot him. He had survived long after both the cynics and the medical professionals predicted that he would. He was promoted to a first-grade detective and was quite active in making speaking appearances and getting involved in causes that he believes in and traveled frequently. I am quite glad that in some way I assisted his returning to an active life.

On January 10, 2017, Stephen passed away, the result of the injuries he had sustained so many years before. His line-of-duty funeral attended by thousands, caused New York City to pause and reflect on the life of a true hero.

The care I rendered for Stephen never warned me that my tasks and involvement with the lives of the members of the thin blue line as a NYPD police surgeon were just beginning.

CHAPTER 2
IN THE BEGINNING

I guess it all started in Brooklyn, but I must admit I don't remember living there. My parents were born in Brooklyn, their parents lived in Brooklyn, they got married in Brooklyn, so it was natural that I was born in Brooklyn. Once the Brooklynites were making a reasonable living, they moved to the suburbs. We moved to Queens.

My father, Murray, had tried to enlist in the Army during World War II. When he was 16, he had worked in a printing plant. He was one of what eventually would be nine siblings, raised in Brownsville, Brooklyn, a poor neighborhood of Jewish immigrants. Printing presses according to him required three steps. The boys would feed the paper, the safety would push across to keep hands out of the way, the press would come down, and then you would remove the paper. The safety notwithstanding, the press would sometimes come down on the operator's hand, crushing fingers. My father lost the middle and crushed the index and ring finger on his right hand. The settlement was routine: $10,000 to the boy with the now permanent injury. I have met people his age with the same injuries. He tried to enlist for World War II in spite of his missing and crushed fingers. But his injuries prevented him from shooting a rifle. Unable to shoot, no army.

Being poor, Murray never finished high school. He had aspirations of becoming a pharmacist, but in view of the need to help support the family, he quit school to go to work. His father, Isidore, was often absent and worked only occasionally. I never knew my grandfather, who obviously came home often enough to have children, but not much else. My father and his grandmother, Goldie, provided support for the family. Goldie's brothers had been killed during the Russian Revolution, because they were Bolsheviks. As a result, the Russian government had provided her with pension checks each month during the hardest of times.

My mom, Florence, was the opposite of Murray. She had been brought up in a wealthy home and, as she always told us, she never wanted for anything. Her parents were Russian immigrants. Her grandfather, Yale Brevda, was a wealthy land owner in Russia and had a large farm with horses. He had gotten out of Russia when it had become clear that he was everything the Czar and the powers that be didn't want. He was a land owner, wealthy, and Jewish. I never learned his Russian name, but apparently on arrival at Ellis Island, they tagged him and the family Brevda. And so it was.

Yale Brevda had brought enough money with him to open a tobacco importing business and eventually a box factory in Brooklyn. This is how it was told to me and explained the fact that Mom was always wealthy. Mom was a tranquil, even tempered soul who loved Murray. They met when she was 16. He was really her only boyfriend. They married in 1938 in a colossal wedding in Brighton Beach, Brooklyn. Murray wore top hat and tails. Mom's family had friends wealthy enough to afford a 16 mm. movie camera, and I actually have a film of their wedding. The film reveals a stern, grim father and mother of the bride, clearly unhappy of the fact that their daughter married a poor boy from the wrong side of Brooklyn.

My mother finished high school, was an enthusiastic reader, and had aspirations of going to college. In those days, girls really didn't go to college unless they were especially motivated, so she let that goal pass. She lived in a very paternal family, run by Nathan Brevda, a tall, stern patriarch who dominated everyone. Mom's mother, Rose, was a short, pleasant lady who lived for Nathan. They lived in an upscale home in Sheepshead Bay, Brooklyn, a wealthy neighborhood. We would visit on Sundays having a standard Sunday dinner of boiled brisket and potatoes. Nathan would end the day by giving each visiting grandchild a dollar.

During World War II, new and desirable items were restricted under rationing. Nylons, silk, rubber items, garden hoses, raincoats were under restrictions, but "seconds", namely floor samples, slightly damaged goods, but not used, were not restricted. Murray discovered that he could negotiate with department stores to purchase these items well below cost, and sell them without restriction. So he originally began his career with a pushcart.

Business was good, so he needed someplace from which he could sell the stuff and, in 1943, he purchased a foreclosed four-story building on Ninth Avenue in Manhattan from the Emigrant Savings Bank for $500 down and $14,000 mortgage. He originally went to Nathan, his father-in-law to borrow the $500, but Nathan would only say "Ich bin nicht ein bank." "I'm not a bank." Murray was from the "wrong part" of Brooklyn, namely Brownsville, while Nathan was from the "right part," the well-to-do Sheepshead Bay neighborhood. Resentful that his in-law refused to back him, Murray repeated this story numerous times during his life, proud of his achievements, and successes in business. The Emigrant lent him the $500.

Setting up a new business, he needed to devise a way to be noticed. He needed a name. Able Furniture would be the designated name of the business which would buy and sell used furniture. He was always thinking. Why Able, I asked him when I was very young. It would appear first (although these days other companies use names like AAA) first in the used furniture listings in the Yellow Pages. He stayed Able Furniture until he finally closed the business.

Murray worked in his store, successfully selling "seconds." Around the corner, on 54th Street was (and still is) the Midtown North Precinct. It was not uncommon for the officers to come into the store to buy things that were not restricted. He became friendly with some of the detectives. One of them, Bill Holzherr, a strapping German-American told him about a great community that could get him out of Brooklyn: Rego Park in Queens. So that's where we ended up. We lived in a rental house across the street from Bill.

Bill retired on a pension that was so small that eventually, after he died, his wife was unable to support herself. Bill, like some of the other cops of that era, had the option to refuse to pay into Social Security from his wages. For a while, an opt-out provision was part of the police contract and often very short-sighted and financially naïve cops preferred the money in hand rather than in Social Security so that their spouses were ineligible for Social Security in their later years. After Bill died, his wife Lucille spent years almost destitute, although Murray and I helped her out. Murray bought Bill's house when he moved. The house is still there.

Murray's business in the post-war period boomed. His business evolved, purchasing not only "seconds", but he also discovered that hotels in Manhattan were replacing their furnishings and refurbishing their rooms. He was there to buy whatever they were discarding. He discovered that a well-placed tip to a housekeeper or low-level manager would result in them telling him to remove all the "junky old" furniture. He could pay for one or two items and take out fifty. All he needed was a place to put them.

Rego Park was a working community during the year, but it was hot in the summers. Somehow my parents discovered Long Beach, New York, the "City by the Sea." Many of their contemporaries took places in Rockaway and I have no idea why we ended up in Long Beach, just east of the Rockaways but not part of New York City. In 1949, they stayed at the Benjamin Franklin Hotel on the boardwalk and Franklin Boulevard in Long Beach.

Summers were significantly cooler in Long Beach, near the ocean, with Murray driving to Manhattan to work in the store. Within a few years, my parents decided that they really liked it there and bought a summer bungalow with two bedrooms, a living room opening into a kitchen, one bath and a car port. Postwar construction on Long Island rapidly created an abundance of small, relatively inexpensive homes to allow people to live outside of New York City.

In 1949, my brother Charles was born. No two siblings could have been more opposite. Fat, skinny, studious, non-scholastic, short, taller, independent, momma's boy, aggressive, passive, healthy, sickly...I think you get the picture. I was the former. We never really got along, and since my parents are gone, we haven't spoken in years.

Two blocks from our house in Rego Park was William Sydney Mount Elementary School, P.S. 174. It was an easy walk through safe streets unless there was a problem. It started with a slight snow storm. In those days, kids had galoshes to cover their shoes. I hated galoshes. My father insisted I wear them. No...yes...no. You'll wear them or else. Off I went with the hated galoshes. About 20 paces from the house, I realized I had left without my book bag, so I turned around and knocked at the door. Explosion. Off came my father's belt (or, as he put it, his strap). Screaming on top of his lungs, swinging for me, he screamed he would teach me a lesson to obey. My mother interceded although a few lunges got through. I went to school without my book bag, but with my galoshes.

My father was a hard-working, supportive person, but occasionally something would snap within him and I guess would recall his hard upbringing struggling for money and position. He quit high school before graduating and went to work. I think his occasional short fuse reflected deep frustrations with some of the things he encountered in life and in business. Getting hit with his strap hurt, but it was his screaming that was more frightening and actually worse.

Mom was always there to intercede and prevent my father from killing me, an important role. She seldom yelled, rarely got angry, and was tolerant of most of my father's craziness. She clearly understood his background and was far more tolerant than one would have imagined. She always remained behind the scenes, allowing my father to have any limelight that was available. She was smart, handled all the family finances, worked the store and the auctions, and balanced the checkbook and was the bookkeeper for the business.

Mom knew education mattered and was the foil for my father who had a general disdain for education, advertising that he had gone to the "school of hard knocks." She read continuously, knitted, did crosswords, went to Broadway shows, had a constant circle of friends and seldom bothered to cross Murray. She would provide the calm when Murray became the storm.

Every time I got a sore throat, my mother would call Dr. Harris who made house-calls and gave me a once over then would flip me over and give me a shot of penicillin. That was back when that wonder drug could cure you of everything from which you might possibly suffer. I also remember that our shoe store had a magic machine that would x-ray your feet with your shoes on to be sure they fit. I never needed that and my mother wouldn't let them. Dr. Harris, however had a fluoroscope in his office and he used to say that if you're not better, he could look inside you and see what's wrong.

I went to PS 174 from kindergarten through second grade until my mother decided that she didn't want me going to junior high school in Rego Park. She thought that the school was too large and overcrowded. The logical conclusion was to buy something permanent and comfortable in Long Beach. The Rego Park house was an easy sell, as was the bungalow, so the combined monies made it possible to buy the house in Long Beach in 1953.

My parents spent the rest of their lives in that house, more than 60 years. When they passed on, I had the linoleum removed from the hall, took off the fuzzy wallpaper, and ripped up the wall-to-wall threadbare carpeting. The house worked for them and it was never my place to tell them what to do with their home, except on rare occasions. When the refrigerator, which had a handle that went clunk when you went to pull it open, left a large puddle on the floor, I ordered a new one for them. The blue rotary phone in their bedroom stayed.

It was a curious house. It was only a year or two old when they bought it and was designed by an architect who was a relative of the owners. The story was that the architect had worked for the firm that designed the Trylon and Perisphere for the 1939 World's Fair. We heard that story for years. The house had a curvy porch, a half basement, which was quite unusual for Long Beach surrounded as it is by water, a large living room and a small adjacent dining room, but had a kitchen that was a bit larger than a roomy phone booth. My mother was happy with the space. All she needed was a refrigerator, a stove, and a sink. The kitchen was so small that the refrigerator had to be put in front of a door leading to the back yard. Somehow a small table also was made to fit. If more than three of us were at the table at one time, someone had to stand to let people get in or out of the kitchen.

East School in Long Beach was exactly two blocks from our house so that took care of the possibility of ever getting a ride. Elementary School was kindergarten through sixth grade. I have only scanty recollections of those days. A few things do drift back. I was a good student, a chubby kid (the "husky" section of Smorack's, the local clothing store), a slow runner and a lousy baseball player, so it was always right field for me.

I was around nine when my mother bought me my first camera. It was a simple brownie with a fixed focus and a flash gun that you attached by screwing it onto the side. I was fascinated by what you could do with a camera. You could capture time, and preserve it and look at it. I ran around taking pictures of everyone I knew and every place I went. I eventually got an eight millimeter movie camera and took silent, faded color movies. I've been photographing ever since. As I look at my accumulated photographs of special people and places in my life going back over the years, I can remember most of the events surrounding the pictures, although the years they were taken seem to disappear. The smiling faces and good times that I've recorded allow me, as Jim Croce said to "save time in a bottle."

My fourth grade teacher was Mr. Gilbert. He liked smart kids. He liked math and kids who could do math problems. He was also quite full of himself. When you were successful in solving hard problems, he'd praise you by giving you a stamp on your paper that said "Lew Gilbert". He sometimes would give you a pen with his name on it. I was mostly one of the smart kids he favored and was mostly well behaved. But not always. I remember the awful food we'd occasionally get in the cafeteria. At one point a lot of trays and a lot of food ended up on the floor in protest. It was what might be considered a fourth-grader food fight. Mr. Gilbert went nuts. Yelling at the group of us participants, he talked about our report cards and how ashamed he was of us. Each of us received a special gift on our report cards, in bold red letters, "Cafeteria Conduct...D".

In those days we rode bikes without helmets, although it took me almost a month and a half to teach myself to ride a two wheeler. We played dodge ball, where you could throw the ball at anyone standing near you and unless they caught it, they were out. We climbed metal monkey bars firmly situated on the asphalt ground without padding. We had fist fights and headlocks. None of us died.

Polio occurred in the Fifties before the Salk vaccine. Everyone had to line up in long lines at the school to get shots of gamma globulin. I was chubby so I needed two. In the fourth grade during Easter vacation (not Spring break) The Wizard of Oz was playing at the Laurel Theater in Long Beach. All the kids who were in town flocked to see it. Most of us in the theater got a special souvenir: the measles. There was no vaccine available at the time. Half the kids were out of school the following week. I recall that I lay in bed with the blinds drawn because the light was so bothersome. When I recovered, I found that I couldn't see as well as before. Perhaps it's a coincidence but from that time forward I was discovered to be nearsighted and have worn glasses.

Fifth grade was English writing and reading some of the classics, while sixth was in Mr. Oberman's class. He was an inspiring and energetic teacher who eventually went on to become principal and then superintendent of the Long Beach School system. He supported, encouraged and inspired us and would ask us to think about what we wanted to do in the future. I thought I'd become a lawyer because all doctors did was give you shots. The school principal was Mrs. Hendrickson, a short, elderly lady who didn't interact much with the students. I recall that I was chosen to be salutatorian at graduation and wanted her to sign my autograph book. "You were honored in scholarship" was the best and warmest wish she could muster.

Junior high, now called Middle School, was where I really began to gravitate towards the sciences. Nurtured by Mrs. Mayer, I discovered that I really found real things, solid, reproducible things most interesting. Tracked in the "smart" classes, I had to take a language so somehow I ended up in Latin. At the same time the Catholic Church was moving away from Latin, I was stuck with it. My Latin teacher was a weird little man who seemed to enjoy touching some of the boys. One day he decided to try me. I had developed a strong hand grip from carrying furniture summers in my father's store and playing the accordion so when I grabbed his hand quite firmly, his face turned red and he never tried again.

In August 1959, I turned 13. Normally, a Bar Mitzvah is held around the date of the boy's birthday and mine was August 27, but my mother felt that too many people would be away and not available to come before Labor Day. Therefore she postponed it until September 19. That gave me the summer and a little more to learn to say the words in Hebrew that had absolutely no meaning to me. I probably could have said it in Latin with the same enthusiasm, but for some reason it was important to do it in Hebrew. Cantor Mendelsohn drummed it into my head for weeks at a time so I didn't embarrass anyone. I probably could have said it backwards for all anyone knew.

After enduring years of Hebrew School and training for the Bar Mitzvah, the religion and I went the parting of the ways. At that time, I decided never to return unless I absolutely had to for social reasons, and I've pretty much stuck to that. I figured if there was a god, he or she didn't need me to chant repeatedly in a language that I couldn't understand to reinforce for the deity that I mattered or that it mattered to me. I figured somehow he or she would know.

Summer times during junior high were transitional. I was too young for working papers and not ready for a real summer job. Many of my friends left Long Beach for sleep away summer camp, a trip to some mountain lake for swimming, sleeping on cots and doing stuff. My father said he couldn't afford sending me. Not that I cared to go anyway. My mother decided that I should spend summer days at day camp. The bus picked you up in the morning, drove you to the west end of Long Beach driving all around the city to pick up the other kids who lived nearby. So the two-mile commute to and from camp took an hour each way. You swam and played baseball all day.

By the summer after my Bar Mitzvah, I had had more than enough of summer day camp. This was perfect timing for my father who decided it was time for me to work in his new store. This is when I began to call my father Murray, because I was working for him and both my parents felt it better that I call him Murray in public rather than daddy. So he would always be Murray to me from then on. My father had needed to expand his business and an opportunity presented itself. A large warehouse was available in Harlem. Cooke's Storage Warehouse was a seven-story building that served as both a storage facility and furniture warehouse. He bought it with a large mortgage but it would be a perfect location to keep all the furniture he had gotten for little cost from hotels which were refurbishing. He would be able to sell high quality used hotel furniture to the neighborhood residents in Harlem, the African-American community in Manhattan. This was terrific and I was actually delighted that I would get to do something productive. I would get on the Long Island Railroad in the mornings with him, commute to Penn Station and get on a subway 1 stop to Times Square, take the shuttle across, then the #4 uptown subway to 125th Street, get out, and walk two blocks.

Murray also became acquainted with quite a few people in similar businesses. He would compete with them for "deals" but would also watch how their sales were handled. Visiting several older people who were also auctioneers, he realized that this would be a way of making quick sales and turn over lots of merchandise. He always had the gift of gab and could talk fast. He became an auctioneer. All it took was a few dollars and you could get a license. He ran auctions every Tuesday.

Why Tuesday? He felt it was a lucky day for him. He bought his store on a Tuesday. My mother, who had trouble getting pregnant, had told him she was pregnant on a Tuesday. I was born on a Tuesday. In reality Tuesday was a perfect day. In many businesses Tuesday is the slowest day of the week, so dealers who were interested in buying used furniture could be available to come to the auction on Tuesday. Every Sunday, the New York Times auction page had his ad. "Murray Fried Sells on Tuesday".

So, what could a 14-year-old do in a used furniture auction house? Just about everything. I could interact with the public, sell furniture, negotiate prices, carry furniture and make deliveries with the men. I could also get filthy, covered with dust and grime which came with the used furniture which came out of hotel basements and hotel storage. I could take deposits from customers during the auction sales.

He also took used rugs from the hotels which he stored in the basement since they weighed so much in piles that there was concern the floor would collapse if they were stacked on the other floors. I don't think a coal mine is much dirtier than used rugs in an unventilated basement. The top rug of the pile would be sold, flipped, folded, rolled and tied and numbered and the next one would be sold. Aided and abetted by two fans, the dust and dirt would waft across everyone in the stifling basement.

I got to know some of the people in the neighborhood. Cooke's was located at 209 East 125th Street. This was just off Third Avenue in East Harlem. On the west side of 125th Street in 1960 was the Hotel Theresa where Fidel Castro stayed and meet with Khrushchev during the summer U.N. session. Adam Clayton Powell, the charismatic and controversial congressman from the district stopped in occasionally during auction days. I remember meeting Maceo Pinkard, composer of Sweet Georgia Brown who would joke that she supported him all his life.

Under the trestle of the subway on Park Avenue, a few blocks west of the store stood Chemical Bank. My errand on Tuesday mornings was to go to the bank and exchange a few large bills for $100 in singles and fives to be used as change after the auction. As I was leaving the bank with the usual bundle, a young Hispanic man approached me and pulled a knife. He saw what I had and told me to give it to him. I don't know why I reacted so quickly, but I took a step back and threw all the money up in the air. He was obviously distracted by this green confetti but didn't feel it necessary to stab me. I took off. He didn't pursue me. I headed for a local Spanish church on 125th Street, where I knew the pastor. I was scared as I hid in the church. The pastor walked me back to the store. It seems that there were several witnesses who had seen what had happened. The young man was caught and apparently arrested, although I never heard anything more about him or the incident.

In those days most of the merchants in Harlem were white and often Jewish. So too was our store with my uncle Phil and my father's friends from Long Beach working there. Our employees were African-American, called Negroes in those days. Our manager Paul and his brother Taylor were African-American. They kept an eye on me. They would take me to hotel basements to clean out the furniture my father had acquired. I would help load the trucks.

Occasionally we would load trailers heading back to the South. The new furniture factories in North Carolina and Georgia would send 40 foot trailers loaded with new furniture to the dealers in Manhattan. Several southern dealers had visited my father's store and would either buy or accept used furniture on consignment to load onto the trailers. This was far better than having the trailers return empty. If we were loading a trailer in an afternoon, we would cruise the neighborhood looking for "coke heads" who would work for a few hours for a few dollars. Since it was summer, hot as hell, they would only last a few hours before wandering off with a few more dollars. But they helped get the trailers loaded before the end of the day.

The auctions were fun to work. There would be the general din and noise. My father was proficient and would squeeze as much as he could out of the crowd. Auctions can be an exciting experience. Many auctioneers have been accused of hiring shills, people who would stand and bid, employed by the auctioneer to push the bidding higher, but Murray never bothered. He'd simply look around in the crowd and point and raise the bids himself. Sometimes bidders would shout "who's bidding", but the speed and the enthusiasm would override their questions. If no one was bidding, he'd simply say "Sold!" and the item would disappear.

Antique dealers would come from all over, since in those days hotels had quality, not ready-made furniture. Customers included dealers from Southampton, Poconos and elsewhere in upstate New York as well as Manhattan galleries. My job was mainly to grab as much money as I could to cover the purchases. When a buyer was unfamiliar, or a newcomer, Murray would shout from the auction stand, "let's hear it there" meaning go get some money from that guy. My job was to ask for at least a 50% deposit: Cash, no checks. My mother did the books and would come in every Tuesday to write the bills and take the money. We'd go out to a Manhattan restaurant, the Jaegar House in Yorkville, the German area at the time in upper Manhattan, after the auctions.

All the furniture and items from hotels would end up stacked in piles in the store. In addition, anything from house buys, from local apartments, from New York City residents would also be up for sale. He would get all kinds of things from apartment buys. He would buy the entire contents of an apartment, especially from estates and from folks who were moving away. In those days, there were few alternatives for disposing of furniture. Although there were charities that would accept donations, the person disposing of the contents would get no money from the charity. Antique dealers were picky in what they would buy and would only be interested in items of real value, since they had limited space. Murray's Able Furniture, would take everything.

Murray would get a call that someone's grandma had died and left an apartment full of furniture. We would drive over and check out the apartment's contents. Often a lawyer handling the estate was there and desperate to get the apartment emptied. Examining the contents, Murray knew what things would sell and what they were worth to him. So he'd find one or two items, figure out what they were worth and offer that amount for the entire apartment. He further offered to empty the apartment within a day or two. As long as the number he offered sounded right—and it always did if only because the Salvation Army and Goodwill would pay nothing—we had a deal.

He would hand the seller an amount in cash, sometimes even the entire agreed upon amount, take a few items along which he considered the "cream", take the key and head back to the store. He would ask the family member if there were items that were special or memorable to them and tell them to take them. Sometimes they would focus on some prized possession or piece of furniture that would remind them of grandma. Often they wanted nothing. If the lawyers or other non-family members were involved, it was often clear that the location had been thoroughly searched for valuables. Most of the time grandma's place was intact. Depending on the urgency of the seller, we'd often be back in the afternoon to clean out the place.

Cleaning out someone's apartment was really like cataloging their lives. Think of all those items that are personally meaningful, especially as one gets older. Think of all the valuable items stashed in secret places, in clothing, in shoes, in closets and drawers that we all have. Dissembling, searching and removing everything was my task. I would find old coins in drawers, false teeth rimmed with gold (in those days a gold tooth sold for six dollars), sometimes small amounts of stashed cash, jewelry, and other things of value.

I also found photo albums, pictures, perfume bottles, clothing by the closet and drawer full, shaving equipment, medication, diplomas, books, letters, diaries, phonograph records, cameras, radios, souvenirs of travel, wedding pictures, awards, the contents of one's life. The families had abandoned it. The owner had died. I certainly had no attachment to any of it. All of it that no one much cared about would end up in large laundry bins, to be carted to the store where it would sit for months and years to be occasionally picked at by a curious customer.

Obviously, one could wax melancholy about the summary of someone's life ending up as meaningless artifacts in a used furniture store. The greater message, however, is that one's life is meaningful to each of us individually and that "stuff" doesn't much matter. As I looked at photo albums of people I didn't know, I was reminded that in the grand scheme of things, we matter to the circle around us, and that the outsiders really shouldn't be expected to care.

The pictures and paintings we'd acquired found themselves hanging on the vast walls in the large warehouse. Every so often at the Tuesday auction, someone would point to a picture they wanted to buy and it would be offered up for bids. It was on February 22nd in 1966 that a fireman noticed a small portrait of George Washington hanging on a wall somewhere in the back of the warehouse. Thirty-eight dollars was the bid for the "copy" which the fireman authenticated as an original copied from a primary source and sold for $20K. I was in college at the time and wasn't at the auction, but no one in the store could remember where the painting had come from. If it hadn't been George Washington's birthday and the fireman hadn't been observant, more than likely it would have hung there for years after. It had probably hung there for years before.

One of the best times in the store was in January. Macy's would unload its broken and open boxes of Christmas toys and they would be thrown onto a large balcony on the second floor of the warehouse. I would go through the boxes of stuff trying to find sufficient parts of toys to assemble at least a few working ones. My Erector Set had a zillion extra parts with no screws with which to assemble them. I had about 100 rubber tipped darts but only one or two working dart guns. I had plastic model kits without instructions so I got good at putting together boats and airplanes without guidance.

I worked in Harlem until the summer of 1964 when the tensions in the street became too great. In mid-July a white police lieutenant shot and killed a 15-year-old African-American boy. That event triggered major race riots, looting, and general unrest across Harlem and then Bedford Stuyvesant in Brooklyn. It was time for me to find another place to work.

That wasn't a problem: My father still owned the store he had first bought on Ninth Avenue in Manhattan. That was the solution to the problem of going up to Harlem. I would commute downtown each morning in the summer to that store. Devoid of air conditioning, it had a straw rug left by the previous tenant. Unfortunately, it was also infested with small biting bugs that caused these itchy welts on my legs. Off I went to New York University Medical Center to be diagnosed. Diagnosis...throw out the rug.

It was in the 9th Avenue store that I really learned to interact with all kinds of people. Everyone who came in to buy something would offer you less than you asked no matter what number you started with. Every sale was a negotiation. I also learned that when gypsies, who would inhabit empty store-fronts or apartments in the neighborhood, would come in, their kids would wander around the store and steal anything they could put in their pockets, even though a lot of the stuff might be totally useless. I particularly remember they had an affinity for finials, the tops of lamps which held the lamp shades in place. They would also steal light bulbs.

Stress or anxiety once again played havoc with my father. He would come home from work during the week angry and sullen occasionally. Nothing anyone said to him was satisfactory. His bad temper led him to scream and yell and threaten. One night I'm certain I must have stepped onto a long planted mine which exploded in the form of his strap. He hit me a few times and screamed at me, but something happened with me. I turned and told him that he could hit me but he couldn't hurt me. I could take it from him. I was big and had gotten tougher. He never pulled his strap out again. If the truth be told, the temper and the noise was far more disconcerting and would show itself although rarely.

I gained confidence, independence and maturity working in the stores. I learned how to relate to customers, deal with all kinds of characters and negotiate prices. I think because of all those years of hondling, I never negotiate price. When I buy a car, I warn the dealer that they'd better start off with their best price, because if I find a lower one elsewhere or it's not what I previously was aware of what the car should cost, I will walk out. I've purchased property, cars and other items of a similar nature, with minimal if any haggling. If I want it and it meets my criteria, I buy it.

CHAPTER 3

CLASS OF '64

In high school, I really changed: I was studious, shy and attentive in ninth and tenth grade. By junior year, I was into the sciences, honor classes and school activities. I was looking forward to college, although I had very little knowledge of what college was really like. My parents, especially my father, had very little regard for college; he claimed to be a "self-made man." He'd go along with it but really didn't see much purpose to it. Having supplied used furniture to a man who owned several private schools, he somehow felt that this experience provided him with sufficient credentials to recommend colleges.

In addition to the science courses and other prerequisites, I had the good sense to take typing class. It was essential for those pursuing a secretarial career and thus it had some of the school's more attractive women in it. I became pretty good at typing and would type exams for teachers who were unable to type very well. Not only did I make a few dollars doing that but I also learned to compose professional business letters and type accurately with both hands at a reasonable speed. This remains a skill that has saved me thousands of hours over the last 50 years.

The school had formed what was called the Future Physicians' Club which met once a month in the evenings under the auspices of Long Beach Hospital. We became volunteers in the hospital and performed the usual menial tasks of refilling jugs of water in patients' rooms or making deliveries of flowers. One of my tasks was as an assistant mopper in the operating room. I would scrub the floor while the real worker did his thing. Since the volunteer work was performed after school, it was unusual for anything to be happening in the operating room. But late one afternoon one of the basketball team members had fallen and broken his arm. He needed to have surgery. The orthopedic surgeon looked at me and asked if I'd like to watch the surgery as long as I promised not to faint. Sure, it sounded like a cool opportunity.

The opportunity for an uninvolved and unqualified observer entering an operating room is long over and nearly impossible today. Legislation and hospital controls over patient privacy prevents any such activity. This is clearly a good thing.

In spite of watching the operation up close, it was not a life-changing event that made me want to be a doctor, much less a surgeon. I didn't mind watching, but I found the plating of a radius, the larger bone in the lower arm, far from exciting. I found that I did more with my Erector Set at home and the fastidious and fussy performance by the surgeon for his audience of one was more than I really needed. As he shouted "scalll-pelll!," I knew the surgeon figured here was someone to impress and he made the most of the opportunity to let me know that what he was doing was especially important. I never went into orthopedics. After having watched the surgery, I got to mop the floor.

October of my sophomore year was a very strange time. On the evening of October 16, 1962, we were told that the President was making an important announcement. We sat in front of the television set that night. I had a reel-to-reel tape recorder which I had always used to record popular songs from the radio that I could play when I felt like it. The Russians had put nuclear missiles in Cuba. JFK had invoked the Monroe Doctrine about non-interference of foreign powers in the affairs of the Western hemisphere and was going to blockade Russian ships from arriving in Cuba. The confrontation, it was said, was coming soon and it could mean nuclear war, although I was naive at the time and didn't fully comprehend what that might mean.

Outside the high school was the Nike missile base. Nike missiles were created with the idea that if the Russians sent ICBM's towards New York City, the U.S. Army would fire the Nike missiles to try to intercept them. It was a shotgun approach to defend New York City. So we all knew we were prime targets. We rehearsed duck-and-cover every day figuring that our desks would prevent nuclear attacks. I guess the rehearsals worked because none of us were killed by nuclear missiles, and 39 years later when Tower Two of the World Trade Center fell on me, I ducked and covered. But we'll get to that later.

Things were pretty tense and most of us were quiet, consumed by the then-current world affairs. "Well, don't you know we're on the eve of destruction..." as Barry McGuire sang in the song. Somehow things worked out and we weren't bombed. Life went on.

High school did not leave me with many notable memories. I wound up in Latin only to discover that I hated learning languages; I couldn't find ways to memorize the stuff if my life depended on it. I should have realized that before I ended up failing German in college, but only hindsight is 20/20.

I had no athletic skills, so mostly all I did was go to football and basketball games and watch. We'd occasionally assemble on weekends informally at the school and play tackle on a grassy field. I was, being chubby, a blocker and a tackle. Most of the honor classes were devoid of athletic team participants, so we really didn't know many of those guys on the teams. We would go to the home games and expect the team to lose. Generally they rarely disappointed us.

Advanced math was boring, tedious and difficult. Unfortunately, the chairman of the department taught the honors class. Mr. Greenbaum was a short, elderly, professorial teacher who taught theory and obscure mathematical concepts to a class of supposedly advanced students. By the second period of the day, his jacket and tie would be covered with chalk. With no regard to standardized testing and the expectations of the regents examination at the end of the year, about half the class failed the regents and the remainder of the class got in the low 70s. At least Mr. Greenbaum didn't have to worry about the chairman of his department firing him. I do know that shortly after our disastrous year, he was replaced.

English was a bit more stimulating. Enduring Jane Eyre, *The Mill on the Floss*, and some heavy Shakespeare, I found laboring through some of the obscure classics both challenging and difficult. I would occasionally stay behind after school to discuss things with Dr. Shanker, the English teacher. I distinctly remember the arguments we would have. I was slowly being drawn towards medicine and would tell him that medicine was the noblest profession. He would always correct me, saying that teaching was. To this day I really don't know which one of us was right.

The sciences seemed to be where I was most proficient. I found that the orderly and reproducible results of many of the so-called laws of nature were quite fascinating. Math was more precise; however, Mr. Greenbaum had managed to turn me off to that. Fortunately, the science teachers managed to inspire and keep me interested.

For most of high school, I was one of the geeks, occasionally going to dances or dating someone. Looking back, I would have had much more to carry to the future if I had the insight to take auto shop or more shop classes rather than honors courses, but only the non-college bound would be seen in those circles. The jocks took shop.

We were all clearly college bound. Competition for college placement was intense but far less than the young people of today have to face. I drifted along as one of the group, expecting to do well, but not standing out in any way from my peers. We all drifted along and knew that someday we'd get into college and somehow succeed. I was content to do my work, expected to read what I was assigned, and hand in my homework when it was due.

Senior year, it all changed. My father came home one day to tell me that he had spoken to his private school owner and advisor who said I should go to Cornell. I went to the guidance office to throw the name out to them and based on my grades, they encouraged me to apply. My parents felt it unnecessary to visit the school or any other one for that matter, so since it would be good enough if I was accepted, I applied early decision. I was accepted to college by the first week in December, so my future was set. I guess it would have been nice to have seen the place, or any other one for that matter, but I was going to Cornell, whatever that meant and wherever that was.

Senior year was made great by the appearance of Ms. Z, a new teacher in Long Beach, the daughter of my father's good friend, and someone who would spoil me with privileges that I guess all seniors accepted to college thought they deserved. She was never my teacher but since we were friends I was her all-around assistant. She had me type her tests, gave me lifts home, gave me her hall pass, allowed me to be her teacher's aide and in general let me break out of the classroom, strut around the halls, and show off. She gave me new confidence. She spoiled me but she also made it clear that I didn't want to be a teacher.

I became a senior wise-ass. Getting into college that early meant I could actually fool around. A hall pass courtesy of Ms. Z helped. I knew lots of the teachers because I was a talented typist by then as I worked for them and typed their tests and papers. The Long Beach High School newspaper was the *"The Tide"*, not named for the detergent but rather the beach community. Some of us "honor" students got hold of the ability to print out an alternative, student-run rag which we called the *"The Edit"* (Tide backwards). Our op-eds, which directly reflected on some of our teaches, put an end to The Edit.

I finished high school with five years of Latin because I felt I couldn't learn another language. Some people pick up languages easily but not me. You didn't have to speak Latin or do much with it except conjugate verbs, decline nouns and adjectives, and translate "all Gaul is divided into three parts." I hated Latin. There was nothing about it that was interesting unless you were Catholic and even they gave it up in the 60s. I probably should have taken that as a sign but I persisted at it. I should have learned Spanish.

I took calculus and couldn't understand it, nor did I care to. My best class was college biology which would allow me to bypass basic biology in college and go onto the next level course. One Friday afternoon, while we were studying the comparative anatomy of some poor creatures that were dissected, there was a commotion in the halls. Something happened to President Kennedy. It didn't take long for people to flock to the few televisions in the school and we all learned that our President, the cool guy with the wavy hair and the classy wife, had been shot dead.

It's impossible to relate to young people who didn't experience the assassination first hand the impact that event had on all of our lives. Clearly, things changed for all of us from those moments in time. The closest analogous situation more recently are the events of 9/11 yet they're also quite different. I was 17 years old. The President was young; he was the first one born in the 20th Century. You would see him on television. He would tell jokes and laugh. We could relate to him in so many ways. He had a young wife. He was vibrant and energetic. He didn't even wear hats. How was it possible or even conceivable that he could be shot dead in public in his car? It stayed with you. That weekend everyone sat around and watched the funeral.

In the middle of the funeral, the news media cut to where Lee Oswald was being transported in Dallas from some jail to another. Suddenly, he was shot by someone in the entourage. This was live, breaking news. It wasn't the six o'clock news report; it wasn't a movie. It was something that no one could really process. To this day, all of us alive and old enough to remember will always remember where we were when we heard President Kennedy was shot. Our generation also lived to see Robert F. Kennedy, Martin Luther King, and John Lennon murdered. Those events were also all part of us. But nothing had the impact of JFK's assassination.

The year before Marilyn Monroe had died. Now JFK was dead. What does death mean to you when you're 17? Some of us had lost grandparents, but that was normal and kind of expected. You couldn't really relate to your grandparents anyway. Buddy Holly had died years before in a plane crash. At 17, death is supposed to be distant and far away, not an intimate part of our lives. Buddy Holly was 23, Marilyn Monroe was 36, and JFK was only 46. Death, somehow, was sneaking into our lives.

The world was a stressful and more sinister place after that. An old southern guy took over the presidency. Kennedy had kept the world out of war by confronting the Soviets over the missiles in Cuba. Now we were beginning to hear about the Communists overrunning the world and starting in South East Asia, in a place called Vietnam. We were all eligible to be drafted, although none of us really related to the draft at that time. We all looked forward to getting our draft cards since it was proof that we were 18. In those days you could drink at 18. You couldn't vote until you were 21. I'd still rather drink than vote.

Something remarkable happened after the assassination that my father retold for the rest of his life. He was called by the manager of the Carlyle Hotel in Manhattan. The Kennedys kept a suite at the hotel and Jackie Kennedy wanted it cleaned out and all of the furniture to be removed. He could take it all but could not publicly sell it as Kennedy furniture, until some time had passed. So he took it all, gave the manager some payment and brought home two original Kennedy rockers. Everyone who came to the house saw the famous Kennedy rocker. He even had a plaque engraved that said "This is an original rocker that belonged to President Kennedy."

One of the rockers was sort of brown and in disrepair with the thatching on the seat somewhat cracked. That one lived in our basement. The second was white, pristine, with white foamy cushions and foamy arm rests. That one had a place of honor in our television room.

Years passed. He decided that he had run out of people to show them to so it was time to turn them into cash. He read in the news that Guernsey's auction house was selling Kennedy memorabilia. He contacted the auctioneer who came to the house and eventually took them for sale. The brown one sold for under $20 K but a bid on the phone for the white one came in at over $300K. The first buyer paid and took the rocker, the second one failed to complete the transaction. My father, the auctioneer insisted that he either get paid or get the rocker back. Guernsey's agreed to return it.

Then my father realized that Guernsey's had failed to get a deposit and should have sold the rocker to the next higher bidder, but didn't. He got himself a lawyer and began a lawsuit. Guernsey's settled the case and returned the rocker. My father kept it until the day he died. After he passed on, I contacted Guernsey's again. "Remember Murray Fried and the Kennedy Rocker", I asked the auctioneer. "Of course I do. He was the only client who ever sued me." The rocker finally sold again for a lot less.

Life went on. True, everything you could think of was named after JFK. Airport, schools, streets, plazas, Cape Canaveral. Yet the general pall that fell over the winter was slowly lifting. It was the Beatles, the Rolling Stones, senioritis, dating, girls, and my driver's license. I had taken drivers education the semester before and passed the driving test on the first try. (I was warned to watch out for the blinking red light in Mineola which caught a lot of the takers unaware.) I could now go wherever I wanted if I could convince my mother to lend me her car.

In '64 Robert Moses had created the World's Fair in Flushing Meadows. That was about 10 miles away and a perfect destination for a new driver. It was also the home of the Mets, the new baseball team in New York. Needless to say that was the chosen destination. I also drove myself and my buddy and our dates to the prom. After the prom, I went to the beach, then home to sleep. My buddy and his date decided to stay on the beach to watch the sunrise, and I picked them up the next day and we drove to the World's Fair. They were sound asleep on the lawn when we came to pick them up around three in the afternoon at the Fair grounds.

More curious than excited, I worked the summer before I headed for Cornell. I hadn't the slightest idea what college was going to be like. I had neither seen it nor was there anyone around who could tell me what to expect. I was leaving Long Beach, leaving Manhattan, and looking ahead. During the Summer of '64 the murder of civil-rights workers preoccupied the newspapers and the airwaves.

CHAPTER 4

CORNELL UNIVERSITY, FAR ABOVE CAYUGA'S WATERS

Cornell University. "Far Above Cayuga's Waters" as its famous alma mater theme song says. Ivy League. Wow! Big deal.

Upstate New York: The trip up there was endless. Six hours, four of which was on old Route 17. You drove one lane in each direction for countless miles until you got to Binghamton. Then more slow, tedious driving through Dryden and then Varna until you finally arrived. Cornell was a land-grant college created during the Civil War under the Morrill Act of 1862 to encourage people to inhabit unpopulated areas. All you had to do is live there and you got free land. I think they overpaid.

Cornell was bigger than I had expected and hilly. It had an incredibly scenic campus, located on large gorges and great scenic terrain. So? My dorm was a mile and a half away protected by bridges, moats, and hills. The six "University" dorms were as picturesque as post-war temporary cinderblock and brick dormitories could be. Drab walls, two beds, a desk on either side of the room with a bookshelf above each desk. Most of the campus buildings were named for some benefactor or wealthy donor. These structures were called University Halls One through Six. The only things missing were the bars on the windows, the toilet and the door that clanked shut. Bathrooms and showers were down the hall.

Freshman orientation in the Cornell College of Liberal Arts and Sciences to welcome the students consisted of a huge assembly where we were told to look to the right and then to the left. One of us would not be there in four years. It was so nice to hear about flunking out in Week One. So what courses does a freshman take? English 101, Calculus (again), some other 101 courses, and whatever else they tell you. Things were mostly predefined because I chose the pre-med course. They required a language and everyone who offered advice for premeds said German was the language to take. To this day, I haven't a clue why. The only problem was the introductory languages took six hours out of your 15-hour schedule. So when I flunked German, I was automatically put on academic probation.

I did well in calculus this time since I had a previous practice session in high school. I also did better in German in the spring repeat since I knew the words and lessons since they were in the same book and from the same materials. One of my most notable memories of German classes was sitting in the basement of Morrill Hall, named for the Morrill Act, in an unventilated classroom listening to the instructor, a native speaker who could properly pronounce the words while half the class smoked cigarettes.

My parents didn't smoke. I didn't smoke. Most of my friends didn't smoke or, if they did, they didn't do it frequently. I couldn't stand all the smoke but no one at that time would allow you to prevent people from smoking in the classrooms. So I learned to smoke DeNobili cigars. These were incredibly pungent foul smelling half-size "stinkers" that made your eyes tear and made you dizzy while puffing away until you became accustomed to them. So I brought them to German class and lit up. It didn't take long before a truce between me and the cigarette smokers was at hand.

Escaping from the dorm on the weekends was often a burden. Freshmen were not allowed to have a car unless you lived in town and commuted. You could take a bus up the hill to Ithaca College, but without a car there wasn't a whole lot of places to go. If you were fortunate enough to know an upperclassman or someone who lived nearby (a "townie") and commuted to school, you could get a ride.

One of the locals knew some of the guys in my dorm and he was happy to take us to Elmira or Cortland, both of which had girls' schools. We did this every few weeks. In early November, an excursion had been planned for a Saturday. But that afternoon I was prostrate with the flu and couldn't join them. It was cold, rainy and nasty anyway, so I opted out. That night two of them were killed in a head-on collision.

This would not be the only time that getting sick seemed to have changed the course of my life. It would happen again with the Draft Board while I was doing my residency, but that's for a later chapter. Maybe I should seriously consider not taking yearly flu shots.

Cornell was not only an outpost of civilization but also a bastion of young people, where touring bands and talents who were crossing the country could arrive and play at Barton Hall and know they'd get a big turnout. The Rolling Stones on their first American tour played there until almost one in the morning. Ray Charles packed the place. Barton Hall was also the ROTC assembly hall. In 1964, the Reserve Officers' Training Corps program was big on most college campuses. Vietnam was just becoming a problem as was the early war protest movement.

Directly behind Barton Hall was the Statler Hilton Hotel School. This was an actual hotel on campus where one could stay. It was also a school endowed by the Hilton people to train future hotel management personnel. Many future hotel management personnel were graduated from the Statler School at Cornell. One day, ROTC was having some kind of assembly. Some of us were sort of hanging out to see and heckle and be as anti-war as you could be in 1964.

Somehow some of the food and trash of the Statler was nearby and became active protest fodder as we sort of shared it with the assembled troops. The Campus Cops rounded up a moderate sized group of unapproved protesters and herded us into Barton Hall into the "lockup" cage where they kept the sports equipment. My first time in jail! As we were paraded in front of the polaroid for our campus mug shots (this was long before the days of ID photos) by the campus patrol, they advised us that they had our pictures and that if we got into any further trouble, we would be the among the first of those one in three who wouldn't be there in four years.

Second semester freshman year, was the time you "rushed" fraternities and the girls rushed sororities. There were innumerable fraternities and fewer sororities because the boys outnumbered the girls by at least four to one at Cornell. These old mansions had been converted to provide room and board for many students. But since I was on academic probation from flunking German, was somewhat antisocial, and realized that it wouldn't be terribly smart to party for a second semester, I chose not to join. So I gathered two other people and looked elsewhere for living space. We found a private three-story house in "College Town" just outside of campus, nearly at the top of the Buffalo Street hill, the steepest hill in Ithaca and something that more resembled a street in San Francisco rather than in Ithaca, New York.

We managed to live there for three years. Above us was a mixed group of guys who were well connected with the local drug trade. There was always someone tramping up two flights of stairs at all hours of the day or night to pick up an ounce or two. There was usually enough pot on the table upstairs to keep one mellow if one chose to be mellow.

Downstairs lived the members of one of the thousands of student rock bands. These students would play at fraternity parties, attend occasional classes, and practice at all hours of the day or night. Nothing beat hearing *"Louie, Louie"* or *"Reachout"* at 2 a.m. It didn't take too long to reach an appropriate truce with the wannabe Kingsmen, a one hit wonder, rock-and-roll group of the 60's.

In the summer of '65, I studied as much German as I could stand, and decided I'd rather not have to commute to Manhattan just to get covered with grime and carry furniture up three flights of un-airconditioned stairs. I went to work for Fortunoff's Department store, at that time a family-owned, high class, upscale department store on Long Island. I applied for summer work and they hired me.

To work for Fortunoff's, I had to submit to a lie-detector test (drug screening was far away in the future). They hooked me up to a machine and told me they would first rehearse the questions before they actually turned on the machine so I could be prepared for the questions. Did you ever steal from an employer? My father was my boss in the past so I never robbed him. Besides, all we sold was old used furniture so what could I steal? Did you ever get arrested? My trip to Barton Hall wasn't an arrest so that was a "no". Did you ever smoke marijuana? Hmmmm…Ever? Well, how about do you smoke marijuana frequently? Nope. You're hired.

I was a good driver and Max Fortunoff was moving his stuff out of his original store on Livonia Avenue in Brooklyn to their new landmark superstore in Westbury, NY. I became one of the designated drivers. I would get into a station wagon with black rear windows with a big guy sitting next to me who provided directions, and drive to Livonia Avenue in a slummy part of Brooklyn. We'd load the car with silverware and jewelry and drive to Westbury where he'd watch them unload the stuff. It was great fun and I learned to drive in the city traffic. This would happen irregularly. For the rest of the time I worked the gift counter, selling beer mugs, wallets and the like. The Fortunoffs were generous and easy to work for. Once in a while they'd send me to their huge house to drive their kids or the nanny somewhere.

Sophomore year at Cornell wasn't memorable except for my trek from the College Town apartment up to campus. It was dark, cold, wet and long. I had an eight a.m. Saturday morning organic chemistry lab in the Baker Lab basement. So if I happened to party or go out drinking late on Friday, it was the longest possible journey. You couldn't have a car on campus, but you could bring it up to school. I got to bring my Chevy back to Cornell as a sophomore, but I still had to trudge to the lab on foot.

The eight a.m. Saturday class was simply a laboratory exercise session where you'd mix this and that and figure out what compounds you were playing with. It was taught by the usual dipshit (an archaic word translated into modern vernacular as nerd) instructor. I'd do my best to get to the class on time and always did my work. I was pretty good at it, but sometimes I didn't make it on time. The instructor I recall was preoccupied with my punctuality rather than concentrating on performance. So I once again was reminded of the one in three that I'd heard about during orientation.

Tired of the constant nagging about tardiness, I felt it necessary to interact in a positive manner with the instructor. Staying after class after the usual discussion of my lack of punctuality, I looked him in the eyes and told him that I successfully did all the work expected of me, passed all of the tests, and did my best to get there.

I suggested that he consider the quality of my efforts instead of his fixation with the clock.

I also pointed out that if he failed me I might be back on some sort of probation, which could lead to my being thrown out of school. If that were the case, I could be eligible for the draft, which was sending non-deferred, non-college students to Vietnam. So in effect he was threatening my life. If that were to happen, I'd be back and neither of us would enjoy the interaction. I passed the lab without any further discussion.

Something peculiar happened with my father during my sophomore year of college. Although he didn't visit me at school and we didn't call each other very often, I began getting a barrage of letters from him. He would obtain stationery from each hotel he would visit, jot a few lines in his scrawling handwriting (remember, he had a missing middle finger and 2 other crushed fingertips from the printing accident causing quite distinctive penmanship) and often would put a $5 or $10 in the envelope. The messages were more of a communication that he was in this or that particular hotel today and not much more. I was quite taken, however, that he would think of me while running around. I knew he didn't really understand my need for higher education, but he clearly missed and respected me.

Cornell was 50 years ago so obviously I only have vague memories of the four years I spent there. As I look back, some things reverberate. Most blend into that soup that constitutes our past.

In those days, all the major buildings on campus were wide-open all day and all night. You could wander into some desolate hall and hide from the rest of the world. You could also stay in many of the libraries until the wee hours and when exams were pending, 24 hours a day. When I was in the freshman dorms, the trek to the library was up the biggest hill on campus so it was not something you'd want to do frequently or in the evenings. The trek into town was a little better.

To get into town, to the local spaghetti joint (all you could eat for a few dollars, although each plate seemed to get spicier), the short cut was through the graveyard. I was always fascinated to see headstones dating back to the early 1800's thinking about the folks who lived up there so long before, and sort of snickering that if they returned then there'd be a bit of culture shock about what had happened to their country since they were laid to rest.

Cornell was so vast at that time that one could easily get lost among the buildings. Marc, my first roommate, was a physics major because his mother felt that was what he should do. She would call us frequently and demand to know how he was doing and what he was up to if he didn't bother to get on the phone. "I don't know" became the pretty pat answer. Marc hated physics.

Marc was into theater and music. He played piano and became facile on the huge pipe organ that was imbedded in Annabel Taylor Hall, the non-denominational chapel with the rotating stage that could accommodate multiple religions. Sort of a convert-a-god situation. The altar would rotate based on the group that was using the facility. One side was Jewish, the second Christian and the third non-sectarian. It was designed to reflect the non-sectarian inclination of Cornell. So, Saturday was the Jewish side, Sunday the Christians had their turn and I guess other days, it was up for grabs. I have no idea if things have changed to reflect Muslim or other religions today. We would go up there at night and he became the phantom of Annabel Taylor. He also had access to Lincoln Hall, the music center, where he'd play away on the pianos or rehearse for some half-baked play in which he was performing or directing.

Williard Straight Hall was and still is the home of the student union and the center of Cornell Activities. It housed a grand piano on an upper floor which Marc would also occasionally play. In my four years at Cornell, I had no idea who Willard Straight was or why the hall was so named. In 1968, the year after I left Cornell, the hall was occupied by protesting African-American students with bandoliers and rifles, one of whom had actually lived above us in our "College Town" house. Major changes including the resignation of the college dean followed the takeover. This was 1968. It's amazing that everything old is new again and colleges are once again facing the same problems.

My favorite hideout was actually in the basement of the Olin Library, a "new" library built in 1961. It was built as the graduate research library to supplement and add space to Uris Library built in 1891 and which was essentially the undergraduate place. You were only allowed upstairs in Olin if you were a grad student or doing a particular research study, but the basement contained the microfilms. They had microfilm of most major newspapers from the beginning of time and you could go to the stacks and take out the New York Times from 1862 or 1929 and see what was actually being written. I guess I was and still am a history buff and it was fascinating for me to spend hours reading current events in the microfilm of old newspapers.

In those ancient days at Cornell, there were no cell phones, no computers, no Google, no printers. Papers had to be typed using typewriters. If you made a mistake, it was White-Out® to apply a small coat of white fluid to cover up the mistake. Looking back, if someone had told me what was coming, it would be the same culture shock for me that would have befallen someone who was resting in peace in our shortcut town graveyard. The campus would be bigger, but parts would be quite familiar.

Our College Town apartment was a good enough place. Each of us had his own private bedroom. We could easily have guests stay over, and two of us had our future fiancés stay. I had started dating Linda after high school. She was from Long Beach and was going to Albany State. She'd travel to Syracuse and I'd drive the half hour north, pick her up and drive her to Cornell for the weekend. I'd drive her back on Sunday night.

Marc was luckier. His girlfriend and eventual fiancé went to Cornell. She would stay much more frequently and we essentially ended up with a co-ed apartment. Our third roommate was slower in development and would spend long periods of time locked in our one bathroom with appropriate illustrated material to keep him satisfied. Luckily, we got along with our upstairs and downstairs neighbors enough so that, if a facility was urgently needed, there was a place for us to go.

We attempted to cook in the apartment. We would make steaks or burgers in the broiler and occasionally would hear strange scratching sounds when we weren't cooking. One day a mouse crawled out of the bottom of our stove. Opening the bottom part, little footprints in an inch of fat revealed that it was necessary to occasionally clean the stove. The stove was unique because if you held the handle of the refrigerator and touched the handle of the stove, you got jolted with a major electrical shock. I guess the landlord had done the wiring and forgot to ground things. Soon enough we learned to hold only one or the other. Pain is a good teacher.

In April 1967, a fire in an off-campus residence hall killed eight graduate students and a 37 year- old professor. The fire had been somewhat contained, but they had succumbed to smoke inhalation and asphyxiation. Multiple firefighters were also overcome with smoke inhalation. Realizing that our own residence was wood, and nothing short of a tinderbox, we harassed our landlord, a local farmer, to provide some fire protection for us. We lived on the second floor and there was only one staircase up or down.

His engineering genius came up with the solution. You could break a window and jump since the window was only 15 feet up. He cut a hole between two bedrooms, covered by a wall which became a door so you could go out through either bedroom to jump out the window. I guess if my room caught fire, I'd have to knock on the wall, open the wall which became a passage way and go into the adjoining bedroom to try to get out. The landlord, sparing no expense, also put a fire extinguisher in the hallway. Fortunately we never had to test the "escape route" or the fire prevention, in spite of the constant smell of pungent smoke emanating from the third floor.

Studying consumed most of my time. Needless to say, I had quite a bit of making up to do because of an "F" in my six-credit German course. Fortunately, it was evident that it was in a language that was heavily weighted in my cumulative average, but could easily be overcome with performance in other subjects. Therefore I concentrated and focused on the sciences. Organic chemistry was the big pre-med course and I memorized every page and compound that ever existed I think. I got the requisite A.

Biology was too broad and one was allowed to major in a subset of biology for premed, so I chose genetics. I found it fascinating. You would go way up to the Ag (School of Agriculture, a state school) campus (about 4 miles away) in the evening and count fruit flies under a microscope and look and chart mutations. You could also sniff the ether we used to kill them. It made the trip doubly worthwhile and you could park on the Ag Campus after hours, although sometimes you had to wait a while to get over the room- spinning effects from the ether.

Not wanting to be the usual pre-med, I avoided courses like comparative anatomy. It was rumored that all the premeds were constantly sabotaging each other and competing for grades. Often the students were so competitive as to actually change the pointers on the specimens used during tests to screw the next student. You didn't do that in genetics. Genetics was in its early throes and Watson and Crick had won the Nobel Prize for explaining the structure of DNA in 1962, although the model had been worked out years earlier. The science fiction of genetic manipulation, of recombinant DNA, of altering genes at that time was only mental gymnastics. This science fiction has become scientific fact today. Boy, it makes me feel old to think that science fantasy when I was in college is science reality today.

At Cornell, I was in the School of Liberal Arts. That was great since I was allowed and in fact required to take a wide variety of courses, including not only the hated language course, but also literature, comparative religion, history, philosophy, and art. Art was my favorite. I discovered that I could sit up front in a darkened auditorium and stare up at color slides and hear about how man interpreted his surroundings, his place in the universe, and the difference between human beings and everything else. Art history became my minor. I must admit that the influence of those liberal arts courses, especially art history, have influenced me to the present day. True, the science and medical courses were important at the time, but they have become obsolete while the broader humanities have remained inspirational and pertinent to the formation of my leisure, perspective and pleasure. Curiously, as I will show in the next chapter, art history actually helped me get into medical school.

Only once in my four years at Cornell did I make the dean's list. I had an undistinguished time but did what was necessary to graduate from Cornell. After four years, I couldn't wait to escape from Ithaca. The scenic beauty of gorges and cliffs and hills and farms didn't do it for me. Exploring the Finger Lakes region once took us to the northern part of Cayuga Lake, the town of Seneca Falls. Seneca Falls is renowned for having held the first Women's Rights Convention in 1848, one of the pioneering sites for the woman's suffrage movement. I think the major difference in 1966 was that the roads were paved and the installation of a traffic light, which on circling the lake late Saturday night, I didn't notice and passed.

Stopped by the local police, I was informed that I had not only passed the light but was speeding, having clocked in at 39 miles an hour. "Obviously you college boys have no regard for our town and think you can zoom through it," he said. I, for some reason, which I no longer remember, was not in my usual jeans, but looked presentable. Looking at the officer, apologizing, I told him that I didn't realize we had crossed into town and hadn't realized the light had changed. I told him that we were heading back to Cornell, were kind of lost, and were heading back for the eight o'clock mass that morning which was being conducted by our friend, the pastor. Clearly the story was so preposterous that it must be true. He gave us a warning that we should send a message back to Cornell that when travelling through the historic town of Seneca Falls, we should be cautious and obey the laws. "Thank you officer."

We were given the MCATS (Medical College Achievement Tests) in junior year, but the results were secret and I never knew what I got on them. The only way to know was to see your advisor (mine was my genetics professor) who would look at your grades, look at you and tell you if you had done well enough to get into medical school. The only way to find out your MCAT score was to sneak a look at the paperwork the advisor held in secret on his desk. Although I don't remember the scores, they were obviously high enough.

Interviews for medical schools were conducted in the fall of senior year. An A in biochemistry was absolutely necessary as were a few other A's to get you a real shot at getting into a top medical school. I absolutely had to get back to New York City. I had done my time in rural America and, while the peace and quiet and bucolic serenity may have been pleasant for the prisoners in Elmira or Attica, it was not for me. I applied to SUNY Downstate in Brooklyn and was accepted without an interview. I thought I should practice my blabbing skills, which had been nurtured in my father's store and perfected as a senior in high school, by helping out the new teacher. Interpersonal discourse became more refined in the summers I had worked at sales at Fortunoff's Department Store. I agreed to go to Hershey Pennsylvania for an interview granted by the medical school being established in Hershey.

I awoke at five a.m. from my apartment on Buffalo Street at Cornell and drove the 220 plus miles to get to Hershey Pennsylvania by the 10 a.m. interview. I knew that this was a new facility, but it was worth the drive just to see about medical school interviews. Hershey was Chocolate Town. You could smell the chocolate when you got near, but the interview and the medical school was in an ancient facility with plans for the new hospital. It turned out that in 1963, according to M.S. Hershey/Penn State website, "the M. S. Hershey Foundation offered $50 million to The Pennsylvania State University to establish a medical school and teaching hospital in Hershey. With this grant and $21.3 million from the U.S. Public Health Service, the University built a medical school, teaching hospital, and research center. Ground was broken in 1966, and Penn State's College of Medicine opened its doors to the first class of students in 1967." I would have been in the second class.

Nothing stood on the site where the hospital was going to be built. The drawings were all there. The plans were real, but there was nothing much more than barns, silos, farms, and a chocolate factory in Hershey at that time. I spent the morning seeing the future, but not much of the present. I toured the campus. I was interviewed and re-interviewed. I figured I'd get back to Cornell later that afternoon because they told me the interviews and tours were going to be done by 3 p.m. They told me they were reserving many spots for in-state residents. No problem. The spots they were reserving for in-state residents really didn't matter to me since I had only travelled there to practice interviewing. I really had no plans nor intention of going to medical school in rural Pennsylvania.

At 2:30, I was approached by one of the suits. He asked me if I'd stay later and see the dean of the school. I met with several of the major officials of Penn State and of the medical school. They told me that they were impressed with me. I guess I was more proficient with gab than the average Penn State interviewee. They said that, although unusual, they were offering me a place in the medical school on the spot. I guess my interviews or grades or both went well enough. I hated Ithaca and its isolation. This place made Ithaca seem like downtown Manhattan. I couldn't accept their offer on the spot, knowing that Downstate, a place I hadn't seen yet, but was in Brooklyn, would take me. I would get back to them.

If I wasn't arrogant enough already, this offer made my day. I was going to go to medical school somewhere. I was going to get a draft deferral, which by this date had become important. Those not in college or non-essential industries were subject to the draft. My future seemed pretty clear and pretty predictable. I would probably become a doctor, get married, have kids, get rich and live in the suburbs, and fade away. Little did I know what was in store.

My next interview was in New York City at New York University Medical College. This was a super place. It is in the heart of Manhattan. It encompassed Bellevue Hospital, NYU Medical

Center, and the Manhattan V.A. My interview there was conducted by several of the attending physicians and finally by one of the female hematologists. Behind the desk hung a large Jackson Pollock print from the Museum of Modern Art. As I walked in, she greeted me and I introduced myself, asking her if she was a Pollock fan. She looked particularly puzzled and I pointed out the print. She was using the office and knew absolutely nothing about the artist she explained. She couldn't understand it as art and said that anyone could do that.

I suggested that he was a quite renowned abstract expressionist who was considered a breakthrough and major figure in modern art, explaining what I considered important about the abstract expressionists. She continued asking me about art and modern art, looking only briefly at my record and the paperwork that she had on her desk. After about 20 minutes, she looked at her watch and said she had taken too much time learning about art and she had to ask me why I wanted to be a doctor. So I told her. She smiled. I was accepted at NYU. Escape from Cornell. Back to New York.

I had one more interview. It was in Ithaca. The (with emphasis on the "*THE*") New York Hospital Cornell Medical School sent a few representatives to Ithaca to interview potential prospects just before mid-semester. We had 20 minutes set aside for the honor of being cross-examined by representatives from The World's Greatest Medical School. Three doctors sat across the table and fired questions at you. Why did you want to be a doctor? Why do you want to go to Cornell? What do you have to offer us? What makes you special?

Most interesting was their interviewing technique, namely to interrupt you as you tried to finish your answer by firing another question at you. So as arrogant as I was, as satisfied with my decision to go to NYU, I felt it appropriate to retaliate with as impertinent a retort as I could muster. Rumors had always abounded that Cornell was a WASP school with quotas for everyone else, although that was never substantiated. In 1967, however, anything was possible. I turned and with a straight face asked, "Is it true you only accept a maximum of 8% of your class as Jewish?" Dead silence as I walked out.

I guess the best part of going to Cornell was the sheepskin. It probably served me well as a passport into medical school, combined of course with some decent grades. I also realized that I wasn't cut out for the serene environment that the isolation of upstate New York provided. Nature is fine to photograph and scenic beauty is great in short doses.

But I can only tolerate only so much of the bucolic habitat. It's sort of ironic that the University was so big, but the area in many ways was so small. I'm not a hiker, a biker, a jogger, a fisherman or a hunter.

The student population at the time at Cornell would have numbered a small city. Living off campus and only attending fraternity parties on rare occasions, I only knew a small group of the thousands of people who populated the campus. Incredibly inspiring and original speeches were offered I think. I have no recollection of who spoke or what they said. This happened at every college graduation since people began attending colleges. I've been to hundreds of testimonial dinners and numerous graduation ceremonies. I've learned that less is more. Everyone knows why they're there. When I'm called upon to speak, three sentences or two minutes is usually sufficient in my mind. I do remember that we sat outside because the auditorium and Barton Hall, a small building that could hold two jet planes couldn't hold everyone. Onward to medical school, back to civilization in New York City.

Years later, my daughter, when thinking about going to college, considered Cornell. We visited multiple schools, including some in New England. Her academic advisors had told her to consider Cornell. I tried to remain neutral but knew that she enjoyed the city environment. Tufts was in Boston and perhaps slightly below the Ivy Leagues at that time in reputation. Cornell was still in Ithaca. With a bit of prejudicial coaxing and some comparisons, she chose Tufts. I still love visiting Boston.

I've been back to Cornell twice since I graduated in 1968, once on my way to Canada and most recently on the way to a wedding in Syracuse. Although they've added lots of new buildings, changed some of the streets in the 48 years since I left, the place looks a lot like it did. Most amazing of all is that the house I lived in for 3 years off campus is still there, essentially unchanged. Even the outside color is the same. I couldn't inspect the inside since the current residents keep the front door locked. Obviously some of the old haunts are gone, but the Arts Quad is pretty much the same, although they no longer smoke in the buildings, and the card catalog in the library is replaced with computers. The rotating altar in Anabel Taylor is still there.

CHAPTER 5

MEDICAL SCHOOL

Medical school, in contrast to Cornell, didn't want anyone to drop out. Apparently they received federal money per student and if someone left before finishing, that money was not received. Now, in contrast to day 1 at Cornell, you could look to the right and look to the left on opening day and pretty much be assured that you'd all be there in 4 years. I am aware of only two people who left and a few who transferred in. Several went on to earn not only a medical degree but also a PhD as well and stayed longer than 4.

I can't say that I'm aware of what the medical school curriculum consists of these days. I've long ago left the academic environment and have no interaction any longer with medical students. I do, however, remember some of what it was like those days. Most of the first two years was replete with useless information, memorization and marking time. There were also many, many tests.

It was an easy trip from Long Beach to Manhattan especially when compared to the trek to Cornell and moving into the dorm was easy. The first year dorm was located at 34th Street and the East River. You were assigned a roommate arbitrarily and the rooms were pretty much the same as the freshman dorms at Cornell. Two beds, two desks, a bookcase on either side and the toilets down the hall. But I wasn't at Cornell. I was in civilization.

Medical school was very different from college. Obviously everyone there had one long-term goal and had decided on their general direction. The differences were, not what we were going to become, namely physicians, but rather the specialties we were going to pursue. Many of the med students had been highly driven, competitive, cutthroat folks in college plugging along in the pre-med route and honed by adversity to become highly competitive. Some of us had escaped some of that. The group who had experienced the high-intensity competition certainly were unable to quickly shake off that experience and came loaded for bear. Most notable among the new medical students were the females who had probably experienced the hardest time getting into medical school, which was still a good old boys' network.

In spite of the fact that the faculty had told us that competition was going to be minimal if at all, and that they wanted us all to succeed, the overdrive that motivated many of us remained. Every examination became a terror-filled experience for a majority of the students, until it finally became apparent that the faculty told us the truth. They really weren't trying to flunk us out. Grades on preliminary examinations were still posted, but it was only for self-assessment. If one did poorly, remedial help was always available.

The curriculum was predefined. The big deal was anatomy lab, which was the first major initiation into the world of humans. Dead bodies were covered with white plastic sheets and you were assigned four to a cadaver. Initiation to the fraternity of medicine was performed by the purchase of the "Manual of Human Dissection" by Charles E. Tobin, which you were expected to bring with you to the lab and learn. Day One was the axilla, dissection of the armpit.

Our cadaver was female. Obviously no history, no identification, she was simply a desiccated corpse who was heavily embalmed to last for the months that we'd be "learning" her anatomy. As a surgeon, I will attest to the fact that there was absolutely no relationship between what I observed in the cadaver lab and what I came to know about the human body.

Cadavers don't bleed, don't have normal colored muscles or other organs, don't provide any tactile feedback, don't teach anything useful to medical students and are far more like rubber exhibits than people. If I didn't learn anything from my cadaver, I can't imagine what anyone going into psychiatry, pediatrics or even internal medicine could have gleaned from standing around and pushing and pulling body parts to find whatever the "Manual of Human Dissection" asked us to locate.

I guess we were still doing this because tradition required you to be hunched over an unfortunate corpse early in your career. When the time came for me to actually become competent with human anatomy, I revisited my books, observed the living surgical patients extensively in the OR, and learned what was necessary all over again. Another major point that became apparent over time was that, although structures were pretty much the same and everyone was essentially reliably the same under the skin, details of each person's anatomy were different. Branches of blood vessels, nerves, and muscles appeared differently and at different places in different people.

Yes, it smelled in the cadaver lab. It was just the pungent, penetrating odor of formaldehyde. Nowadays formaldehyde is suspected as a possible carcinogen by the EPA, so they don't use it anymore and don't expose medical students to it. Yes, we spent months with visits to our dead lady with the formaldehyde perfume. It's never been clearly established whether she really could have caused leukemia, but I'm sure it's better to err on the side of caution. I know they no longer use it.

Yes, we wore white coats and gloves to "protect" our own clothing. Clearly you didn't need to dress up to go to the lab. Or so I thought. After showing up several times without a tie, I was taken aside and told that it was necessary to come wearing a tie. I guess you never know who's going to visit you while you were hunched over a dead person who was now in multiple parts and reeked of formaldehyde.

In those days, Manhattan had an abundance of Tie City shops that sold discount ties. I chose the blue one with the red strawberries and pink flowers and wore it pretty much every day to the lab until the tip turned brown as it repeatedly dipped into my deceased lady's fat and other conglomeration of liquids that welled up as we continued our dissection. The trend spread to others in my class and we had a bright array of absurd ties displayed for the dead who were supposed to instruct us in anatomy. I guess it was our impression that certain things were more important than wearing a tie to anatomy lab.

The remainder of the curriculum was even less useful than the human dissection lab. Hours wasted learning the Kreb's Cycle and Cytochrome system, theoretical facts relating to energy transport in the cells, certainly laid the foundation for a surgical career. Looking back, it seems that medical education in those years was based on filling the first two years, the "basic sciences" years with theoretical information of little use, but founded on some ancient idea that knowing or hearing about this stuff made you a doctor. The good news is that, today, there is less filler and far more practical knowledge that needs to be imparted.

Most of the drugs and medications we were taught about have long passed into history. Memory was the key to pharmacology. The teachers all used generic drug names so it became impossible to translate the popular brand names into useful information, unless you read their labels.

Histology, I guess, was supposed to teach you to read slides and figure out what was muscle, what was cancer, what was inflammation and what was just a smudge from bad stains. Everyone was expected to purchase a microscope and use it in our classes, although, as I recall, the slides were also projected onto a screen. I guess it was a way to engender interest in those who were more science-oriented and were considering pathology. During my career as a surgeon, I spent many an hour looking through microscopes with a real pathologist telling me that those dots and pink things were or weren't cancer.

Looking back, the most amazing part of the first two years spent in medical school was how totally useless the information memorized would be in my future. I have become acquainted with the new Hofstra Northwell School of Medicine recently opened on Long Island where they're taking a totally new approach to medical education. I guess it's taken medicine 50 years to get the message, but finally the word is that teaching someone to be a doctor should rely on practical clinical experience.

Wasting years learning things that can be gotten from publications and the Internet seems to finally have been put to bed. New and current teaching in modern schools relies far more on critical thinking and clinical interaction. Medical students at Hofstra are exposed to patients in the first year, are trained as they ride ambulances, become EMT's and have much earlier personal interactions with patients. Maybe if I hadn't clogged up my head with so much useless and obsolete information in those earlier years, I'd be able to remember more today. Probably not.

In late 1969, I received greetings from my Uncle Sam. The Vietnam War was on with large numbers of injured and killed American soldiers coming home. We would see them at the Manhattan V.A. with terrible injuries from AK-47's and mines, suffering from drug abuse and PTSD. Medical students were deferred from the draft, but the draft board apparently didn't know who we were. Nor did it care what we were doing. All the physicals were performed at 39 Whitehall Street, Manhattan and a large number of the medical students were sent notices to report.

The morning I was supposed to report, I was sick with the flu. Flu shots were a thing of the future. I originally thought I'd drag myself down there and be classified 4-F but, for one thing, the flu didn't make you 4-F and, for another, I couldn't get up enough energy to get out of bed except when I was coughing, and shaking. So I stayed curled up in bed in the dorm. I really couldn't get there, so I thought I'd have another chance to go for a physical.

I took about 3 days to recover from the flu. I asked many of the guys in my medical school class what Whitehall Street was like. There is a stanza from *Alice's Restaurant* by Arlo Guthrie that best sums it up:

> "I'm here to talk about the draft. They got a buildin' down in New York City called Whitehall Street, where you Walk in, you get injected, inspected, detected, infected, neglected and Selected!... Proceeded down the hall, gettin' more injections, inspections, detections, Neglections, and all kinds of stuff that they was doin' to me at the thing There, and I was there for two hours... three hours...

four hours... I was There for a long time goin' through all kinds of mean, nasty, ugly things, And I was just havin' a tough time there, and they was inspectin', Injectin', every single part of me, and they was leavin' no part untouched!"

But the Draft Board also offered you a deal. It was called the Berry Plan. It gave doctors who were doing their residency a deferment but obligated them to serve after they had finished their specialty.

Many of my fellow medical students examined that day enrolled. But I didn't go to Whitehall Street. So I wasn't given the opportunity to enroll. Within a month of not showing up for my draft physical, I received notice that I was classified 1-A, available for military service at any time.

In December 1969, the US Selective Service created a draft lottery. Three hundred and sixty-six dates were placed in a hopper and chosen at random and 195 dates were chosen and assigned to groups who would be drafted. This first lottery was for people born between 1943 and 1950. I was born in 1946. My birthday got number 355. Since it was anticipated that only those up to number 195 would be called, there was no need for me to go any further. I remained 1-A but was never called and never needed to avoid the draft. Again, sometimes it is not so terrible being sick at the right time.

It is also sometimes too easy to make life decisions. I had been seeing Linda pretty regularly on weekends. She'd come down to NY from Albany and we'd stay together in the dorm. I had moved into a private room during my second year of medical school directly adjacent to the FDR drive on the second floor. It was almost like living on the highway. You get used to the traffic noises. They reminded me of the ocean and gently allowed me to fall asleep. The only things that would wake me up were fire trucks blasting their horns, police cars and ambulances with sirens or the rare occasion in the middle of the night when the traffic noise would stop completely for a few minutes.

I also had another diversion in my second year of medical school. Anyway, at some point in our relationship, Linda suggested that if she finished school early, we could get married. Being a hopeless romantic, I remember I said something like I guess so. We would get married on the condition that she started a job so my parents wouldn't be supporting us.

I had moved out of the dorm with the anticipation of getting married and got an apartment a few blocks away, easy walking distance to the hospitals. Apartments were, even in those days, hard to come by, especially in Manhattan, unless of course you met the super or rental agent and gave him the initiation fee, namely a month's rent for his troubles.

We were married on February 1st, 1970, a Sunday. The next day, Linda went to work and I returned to medical school to the applause of general glee of my colleagues. I was not alone in the decision to marry during medical school. Although there are no hard statistics about divorce rates, the number bandied about approaches 60% of those married in medical school end up in divorce. I ended up in the 100% segment.

Since time only goes in one direction, I can't undo what happened. I can only look back at lessons learned: Don't get married too young. Don't let infatuation dictate major decisions especially about marriage. Don't get married in medical school. Don't get married until you're mature enough to have some idea of what you're doing.

Second year of medical school dragged on until May 4, 1970, when four students were shot dead at Kent State University in Ohio. This became a rallying cry for student protests across the country. Colleges were being occupied by anti-war protestors and final exams were interrupted. On May 11, 1970, a large group of anti-war protestors marched down towards City Hall in New York City to protest. Some of the medical students felt that wearing white coats and Red Cross armbands would make them above any fray that might ensue. I never thought an elitist "I am a Doctor" attitude worked for me so I sort of dragged along in my blue jeans. I also didn't think that marching towards City Hall would end the war or make much of a difference.

One of the white-coated, longer-haired medical students noticed a red Con-Edison warning flag at a site where there was electrical work being done. Grabbing the flag, he proceeded towards City Hall in New York City, waving his red flag. Unimpressed with waving a red flag, a group of us lagged behind.

White coats didn't seem to matter much to the hard hats who were working at a building site in lower Manhattan. Waving a red flag, however, became quite noticeable by the workers who had come down from the various construction sites to render their displeasure with the gaggle of protestors.

Since we were only medical students, the ability to render aid to anyone really injured stopped with ice packs and Band-Aids®. None of the group of white-coated, Red-Cross arm-banded, red flag waving individuals did much to help the situation except to show the construction workers on Wall Street exactly which ones were the easiest to beat up. I guess the Geneva Convention regarding medics hadn't had much effect on people who actually worked.

The turmoil in the latter part of 1970 spread, causing classes and final exams to be cancelled for the duration of the semester, as they were throughout the city and in many parts of the country. This was the so-called student strike protesting the war. I didn't really think that staying out of school would end the war. The frustration with the ongoing war was palpable in those of us who were directly affected by the potential of going to war for a cause in which no one believed. The daily news reports were filled with ongoing demonstrations and violent protests, but each of us had our own very personal feelings as well as our collective opinions.

I had always been attracted to photography as a hobby and a way of escaping ever since my mother had bought me my first Brownie™ camera with the screw on flash. Now I was in the real city and there were great things to photograph. I bought myself my first real camera, a Nikkormat™. I would walk around weekends taking pictures of just about anything. I have pictures of the Twin Towers being built, of life outside of the hospital, and of my fellow students enjoying themselves in Central Park. All in black-and-white.

I also learned to print and develop my own film. I had trays to do black-and-white printing, which I printed in my galley kitchen occupying the sink for hours on end. I found a perfect outlet for my energies. I took a large portion of the pictures that were destined to be used in the 1972 NYU School of Medicine Yearbook. This gave me an excuse to walk around the hospitals with my camera. In those days, things weren't as restricted as to limitations on photographing patients, although we were still protective of patient privacy and it was tacitly understood that you didn't show faces. None appeared in the yearbook. I guess in those days privacy rights were instinctive in those of us studying to be physicians.

In the third and fourth years of medical school, everything changed. We actually went into the hospitals and saw living patients. In those days, privacy was a rather remote ideal since the wards at Bellevue built in the 1930's were pretty wide open and had only draw curtains separating the beds. Occasionally a confused patient would reach for the wrong nightstand and drink from his neighbor's urinal.

Senior residents would walk the students around and demonstrate how to examine patients. Regularly scheduled rounds were made daily with attending physicians. These were the famous "teaching rounds" when a small group of white-clad students and physicians-to-be would approach each bedside, review the history and the chief complaints of the patients, and any progress that had been made since the day before. Rounds on the medical service would last for hours, allowing the chief and senior residents who were in charge of rounds to discuss erudite and brilliant diagnostic possibilities.

Seldom did anyone actually talk directly *to* the patients. Few attendings at Bellevue bothered to interact with those in the beds except to use them to demonstrate some condition or illustrate some sort of major laboratory finding. We and occasionally some of the residents, however, looked at and actually examined them, something that has significantly changed in the current hospital "rounds" situation. Now, most rounds are conducted outside of private rooms where computer screens and lab findings serve as patient surrogates.

Rounds were always accompanied by the chart racks. These were large rolling metal structures on which would hang the patients' charts. Charts were stacks of paper clipped and supported by the vice-like grip of the enfolding metal holding the records. In other institutions, charts were notebooks, but at Bellevue, they were the alligator-jawed charts with the contents hanging vertically. Just like in the movies.

After a twenty minute discussion at the bedside, with one or two of the group drifting off and looking at their shoes, the senior resident would impart his wisdom and tell us the truth about what the real diagnosis was and throw in some major diagnostic surprises that each of us students had so clearly and obviously missed in the workup. Occasionally, senior attending physicians would accompany us on rounds. They obviously knew just about everything in medicine, wore long white coats and would give us the ability to focus on the correct answers. Sometimes they were even right.

It was on morning rounds that the daily fate of the patients would be decided. At each bedside, a scut list would be generated, dictating what blood tests and other tests would be ordered during the day to help determine the nature of the patient's malady and allow his cure to progress. Most of the tests were blood tests, sometimes x-rays and occasionally consultations by outside services like cardiology, gastroenterology, pulmonary, infectious diseases or our favorite, psychiatry.

It was from the rotations through the various specialties that you would decide which direction in medicine you were going to go for your residency. But you had to rotate through all of them before choosing. You know, like being forced to taste everything on the menu before you could know that you hated meatloaf.

I started my medical rotation at Bellevue with the unfortunate Mr. L. He had huge veins and the first task was to draw blood from him. Third-year students can't get water from a garden hose, let alone draw blood. So it was my daily chore to apply the tourniquet and apologize to the poor Mr. L when I, covered in sweat, had to stick him more than once. He didn't seem to mind or complain, but maybe the strategy was to stick him enough times so that he'd recover and go home. I think he had pneumonia.

Bellevue patients were often homeless, sicker than the average patient, and often suffered with multiple medical problems. Many of them also had lice, were unwashed and some were also psychotic. Most were charity patients, but we actually did our best to care for and about them. Never was the word "insurance" mentioned regarding any patient. Sometimes discharging them, sending them home was a stretch since some of them had come from the street and would be returning there. Upon discharge, the patients were given a clinic appointment where supposedly they would receive ongoing medical care. A few of them actually did.

From these patients you were to learn how to take a medical history, learn differential diagnosis, and learn physical examination. You could practice these skills and learn how to listen to heart sounds using prerecorded tapes. One obese Hispanic female had been admitted for pneumonia. I listened to her lungs and heard nothing particularly extraordinary, but on listening to her heart I heard a faint but clear murmur. I reported it to my resident/boss who told me I was hearing things. The attending reconfirmed the resident's opinion that there was no murmur. But since I continued to hear it, all agreed we would settle the issue and prove me wrong with an echocardiogram.

Of course, everyone heard the murmur when it turned out that the patient had mitral stenosis, a serious heart condition where one of the valves in the heart is stiff and small, eventually causing heart failure. The findings were so classic that she was sent for cardiac catheterization and subsequent open-heart surgery. She survived and went home.

It is sometimes quite easy to decide which specialty pathway one wants to pursue. Sometimes it even becomes obvious. In medicine, if you're satisfied to ponder, postulate, consider all options, mention all pathways, you go into internal medicine or a related field. If you're a first-born who insists on the immediate gratification and solution to a problem, you head towards surgery. At least that's the way it used to be. Now, with new subspecialties, with interventional cardiology, endoscopic gastroenterology, Emergency Room doctors, and other doers, the lines of the thinkers and the "do-ers" have become blurred. A multitude of "medical" subspecialties has evolved into actually performing procedures and seeing reasonably quick results.

Most ironic is the fact that sometimes the "do-ers" can't fix what they have done. The gastroenterologist who performs a colonoscopy on rare occasion (thankfully) perforates the colon and must call the surgeon. The ER physician who puts a chest tube in and encounters positioning problems causes bleeding and needs help calls the surgeon to fix the problem. The interventional radiologist, who has problems with the angiogram, can usually stop before disaster strikes, but in the event of major blood vessel problems, is on the phone to the surgical backup. So today, as in my day, when a "do-er" sometimes encounters a disaster and cannot undo it, he calls the surgeon to rescue him.

I did my pediatrics rotation. I find kids a bit difficult and don't deal well with really sick kids. I did Ob/Gyn and was actually thinking of that as a possible future until abortions became legal and very popular. On January 22, 1973, the Supreme Court ruled that abortions were legal. Immediately following that decision, the back-alley and self-induced abortions causing terrible deaths and destruction to desperate women ceased. I felt that abortion would be the next biggest part of an OB/Gyn practice and I just didn't want to embark on a practice that depended on abortions to make a living and turned away from that.

My worst rotation was psychiatry. In those days, psych consisted of going into the wards at Bellevue and listening to the group therapy sessions of patients who were hard-core psychotics, often long-term addicts, usually on locked wards. It was my last rotation. It was hot, confining and terribly boring. Again, as a first-born and eventual surgeon I was interested in the quick fix, the successful outcome. I still am. In addition most of the patients were on Thorazine® or Stelazine®, and walked around heavily sedated or zombie-like. Words would come out in slow dribble, making little or no sense. At the end of this rotation, I was off to a cross-country delayed honeymoon. Needless to say, the psychiatry rotation was interminable. I wasn't going to be a psychiatrist, but more likely would need one if I were to survive Bellevue psych.

I did my best to sit and endure these sessions in psych. As had happened several years before at Cornell in my chemistry lab, my professor advised me that my attendance was somewhat scanty and that continued absences might cause me to be required to repeat the experiences. Once again a private discussion between me and Dr. A. resolved the matter successfully—and this time without threats. I'd do my best. So would he. I suggested that he could analyze my reluctance to attend and spend hours listening to things I couldn't stand. He could get his head around my lack of motivation. All I needed was a passing grade and I could go off on my honeymoon. I passed. Off I went.

Fourth year of medical school was really more of a group of electives to allow you to choose more clearly what discipline you would choose. I was a surgical "sub-intern" and worked as much and as hard as I could to prove myself to the powers that be that I was suitable to be chosen for the surgical program at NYU. At that time it was considered one of the best in the Northeast and probably in the country. Besides, I wanted to stay in New York.

Match day for residencies was in April. Match day was when medical students were informed where they would be attending in the following year (actually beginning in July) to subspecialize in their chosen fields of medicine. This was different from college acceptance which is a much more fluid and ongoing process. Match day happens all at once on a designated date in April. Applications are sent to a clearinghouse by medical students and separated based on sub-specialty rotations. The student designates the particular program he would like to be placed into in order of preference. The programs designate whom they want. Thus they match. I think it's still done that way, except far more efficiently I'm sure.

I was very confident that I would be staying at NYU and that's what happened. Several of my fellow NYU graduates would be staying, some in surgery, others in other specialties. I knew what it was going to be like as a surgical resident. I was delighted.

Sometimes the match didn't work out well. I applied to places in New York City with no plans to go out of state. The match is supposed to be an untainted process with no inside information provided, but of course that's in an ideal world and actually makes little sense. If they want you and you want them, what's the big deal if they let you know? They made a big fetish about non-committal and secrecy but I was very confident about where I'd end up.

Clearly Murphy's Law can kick in and there are sometimes unhappy campers who are headed for Cincinnati when they thought they'd be in Virginia. None of the matches are irrevocable and sometimes some folk don't even match. So they have to struggle to revisit their choices, or find sites that they want. Obviously sometimes the medical students realize they've chosen the wrong specialty so the match is simply a beginning of the next phase of the career path.

The other consideration for the future was the pyramid, the winnowing down from a large group of junior residents to a small number of Chief Residents. In those days, competition was fierce in surgical residencies. NYU/Bellevue was notorious. It was, however, far too soon to begin worrying about five years or so in the future, I was happy to be staying there. Come July 1, 1972, I was going to be called "doctor".

CHAPTER 6
RESIDENCY IN SURGERY

Before you could practice surgery, it was necessary to complete a residency and serve as a chief resident. This was a minimum of 5 years of training, graduating from what was an internship in the old days through each subsequent year of training. Internships had become obsolete since in the past they usually meant rotating through a series of specialties. Now the surgical intern was really PGY-1 (Post graduate year 1) and subsequent years numbered PGY-2 through 5, PGY-5 year traditionally the Chief Residency. Realistically, it is essential that the surgeon-in-training receive the broadest experience with the widest variety of surgical cases and learn about patient care. Neurosurgeons needed to complete at least PGY-7 and beyond. Cardiac training was 2 years additional after Chief Residency. Residency was a good name for the training since you literally lived at the hospital and put your real life aside.

July 3, 1972. The most dangerous time to be in a teaching hospital, a hospital with residents and medical students, is at the beginning of July. That's when the new medical school graduates become doctors. A month before they were called students, this month they're doctors. Unlike rookies in many other professions, there are no indications as to who knew what or for how long. *I always remind people that the person who placed last in the medical school class is still called "doctor".*

I started on the tumor service at Bellevue. This was located on the top floor of the old hospital, no air conditioning, built as a WPA project in the late 1920's. It was the time of open wards with high ceilings to circulate air. The patients were mostly uninsured, charity patients. All patients on the first day of the new rotations were postoperative because previous residents realized as July approaches, they wanted to get as much experience as they could, performing all the surgery they could squeeze in during the last months. In addition, few if any pre-operative patients would be admitted because that would leave loose ends and would require some extra work. Most of the patients remaining on the ward had undergone major surgical procedures, generally with breast or neck cancers, many with infections. It was hot as hell, and in spite of the high ceilings, and open windows, no air circulated.

Our surgical on call schedule was every other night on call. It's almost hard to believe, but it was the way surgery was taught. In at 6:30 a.m. on Monday, home by 8p.m. on Tuesday; in 6:30 a.m. Wednesday home by 8 p.m. Thursday evening; in on Friday 6:30, home Friday night by 7 p.m. usually. In on Saturday 7:30 a.m., work all day, all night Saturday and Sunday and Monday until around 6 p.m. Back on Tuesday 6:30, home Wednesday at 8p.m., in Thursday 6:30 a.m. home Friday 7 p.m. back only for rounds on Saturday around 7:30 and home Saturday afternoon by around noon. Then back on Monday morning again.

This call schedule was brutal and you essentially lived and worked at the hospital. You would catch naps when you could, sleep in fits and starts and were assigned a small shared dorm room in the hospital administration building built in 1930's with a small window that faced a courtyard so it was totally without any ventilation. You would head up to the room and stretch out naked on the bed after taking a quick shower and fall dead asleep, only to be awakened by a hospital operator telling you to call someone about an emergency admission or that one of the patients was having a crisis, a high fever or needed their sleep medication renewed.

It was in my first year that I met Anne. She was a new graduate nurse and was working in the Recovery Room at Bellevue. She was a pretty, enthusiastic young nurse with an ultimate Irish face. She was born and bred in the Bronx with a very distinctive Bronx accent. Needless to say, I found it quite entertaining to imitate her. I was married and at the time was content with that situation, so I was not among those residents who needed to fool around. That didn't mean that I couldn't become friendly with the nurses because it was clear to me that my fate would soon intertwine with the care the nurses would offer the patients.

So it was Anne, Roberta, and Mercedes during the day and Leah, Josephine, and Angie at night in the Recovery Room and Susan, Christine, and Laurie in the Emergency Ward to name just a few. We were colleagues and friends. We looked out for each other at work and socialized when we had a few minutes off. Linda, my wife, was home but would come to the hospital occasionally and knew most of my friends. I would admit that my nurse friends probably contributed to Linda's insecurities and certainly didn't help my marriage, although I can say that I never strayed. Maybe I was just too tired?

Malcolm Gladwell says that one needs 10,000 hours of experience to become proficient at anything, although I didn't know it at the time. All of the residents who were going into surgery wanted to experience and learn as much as we could. I think it was the spirit of the time, the pressure from peers and the motivation for success that kept us going. Most of the residents who were destined to become surgeons objected to the schedule because when we left, we'd miss half the cases. You only had so much time to learn everything you needed to learn.

NYU had what was affectionately referred to as a "pyramid program" in surgery. Forty interns were whittled down to eight chief residents. You would not be eligible to practice surgery unless you completed a chief residency. A surgical residency in those days was 5 years. We still referred to the first year as an internship; however, it was concentrated essentially in surgery.

Some of the 40 interns were only staying for a year or two and then heading for subspecialties like orthopedics or urology. Some were planning only a few years and then heading for plastic surgery. The rest of us were hoping for careers in surgery and hoping to become chief residents. So it was like Day One at Cornell. Look to the left and the right: One or even two of you won't be here in four years (or in this case five).

Frank Spencer, M.D. was the recently hired Chief of Surgery. He had arrived at NYU to run the program several years earlier and was intent on creating the best surgical training program in the country. He was a cardiac surgeon, a brilliant educator, demanding excellence and setting a striking example of discipline and dignity. If we survived the residency, we would become outstanding surgeons. The program he created at NYU was one of the major incubators for future surgeons, some of whom would go on to greatness across the country as program directors themselves. Most of his trainees, myself certainly included, retain a warm regard and enormous respect for Dr. Spencer.

He had honed his surgical and educational brilliance while serving in Korea.

The American College of Surgeons in one of their publications said the following of him:

Dr. Spencer's residency training was put on hold by his service in the U.S. Navy during the Korean Conflict. During his two years of service to the U.S. Navy Medical Corps, Dr. Spencer's knowledge of artery repair led him to request permission from the Navy to attempt repair of injured blood vessels in the legs. The practice Dr. Spencer suggested was in strict contrast to the course of treatment at that time (arterial ligation of the injured vessel), which often resulted in gangrene and amputation. In spite of a denial of his request to change treatment protocol, he took the initiative with performing the repairs anyway, which resulted in Dr. Spencer facing court martial. However, with more than 150 repairs being performed and an 80 to 90 percent success rate, Dr. Spencer was not court martialed, but awarded the Navy's Legion of Merit Award for exemplary service. Of his recognition, Dr. Spencer said, "...arterial repair in Korea benefited more people than anything I've ever done."[1] He returned to his surgical training at Johns Hopkins in 1953, completing his residency in 1955.

I was certainly enthusiastic and energetic, in spite of not fully knowing exactly what was in store. Dr. Spencer had interacted with us while we were medical students. He would meet the incoming students who were rotating on the Surgical Service and had made it a point to memorize every rotating student's name. He would go down the roll call on Day One calling each of us by name. It was the same with the interns. He knew our names and where we had been students. He immediately made us part of the team, incorporating us into the Surgical Service.

Dr. Spencer would round with the Bellevue services every Saturday morning. Originally there were three surgical services at Bellevue so it was every third week. Rounds with Dr. Spencer became the ultimate show-and-tell where the patients were carefully picked based on difficulty of diagnosis or triumph of surgical treatment. He would interact with everyone on the team.

Because of his military background, Dr. Spencer believed in the hierarchy of responsibility for each member of the surgical team. The Chief Resident was the obvious captain of the team, responsible for the overall performance of every other member. At each level of the team from intern on up, there existed certain expectations of performance. The intern was expected to work up and write up the admission of the patient. He was expected to call for help and would only be criticized if he failed to do it. The senior residents were the supervisors and teachers and the Chief Resident would be expected to interact with the attending surgeons when necessary and report to them all the surgery being contemplated.

All you did as the intern was eat when you could, sleep when you could, go to the operating room, see new admissions and do the "scut" work, that is, drawing bloods (I got better at it after my first experiences as a student), scheduling x-rays, obtaining consent for surgery, getting the patients ready for the operating room, and being sure the lab work was available. You would also be a messenger, wheeling patients for tests, bringing blood samples to the lab and sometimes wheeling your own patients to the operating room.

As an intern you would rotate through the various hospitals and various services, and do a month on Dr. Spencer's cardiac service. I had no interest in becoming a heart surgeon. An intern would be expected to spend countless hours in the operating room assisting at open-heart surgery. Pre-rounds would start at 5:30 a.m. for the interns and the fellows. The intern got to carry the "numbers book" where the current information regarding the patients' lab values were entered before rounds so that when real rounds began at 6:30 A.M., when all the latest values were available.

When you scrubbed into an open-heart case as the intern, you had a two-fold mission. You would be expected to help "harvest the vein." This would involve making a long cut in the patient's thigh and removing intact the greater saphenous vein, carefully tying off all the branches because this vein would be used to bypass the clogged arteries in the heart. Once this was accomplished, Dr. Spencer would usually appear and provide you with a white glove with which to hold the non-beating heart so that a bypass could be attached to arteries that were either below or behind the heart in an area that was less accessible unless someone provided traction.

I discovered that holding the heart was endless and would cause your hands to cramp, so that if you could get out the vein before Dr. Spencer would appear, you could occasionally escape. I got quite good and quite fast at getting out the vein.

It didn't take me very long to get into controversy during my internship. One of the least favorite rotations for the intern was the "Head Trauma" service. Before CT scans, before MRI's, the only way to assess patients who had fallen was by "skull films" (x-rays of the head), and repeated neurological exams. An intoxicated lady had fallen down a flight of stairs and was brought to Bellevue by her husband. Clearly, she was in extremis with no neurological activity. I had just finished a rotation at the Manhattan V.A. where I had watched a very early kidney transplantation. This patient would be a perfect opportunity to obtain a kidney donation, although the appropriate protocols for declaring brain death were not fully in place in those days.

I spoke to the husband and asked if he was willing to donate his wife's organs. He agreed that it would be appropriate. I spent countless hours calling for guidelines, assistance and eventually obtaining the appropriate information to allow organ donation. There was only one doctor at NYU who was involved with the transplant service, still in its infancy. I finally reached him after numerous attempts through the switchboard, pager and direct calls. He was somewhat interested but didn't have the ability or time or inclination to perform organ removal. Obviously stubborn, since I had spent so much time convincing the husband to donate his wife's organs, I wasn't about to let this go by the wayside without a fight. I called everyone I could think of, finally getting to Dr. Spencer. He made a few phone calls (I think) and reached a transplant team at Downstate Medical Center rather than a team at NYU where organ transplantation was being done more regularly. The team from Downstate harvested the organs, using Bellevue's operating room.

The following week I heard from the doctor supposedly in charge of the new NYU transplant service. He was very disturbed by the way things had transpired and angry with me. I figured I was already in trouble. I was summoned to the surgery office where I thought I had overstepped the attendings in pushing for the organ transplant, but felt I was justified in making numerous phone calls. Dr. Spencer agreed. I was safe. He indicated what the new protocols, guidelines and supervision would be. He also indicated that he would discuss things and change the service, and eventually change the physician in charge. I'm sure he did since I never heard from or about the transplant surgeon in charge again.

Internship (PGY-1) blended into residency. PGY years are sort of a blur although obviously I can recall incidents and events. Looking back, lots of cases, unique patients and events come to mind. I can't recall all the details but some of the patients will always remain in my memory:

- The young man who decided to torch his pizza shop in Brooklyn, on New Year's Eve during the oil crisis of 1974. He got himself soaked with gasoline and sustained massive burns. At the time Bellevue received the burn patients and we were notified of the transfer. The ambulance ran out of gas en route and it took 6 hours to get him to us. He died several weeks later of sepsis.

- The gang member whose nipples had been blowtorched by rival gang members who had an anoxic episode during routine plastic surgery and was brain dead. Clearly an anesthesia mishap, the anoxic brain death was still a surgical mishap. Dr. Spencer wheeled the patient into the Morbidity and Mortality conference, on a respirator, to bring home that the surgeon was captain of the ship and responsible for whatever happened.

- The street prostitute who had been stabbed multiple times and required a colostomy to repair her colon. She began plying her trade on the ward, using the new orifice we had created.

- The 15-year-old anorexic patient who, in spite of every attempt at feeding, slowly faded away and eventually starved before our eyes. None of us could understand how she was able to starve herself to death in spite of tube feedings and all attempts at nutritional support.

- The Bowery patient who had weeping leg ulcers, an unwashed denizen of the streets admitted for infection, crawling with maggots, who was sitting in an ancient wooden wheelchair and produced a large amount of sputum which he shared with one of the residents. When the resident pushed him, the patient fell on his face, crashing to the floor. The resident was fired. Patients were patients. Aggressive patients were not unusual but as a doctor it was totally inappropriate to respond to aggression with aggression. Although sometimes obviously difficult to restrain yourself, it was essential to use alternative methods to defend yourself, even if you just walked away. You didn't hit patients. You didn't push patients. You didn't knowingly hurt patients.

- The aggressive Hispanic who had been shot but was awake and alert on being rushed to the trauma slot in the Emergency Room. Resisting and fighting, we pointed out a large hole in his right side gushing blood. "Cheet, I'm chot" was his comment before he lost consciousness.

- The young lady travelling as a passenger down the FDR drive who was the victim of a young man who threw a Belgian block from an overpass crashing through the window of the car and hitting her in the abdomen. Ghostly white from blood loss, her last words were "I don't want to die", but she had her liver torn out by the stone and could not be saved.

- The child molester in the prison ward who had been in traction for multiple fractures who each day was assaulted by the other prisoners who knew what his crime was. They would twist his legs and remove the splints in spite of his crying out each time. This required the residents to replace him in traction until he was finally placed in isolation.

- The transgender patient who was in the midst of being transformed from male to female, whose breast implant had migrated into the middle of his/her abdomen. In those days, the large open wards were separated by gender, and it was actually unclear where this person actually belonged but each ward had isolation rooms so since she had expressed a preference to female, we put her with the ladies, but isolated because the hospital gowns often exposed the determining organs.

- The former minor league baseball player who had undergone extensive head and neck surgery for throat cancer secondary to heavy smoking and chewing tobacco. One early afternoon his carotid artery, which had been under neck flaps that were infected and eroding cut loose in the isolation room, the blood hitting the walls.

- The 22-year-old pretty redhead whose melanoma had invaded her spine causing paraplegia, who finally died in agony of the incurable disease. Obviously she imprinted quite significantly on all of us who were just slightly older than she was and had a hard time handling her death. In those days, PTSD and debriefing was a concept far in the future. You just went on.

- Vega, the young man who had been shot while in Lincoln Hospital, in the Bronx, in police custody for gang activity. He was transferred to Bellevue for protection and further care. He required hyperalimentation, specialized nourishment via vein that hadn't yet been standardized. Each morning I went to the prison ward and mixed up "Vega Juice" to give him sufficient nourishment for the day. Now hyperalimentation is created under sterile conditions under special vacuum hoods in the pharmacy. In those days, it was one bottle into another with an injection of foul smelling, yellow vitamins.

- The bank robber and militant Black Panther H. Rap Brown transferred into the Bellevue prison ward for security and felt it necessary to ask if I knew who he was. He was a scary, angry patient. He remained heavily guarded at all times in an isolation cell and I never went into his cell alone. We did little for him, since he had already undergone emergency surgery. The experience with someone as notorious and clearly threatening was a very early dose for me of another world that I had not experienced before.

- The Chinese gentleman who worked as a cook who had come to this country without papers and was working 12 hours a day when he spilled hot oil on his lower legs, sustaining second and third degree burns. He was brought to Bellevue for treatment and he was assigned to our care. Each day we would change his dressings, send him for whirlpool treatment and eventually give him skin grafts. We also taught him some English. When we discharged him, he thanked me and told me he'd never forget what we had done for him. He said if he ever got back to China he'd send me something. OK. 5 months after he was discharged, a world of patients later, I got an envelope addressed to me at Bellevue. In a hand printed card, he thanked me and enclosed a silk weaving which he wrote to me was a depiction of the Forbidden City in Peking. I framed it and have it to this day.

- The "prince" of the gypsies who lived on the lower east side. He had been stabbed and rushed to Bellevue accompanied by a contingent of hundreds. His father, the "king" had approached the chief resident who was taking him to surgery with the admonition "he die, you die!" Our chief resident at the time was a wiry, aggressive surgeon who had been born in Africa. He'd seen worse and wasn't one to fear very much. Screaming at the father, he indicated his displeasure and readily informed him that his threat was of absolutely no consequence. He told him that he would always do his best IN SPITE of the father. The young man survived, probably only to be stabbed or stab someone another day.

I became the prison doctor and would take a monthly trip to Riker's Island, the New York City massive correctional facility. It was quite the experience, with constant noise and motion, but the inmates would line up to show you potential surgical problems so they could get to Bellevue and then after surgery possibly be released early because of the pain and suffering attendant with an operation. Rikers generated many, many patients.

As the prison doctor, I would make rounds alone on the prison ward. The Bellevue prison ward was a large open ward shaped like a large "T". In the front were the more acute patients; in the back, the ones recovering or less acute. One night I was called and responded because someone in the back had used the sheets to hang himself. Clearly, all of the other patients back there had seen what was happening but had not interfered. Asked what they should do about this person who was quite blue, I suggested cutting him down.

Thursday afternoons at 4 p.m. was M & M, Surgical Morbidity and Mortality Conference. The residents, usually the chief resident, would write up complications and deaths that had occurred the previous week in all of the different hospitals. We rotated through Bellevue, New York University Hospital, and the Manhattan V.A. In each facility, residents would participate in surgery to varied degrees. Patient care, pre-op and post-op was also obvious part of the responsibilities. If a patient had a complication or died, you would be expected to report the event with facts at M & M. Usually the chief resident on the service would be expected to discuss the case.

M & M created incredible trepidation and fear in the residents. You would stand before attending surgeons, other residents, medical students, nurses, and, worst of all, Dr. Spencer and be expected to explain what happened. "What would you do differently? Why didn't you just take a gun and shoot the patient? What did you learn? What did you have against this patient that you failed to pay attention to his pulmonary status? When you're hunting bear, you have to be ready when you find a bear. This is a yellow wolverine, you'd better stay away from yellow wolverines." These were some of the comments often heard at conference.

The chief resident was usually considered the captain of the ship, as was the attending surgeon in the operating room. He or she was five years into training, preparing to finish that June, take the surgical boards and consider going into practice or into a surgical sub-specialty like cardiac surgery. Dr. Spencer expected anyone presenting at M&M to be aware of the case, to come prepared with answers and have appropriate explanations. M&M in the early days was so intense that as the reputation of Thursday afternoons spread, candidates for surgical residencies would avoid applying for residencies at NYU. Over time, M&M became tamer but also became more universal, spreading to other medical disciplines and becoming one of the major hallmarks of quality assurance practices. As an intern, you generally didn't have to worry about being hauled before the group and cross-examined.

During my internship and early residency, I lived in a one-bedroom apartment two blocks from the hospital. It was convenient, but small. After a renewal of my lease, we were entitled to a paint job. I pushed all the furniture into the middle of the room and realized that it would be quite simple to move someplace larger. I also relished the idea of escaping from the hospital occasionally. I found a full 3-bedroom house in Queens with rent that was the same as I was paying in Manhattan. Since I was coming in by 6:30 a.m., traffic at that time wasn't a problem. My wife and I moved to a house. We even bought a dog.

Furniture was never a problem, because my father had warehouses filled with used furniture from hotels. His truck men would fill the house as needed and exchange anything I wanted whenever I wanted it. Sometimes my father would call me and tell me that he had bought a unique item at some hotel and that I should go and look at it. To this day, I still have a huge antique server that lived for years in the kitchen of the St. Moritz Hotel. I sometimes miss the luxury of being able to change furniture as often as seasons change.

I was still on call every other night, but I could get in early and usually go home fairly late, after traffic. I drove the Long Island Expressway day and night. Once in a rare while, I would barely make it home, being overcome with sleepiness from the grueling schedule. Generally, I would catch a nap if that were the case and would commute after the traffic left. I lived in Queens, no longer walking distance to the hospital. The trade-off of convenience for lifestyle was worth it to me.

Even doctors get sick occasionally. I found my feet swollen and painful and needed to round using a cane. I had fasciitis because of the long hours standing and walking. Dr. Spencer saw me hobbling around and actually said I should go home and take a day off. One whole day. I grabbed one of my friends who was headed for orthopedics residency and he got a hold of an ortho resident who said with an injection into my feet of lidocaine, to numb the pain, and steroids, I'd get better quickly. I got injected, but I was still hobbling around for a week.

Training and studying and operating and being married and sleeping became my life, not necessarily in that order. As you progressed from year to year, you performed more surgical procedures, got increased responsibility for patient care, and supervised junior people. PGY-4 year was a special time. There were two major "services" at University Hospital. A "service" was a group of attending surgeons organized loosely by either specialty or choice who would be serviced by a designated group of residents. Each of the two "services" were named for one of the two designated senior attendings, namely Dr. Localio and Dr. Slattery. They were the busiest surgeons at the time, although Dr. Localio had the larger practice. The Slattery service had more surgeons assigned to make up the difference in case load. It was expected that the attending who was performing the surgery would mentor the resident who scrubbed, assisted or was allowed to actively participate in the surgery on the patient.

The residents would change every month or two but as a PGY-4, you would spend six months working on one of the two "services", and have the opportunity to scrub on any of the cases performed by Dr. Localio or Dr. Slattery or any other attending surgeon who was assigned to the particular group of designated surgeons. You would be chosen to be on the "Localio" service or the "Slattery" service and spend six months there.

The Localio service was considered the prime service. Dr. Localio was a short, somewhat round attending who was known throughout the Northeast and performed three major surgeries twice a week. His practice included colon resections, stomach resections, gallbladder surgery and other general abdominal surgery. One of his more common surgeries was removal of a portion of the stomach to cure ulcers. Another surgery was removal of cancer from the most distant part near the rectum that often required a colostomy, a diversion of the colon onto the abdomen. He had invented an operation to try to avoid this, the abdominal sacral resection. Patients would flock to NYU to have the opportunity to possibly avoid a permanent colostomy after the dreaded diagnosis of rectal cancer.

The only problem with the abdominal sacral surgery was that many of the cases would get infected. In addition, a temporary colostomy was also performed at the time of the abdominal sacral procedure. The patient had to go back into surgery for another operation to close the colostomy. Once the area got infected, the tissues were in jeopardy anyway. This operation has been supplanted by effective and more precise stapling techniques. The removal of the stomach for ulcers has been supplanted by medication. Stomach surgery for ulcers, complicated and fraught with post-operative side effects, has been effectively eliminated with medication. Both of these surgeries are obsolete today.

Dr. Localio's service was quite intense. On Localio's service, you watched and performed very little. He was the master and would instruct you while he performed the surgery. He showed you how he did it. Only after several months did you earn the privilege of doing any sort of surgery. I wasn't chosen to be on his service.

Dr. Slattery ran the other service. He was a charming southern gentleman. Tall, with long fingers, he was quite different from Localio. He taught you technique, speed in the operating room and how to accelerate the procedure to avoid lengthy anesthesia time. He would say, if you take too long, you'll never get home to see your grandchildren. He would often finish his surgery in the early afternoons and retreat to his private box at a local racetrack. He let you participate and perform more of the surgery. He gave you confidence while teaching you. He stood by and let you do procedures once he was confident you could accomplish what was needed. I was delighted to be on his service.

Both services, after six months of mentoring, trained skilled and highly competent surgeons. The major difference was that, as in most other activities, there were two was of achieving the results. Both services provided vast clinical and surgical experience. When the year ended, you were a well-trained but new surgeon. The following year (PGY-5) was the Chief Residency.

In our fourth year of residency, we rotated to Booth Memorial Hospital, a facility affiliated with our residency and located in Queens. This was great for me, living in Queens. Dr. Jameson Chassin oversaw the teaching at Booth. He was a superb surgeon, excellent teacher, and true gentleman. He also taught you how to use surgical staplers with which to perform complicate bowel surgery and repairs.

Staplers had actually been brought to America after World War II and developed in the USSR to allow technicians to perform complicated bowel surgery and repairs when so many Russian surgeons had been killed in the war. The staplers invented in Russia were actually hand-loaded devices that could be used by Operating Room technicians to perform high-tech bowel surgery with some success. It was rumored that they had been smuggled out of Russia by an American entrepreneur and a surgeon.

The surgical attendings at NYU and most other academic programs were originally skeptical of staples, stressing the need to learn suturing techniques in complicated procedures. Dr. Chassin could sew as well as anyone, but also embraced the new staplers. He taught those of us fortunate enough to work with him how to use them, dissemble them and load them. I was delighted to spend time with him. Dr. Slattery had also incorporated stapling as part of his skills.

Ironically, without stapling techniques, advanced laparoscopic surgery being done everywhere today would not be possible. The staplers allow the bowel to be reconnected internally without large cuts. No one in the 1970's could foresee this, or even thought surgery could be done without opening the abdomen with a large incision, but the staplers saved time. Once you mastered the stapling techniques, you could perform the same surgery as could be performed with sewing in much less time. Stapling was reliable, but as with any technology, a learning process accompanied the techniques. We learned the skills at Booth with Dr. Chassin.

My Bellevue training years in the 1970s occurred at a tumultuous time in New York. Vietnam was a primary concern with the city and the country. The anti-war movement gave rise to numerous other social tensions. My own involvement was limited by my extensive work schedule, although there was absolutely no possible way to remain apart from everything that was going on.

During the 1970's the anti-war, anti-establishment demonstrations across the city and the country had created an adversarial relationship between the young people and the police. To make matters worse, the Black Liberation Army—a radical group—had declared war on police officers. On January 27, 1972, the BLA ambushed Rocco Laurie and Gregory Foster, two police officers who had previously served together in Vietnam, on Avenue B and 11th Street in Manhattan, about half a mile from Bellevue. Both were rushed to Bellevue, Foster had been shot in the head and was pronounced dead. Laurie had some trace vital signs and was taken immediately to surgery. I was a fourth-year medical student, and an aspiring surgical resident, and I vividly remember the scene with cops everywhere. I took trips to the blood bank to bring up units to be transfused during surgery. Rocco Laurie died in surgery.

Bellevue was a designated outside post for officers in the 13th Precinct, which was only a few blocks away. Burt Morris was our in-house cop. As my residency progressed, I became friendly with officers who would be in Bellevue with prisoners in tow. Officers injured in the line of duty knew that Bellevue would offer top notch and expedited care, so they would head there from all parts of the city. I saw in the officers young people like myself who were doing the best they could, but were facing mortal danger. I never felt animosity nor could I be hostile to the folks who protected us and allowed us to function and get to work safely. Besides, who would you rather party with? Cops or doctors?

So the officers were welcome whenever I was around. It got to the point at the end of my chief residency after recovering from hepatitis, that I would hang out with them when they were at Bellevue. We'd go across the street for coffee and they'd get a radio call about a shooting. "Wanna go to the scene, doc?"

At the end of my residency, the police officers who frequented Bellevue and some of the other officers I had already befriended told me of a job called police surgeon. "Doc, you'd be perfect for that job." I had no idea what a police surgeon did, thinking that perhaps it was a position that paid you to operate on officers. I found out that the police surgeon was the supervisor of sick leave for the officers and that the surgeon's office was run out of the Police Academy. I was finishing my residency in June, and the Police Academy was down the block from Bellevue.

I discovered that the Chief Surgeon for the NYPD was Clarence Robinson, M.D. He was a soft-spoken internist who was glad to speak to me, especially because I came with references from the 13th Precinct, which was attached to the Police Academy. I told him of my interest and involvement with the local police, and inquired about a position. This was 1977. Abe Beame was Mayor and there was a hiring freeze. More importantly, cops had actually been hired and laid off. Dr. Robinson said he was interested in me, that he would keep my C.V. but that I had to be Board Certified in Surgery before he could hire me. He told me to come back when I got my boards.

CHAPTER 7

HEPATITIS: I NEARLY DIE

In August 1976, I was Chief Resident at NYU/Bellevue. I was on call for the trauma service and was both a skilled and a well-trained surgeon. I had pretty much put in my 10,000 hours of learning (as per Malcolm Gladwell) although I hadn't yet finished 10,000 hours of surgical training. A patient with a point-blank shotgun blast to his upper chest was rushed into the Emergency Room, bleeding to death.

The only possible way to save him was to open his chest. I had performed this sufficient number of times to be comfortable with this radical procedure. This was performed using a Lebsche sternum chisel which is about 10 inches long, has a thick handle and in conjunction with a steel mallet allows the surgeon to split the sternum from top to bottom with a few hammer blows. This opens the chest in the middle like 2 shutters on a window when the ribs are spread. Both lungs are on either side and the heart sits right in the middle, easily accessible. This is the best exposure for the heart, the great vessels and allows the most access.

Opening the chest, splitting the breastbone is the most exciting thing that ever happens in the Emergency Room. An open chest is a legendary procedure and seldom actually saves a life, but occasionally does. If an Emergency Room physician did this, he'd be standing there with limited skills to repair whatever he found, so it's pretty much the surgeon who does this. If by some miracle the patient survives, he must go directly to the operating room to finish and repair both the damage for which the chest was opened and the damage done by opening the chest. It's a maneuver that requires the trauma surgeon to have lots of experience before embarking on this. As Dr. Spencer used to say, when you're hunting bears, be sure you know what to do when you find one.

On splitting his sternum, it was apparent that he hadn't sustained a heart wound but rather had sustained an injury to his subclavian artery, a highly lethal injury. (According to the published death certificate of John Lennon, this is the same injury that killed him.) The subclavian artery is a large finger sized blood vessel hidden under the collarbone. We put pressure on the injury, took the patient directly to the operating room on the eighth floor of Bellevue and saved him.

Everyone wants a piece of the action when you open a chest. Everyone flocks to see what's going on. Sure enough, one of the junior residents, in his overly enthusiastic need to be a part of the scene, had pushed my gloved hand into a jagged edge of the patient's sternum and both the glove and my hand got cut. In those days, hepatitis B was part of the job and there wasn't much you could do about it and although at the time we didn't know that the patient had hepatitis, the risk was always present. Six out of eight chief residents had gotten it. In those days there was no vaccine.

Towards the end of October, on a Wednesday, I got sick. I felt like I had a very bad flu, but this time it was the worst I'd ever had. I couldn't move. Everything hurt. I was throwing up, experiencing diarrhea, and ran a 106-degree temperature. I had completely forgotten about the exposure the previous August. I took cold-water baths to bring down the fever and dragged myself into my internist friend Dr. Weiss's office on Friday, thinking I perhaps had severe gastroenteritis or a bad flu or something else pretty awful. He drew a battery of blood tests, made the tentative diagnosis of gastroenteritis and sent me home.

Continuing to throw up, I became progressively dehydrated. I called my close friend Dr. Sharon Drager, a co-chief resident and dear friend, and related the symptoms of my illness. She came out to the house, armed with an intravenous for hydration. I spent Saturday and Saturday night running my own intravenous in my house. My wife, Linda, had no nursing skills and didn't want to be responsible for anything that was going on, so was of no help. There I sat in the bathtub of cold water, with intravenous bags hanging from the shower hooks. By Sunday morning, I had gotten to the point where I could no longer stay home and headed for the hospital.

On admission to the hospital on Sunday afternoon, I was pretty sick. My BUN was 90 (normal being up to 20) indicating either kidney failure or dehydration. My creatinine was 8.4 (normal is around 1). That indicated kidney failure. My eyes were yellow. My clotting factors returned significantly abnormal, measuring less than 10% of normal. I was admitted to NYU Medical Center on Sunday evening, to the medical service. The diagnosis was severe gastroenteritis and Fred Bevelacqua, a medical resident at the time, who had actually rotated on my surgical service, came by to do the initial admission assessment.

Fred, now a senior resident, came to examine me. Originally smiling and greeting me, his demeanor soon changed and I could tell by his expression and his reaction to my laboratory work that he was alarmed by what he saw. He admitted that he was puzzled especially by the kidney failure, but it was also clear that I had turned a bright yellow, indicating liver failure.

Being a chief resident-in-surgery, I knew most of the nurses in the hospital. Word had gone out that I was being admitted and that it would be appropriate that I receive private nursing. Kathy, who was there from the day shift heard I was admitted, volunteered to provide me with private-duty nursing before anyone knew what the cause of my illness was. During that evening shift, she was warned to be careful and wear a mask and gloves. She later told me that the supervising nurse had told her where the shrouds were kept in case I died that night.

By Monday, all signs pointed to liver failure and secondary hepatorenal syndrome. In other words, kidney failure secondary to liver failure. Liver function blood tests confirmed liver failure. I became disoriented, confused, the medical term being encephalopathic. I was treated for liver and kidney failure and for the inability to clot blood.

My serum potassium reached seven. This is considered a moderately life-threatening emergency. This required emergency treatment with extreme measures to rid some of the excess potassium because excess potassium in the blood can stop your heart. I wasn't fully aware of how quickly things were deteriorating, but knew that something bad was happening. I felt awful. I'd never felt that sick before, even when Dr. Harris would come to the house when I was a kid and give me a shot of penicillin. Even semi-conscious, you can tell you're in trouble when people keep frantically walking in and out of your room looking pensive and frowning. They didn't even give me flak about being sick and using this to avoid being on call.

So not only was my potassium too high but the liver failure required treatment with other noxious compounds to decrease the amount of protein in my body. By Tuesday, November 2nd, the consulting group taking care of me decided I needed dialysis. John

Ranson, M.D., a well-respected surgical attending and someone I had known for years came to tell me that I'd need dialysis. Liver failure, which causes kidney failure, was not generally treated with dialysis but there was nothing much else to do for me. Not in a position to argue or even think about it, I became resigned: "Do what you gotta do."

My care became a team effort. I remained on the medical service but Dr. Spencer himself got reports three times a day about my condition. Dr. Weiss was my attending physician and rounded on me several times a day. Sharon Drager, my close friend, and another chief resident posted herself or another senior resident outside my door to be sure that everything and anything that was going to be done to me was warranted and appropriate. She and the other surgical residents and attendings who visited me would also report to Dr. Spencer.

I had been at NYU for nine years including medical school. In the five years of surgical residency, I had gotten to know most of the intensive care and critical care nurses. They were friends. We were colleagues. I respected their skills and depended on them to care for my patients. They stepped forward and volunteered to take care of me by performing private duty. I looked around and figured I was in the best of all possible hands. The residents and attendings would visit me frequently, but the nurses were there 24 hours a day.

Although I had always appreciated the importance of nursing care and respected their participation in the care of my patients, I know that the care they gave me during my siege cemented forever for me the fact that nurses saved your (and my) butt when the chips were really down. The physician starts the car and picks the route so to speak, although in my case, there were numerous hands trying to operate the car, but the nurses get you there alive. This, however, wouldn't be the last time that dedicated nurses saved my life.

On Tuesday, the chief of the dialysis service inserted catheters into my veins and I was taken to the dialysis center. My friend Maggie was the nurse in dialysis taking care of me. I remember seeing the blood extracted from my groin and could feel it flowing back into my arm. Then I went into coma. I woke up somewhat disoriented but could see Susan O'Neill R.N. wearing gloves and a mask and looking terribly upset. Susan and I had worked together for years, but she was clearly there to take care of me. She was delighted to see me awake.

"What day is it?"

"It's 3 a.m. on Wednesday."

"That means the election is probably over."

It was Election Day 1976 and plugged into the foot of my bed was a TV set on a pole.

"Who's the president?"

Susan had neither time nor opportunity to find out, so I suggested we turn on my television. Jimmy Carter was on television making a victory speech. I went back into coma, waking up the following morning.

I sort of regained consciousness to pretty vivid hallucinations. I was walking in the graveyard where many of my family members were buried. I was there to see where I was going to be but as I walked towards what I felt would be my grave, the graves of long-deceased relatives were open and they were awake. As I passed my Uncle Bob, he chastised me angrily telling me I didn't belong here. So did my Grandmother. I guess if they didn't want me, I'd have to leave. I half realized that this was a vivid dream as I woke up some more.

Then I pictured myself floating above the room. I could see the people attending to me as I lay there naked. I had so much misery that I couldn't even stand putting on the hospital gown. It didn't much matter that I was naked, since everyone was concentrating on taking care of me, and I really had nothing special that they hadn't seen before. Then the pain went away. I felt calm, but was looking down at myself. I felt like I was dreaming but was sort of awake. When I got more awake, the pain came back.

Treatment for liver failure at that time was still quite new. Most patients died. Some of the newer therapies included ultrafiltration of the patient's blood using charcoal columns to extract impurities, or as an alternative, cross circulation of the patient's blood using baboon livers, and liver transplantation. The use of charcoal columns, an experimental procedure, was ordered by someone at NYU and were sent up from the National Institute of Health in Washington, D.C. and kept in reserve. The baboons weren't in the running and Thomas Starzl, the foremost liver transplant specialist in the country, working in Colorado at that time, was personally called by Dr. Spencer in the event he was needed.

Dr. L., M.D., a year ahead of me in training who eventually became Chief of Surgery at NYU, had a novel but ancient Israeli solution. It involved placing a live pigeon on the patient and saying some magical prayers to allow the disease to flow from the patient to the pigeon. The pigeon is supposed to die and cure the disease. Obviously, I'm glad we didn't get that far, but the Internet actually confirms that this is in the less-than-standard armamentarium for hepatitis patients.

Another run of dialysis was performed the next day, during which I was mostly awake. I continued to improve. Numerous attendings, residents, and nurses came by. My wife sat nearby, keeping busy doing crossword puzzles, but at a loss to ask anyone about the outlook for me. At one point she realized that I might die and apparently became concerned with whom she should contact regarding a funeral. Even then our relationship was both strange and distant.

One of my nurses who did voluntary private duty on me was Anne from the Recovery Room. We had been friends for five years by that time. Originally not knowing that I was even admitted to the hospital, she had met one of the medical residents who asked her if she knew what was happening to me. He casually related that I was as good as dead with liver failure. At the time, I never imagined that she would become my future wife. I didn't really think at that point I had much of a future or expect to recover.

When a resident got hepatitis B, it was presumed to be from a patient contact. Medical insurance completely covered the hospitalization and the consulting physician fees. If a nurse contracted hepatitis B, he or she was obligated to provide evidence of a patient who had the disease and that he or she had cared for the patient. Two Bellevue nurses came down with hepatitis B shortly after I did. They identified our common patient, the gunshot wound victim who had been admitted the previous August. He had evidence of hepatitis when we reviewed his chart.

One of the nurses developed rapid liver failure and the charcoal columns from the NIH sent for me were used for her. She died. The other nurse suffered for numerous years with chronic hepatitis and eventually succumbed to the disease developing liver failure before she could receive a liver transplant. I am without any residual evidence of hepatitis. I am not a carrier nor am I in any way infectious.

As I began to recover, I became a focal point for rounds, students, residents, and attendings. They came to see me in droves. I needed blood tests several times a day but as I recovered, the ones drawing blood were less experienced. By the end of the week, the interns would come by. I would caution them to be careful with a needle stick, since they might end up like me. Or worse. There was no vaccine or cure at that time.

During the multiple endless visits of friends, colleagues and the curious, Anne came by. Sheepishly she had to tell me something and hoped I wouldn't be angry. Because I was so sick, in coma, she had proceeded quietly to baptize me. She also prayed for me because she felt that every little bit might help. Her little sisters, now my sisters-in-law were in Catholic school at the time and had their classes saying prayers for my recovery. I guess when there's nothing else to do, don't just stand there: PRAY! They all apparently prayed and often to this day remind me of the major parts this played in my recovery. I never had a problem with any of this, although I'm a non-believer. I always figured that if there were a God, he'd be all knowing and pretty much could have guessed I didn't want to die at 30. But, magic is magic, so go with it.

I was discharged home after 12 days. The weather went from fall to early winter. I left the hospital with an elevated amylase, indicating inflammation of the pancreas and post discharge I had to curtail what I ate to prevent flare-ups and pain. November and December were spent recovering at home. My case was discussed at Medical Grand Rounds. At that time, only 15-20% of patients with fulminating hepatitis survived.

Prior to my discharge, I needed to satisfy my curiosity. Dr. Localio had visited me in the hospital every day. I got into a bathrobe and paraded down to his office, which at that time was located on the second floor of NYU Medical Center. He was delighted to see me and invited me to sit and chat.

"Tell me something. You knew I was a good surgeon, why was it that you didn't choose me to be on your service last year?"

"You have a big mouth and I have a bigger one, and I knew we'd never get along. I knew Slattery would have a much easier time with you. When you got sick, it was like one of my kids got sick, so I had to keep an eye on you."

Dr. Localio was neither warm nor fuzzy, but he had class and did the right thing.

Dr. Saul Krugman was a pediatrician who was conducting controversial experimental studies at Willowbrook, a facility that housed large numbers of severely impaired children. Most of these children had contracted hepatitis B while housed there. Hepatitis B was spread by blood and body secretions and was rampant at Willowbrook. Dr. Krugman, under the sponsorship of The Armed Forces Epidemiological Board, Office of the Surgeon General, U.S. Army and approved by the New York State Department of Mental Hygiene conducted studies in an attempt to create a vaccine. These studies have been severely criticized by medical ethicists but did produce important results.

Dr. Krugman, an attending at NYU at the time, visited me multiple times, drawing bloods to compare with his other patients. He noted that I had extraordinarily high antibody titers compared to his patients who had a much milder form of the disease. He postulated that perhaps I had been exposed to the virus in the past, and had some limited form of immunity. According to Dr. Krugman, I had the worst case of hepatitis anyone had ever seen at NYU in a survivor.

I returned to finish my residency in January 1976, but obviously I wasn't 100%. I was terribly tired but I was protected. The staff in the surgery office knew that I couldn't resume full night call, but each day I would nap in the innermost office of the department, undisturbed by beepers or calls until I woke up. Napping became a very important part of my day, allowing me to follow through with the expected night-call duties. I still take occasional naps in the afternoon, 40 years later. They still help me get through my day.

Assured that I had no residual hepatitis B antigen in my blood, that I was not infectious, and would not transmit hepatitis to my patients, I resumed performing surgery in January. I was the golden boy in the residency. When I attended my first M&M conference on a Thursday in January, everyone stood and applauded. For the remainder of my residency, I led a charmed existence.

This was the final year of residency and some of us were going into practice while others were moving into additional subspecialty training. Of eight chief residents six of us had gotten Hepatitis B at some time during the course of our residency training. I had the dubious distinction of getting the worst case. A generation before, the scourge of the residencies was tuberculosis. Now it was hepatitis B. In the years to come, the great fear of the residents would be HIV, AIDS, and hepatitis C.

The day I was to be discharged from the hospital, my wife was supposed to be picking me up, when the Gremlin I had bought to save gas on the commute died. (One reliable thing about American Motors, the proud manufacturer of Nash, Ramblers, and Gremlins was that every car they made seemed worse than the previous model. So, too, with Gremlins. It was certainly a great choice of names.) It wasn't until late afternoon I remember that I escaped. I've been hospitalized numerous times since then, and the greatest gift is the ability to go home. Needless to say the wait was agonizing. There were no cell phones to use for contact and no way of communicating the Gremlin's death. Eventually AAA recharged the dead battery.

Some of the residents were going into open heart or vascular fellowships and staying at NYU. I had no interest in a fellowship. Back then, there were only limited fellowships for specialty training. Today, there's laparoscopic, bariatric, colo-rectal, biliary and even breast fellowships, but we had performed so much surgery and had such a wide variety of experience that we could go into practice. Recently with less surgery being performed during residency, it becomes much harder to become proficient in the time allotted to become proficient, so sub-specialty fellowships make sense. In my time, it wasn't really necessary.

In June, Dr. Spencer called us individually into his office to ask what we thought and to give us advice. He always stressed the three "A"'s of surgical practice: Ability, Availability, and Affability. Not necessarily in that order. Dr. Spencer told me that I had outstanding ability, and that he knew I would work continuously until I achieved what I had to. He expected that with a little effort, I would be affable or at least make a concerted effort at it. In his office, he cautioned me that I was a skilled surgeon, but my big mouth might get me into trouble. I smiled and said, somehow in spite of it, I had made it through the best surgical program in the country. He had to agree with me.

Prior to my getting sick, we were living in a rented house in Queens. I had put aside enough money and it became apparent that it would be appropriate to buy a house. I looked in different neighborhoods in Queens and found a lovely home around the corner from the house in which I had lived as a child. It was just a block away. The streets in Rego Park were alphabetical and I had been brought up on the "E" block for Elwell. The house was on "D"ieterle. I showed it to my parents who thought it a good idea to buy property. I had no attorney so my father suggested I use his, a fellow I'll call Mr. Z, whose daughter had been such a formative influence on me in high school.

We went to contract and I began the process of obtaining a mortgage. Then I got sick. I guess if I had died, the process probably would have stopped. I didn't, but in my two-week absence, the process had stopped. When I got home, Mr. Z told me he had good news for me. It was his opinion that the house was overpriced and he engaged the seller's attorney and found all sorts of faults that were technical but the deal was off. I needn't worry. He had broken the deal.

Two days out of NYU, I took it upon myself to ride to the house, sit with the owners and assure them that I still wanted the house, that the price was acceptable, and that the nonsense that the lawyer had brought up was not of any importance to me. Nothing had changed except I would keep the lawyer in line. We shook on it, resumed the deal, and, needless to say, I let my lawyer know what I thought of his interference.

Ironic that I learned my lesson but my father didn't. He subsequently used Mr. Z to negotiate a lease with Burger King. My father had purchased a defunct bowling alley and several other foreclosed stores in Long Beach to store his stuff. A seven-alarm fire had reduced the stores and furniture to an empty lot. Burger King was interested in building on it but would write its own lease, which my father would show to Mr. Z, his crackerjack lawyer. Burger King got a 20-year lease with no elevation in rent and two more 10-year options with less than 1% increases over the next two leases. They are paying 1983 rents until 2023.

And so my chief residency ended on a positive note. I owned a house and a mortgage, and had become a legend at NYU for years because of my hepatitis. Dr. Spencer told my story to the residents, as both a warning of the hazards of the chosen profession and a triumphant declaration of my recovery. I could have been quite happy to be under the radar, but was optimistic and looking forward to my practice. I was a survivor. Little did I ever expect that this wouldn't be the only time I would be a survivor.

CHAPTER 8

A NEW SURGEON

Not long after I had finished my residency and moved to my first house in Forest Hills, a middle-class section of Queens, big things happened. Prior to the hepatitis, Linda and I had been trying to have a child but in spite of all the temperature-taking and monthly timing, things hadn't been happening. She went for testing and so did I. Suffice it to say, it seemed that I was shooting blanks. Diagnosed with a varicocele, a series of veins that are thought to surround the testicle and prevent fertility, I had a repair done a few months before the hepatitis almost killed me.

Coming home, after a six-month hiatus, apparently things worked, because Linda became pregnant. Happily anticipating the prospect of a child, we were in New York City on July 1st. We were there to see the famous Broadway show, *The Best Little Whorehouse in Texas*. During intermission, someone came to my seat to tell me that my wife had collapsed in the bathroom. An ambulance transported us to NYU where she miscarried. Although July is the worst time to be in the hospital, everything was ok.

Advised to wait a few months before trying again, we resumed activities without much delay. Linda got pregnant again within a few months. It was the middle of the night and Linda had gotten up and was "nesting," putting things together when she decided that she was actually in labor. Calling the obstetrician, I warned him that we were on our way. Driving from Queens to Manhattan, the trip was easy because it was late at night. Besides, the first baby is supposed to take a long time. Calling ahead to the obstetrician, we arrived with Linda in active labor. The nurses, knowing it was her first child, smiled and slowly took us upstairs. Our newborn's head was almost peeking out. A very short time later, we just made it to Labor and Delivery and Sandra came into the world, several weeks premature. Now it was all coming together for me. I had a new house, a new baby, and had survived my first major glimpse of the other world successfully. I needed a practice.

In order to practice surgery, you needed privileges at a hospital. I also needed a job to make some money. Late in my chief residency, after my hepatitis adventure, I was approached by Dr. Ray Laraja, who was a surgical attending at NYU and had recently become Chief of Surgery at Cabrini Hospital, which was located about a half mile from Bellevue. Ray was a terrific guy, easy to get along with, certainly not full of himself and was really responsible for allowing me to begin a career. I will never forget the fact that he gave me a great opportunity and feel the gratitude towards him that anyone must feel towards the person who gives you your first big break.

Cabrini, between 19th Street & 20th Street in Manhattan, was an unusual community hospital. It was located across from the Police Academy and also very near to NYU Medical, Bellevue, the Manhattan V.A., Beth Israel Medical, and, at that time, near the New York Infirmary. The concentration of medical facilities in those few blocks was greater than the total found in many cities, especially since each of these facilities were independent of each other and theoretically in competition.

Cabrini had some peculiar characteristics. Although a Catholic hospital (crucifixes hanging in each room), it had no affiliation with the New York Archdiocesan Hospitals but was supported directly by contract with the Vatican. It was once in a previous incarnation known as Columbus Hospital, founded originally in 1892 with participation by Mother (now a Saint) Frances Cabrini and by immigrant Italian doctors who were excluded from practicing at other hospitals in New York City. The upper floor of the original Columbus Hospital had a suite where Mafia characters such as Carlo Gambino, who were being brought to court, would check in as "heart attacks" to avoid court appearances. Father Vincent and Sister Josephine were the administrators and one or the other would make yearly visits to the Vatican to bring back funds. Eventually, the funding ran out the direct connection disappeared, and the hospital couldn't sustain itself. It closed its doors in 2008.

Columbus Hospital became Cabrini in 1973. At that time, most of the facility was modern and new. Ray had brought me over after my training to teach the residents in training as well as bring some discipline to the program. They actually had a freestanding, unaffiliated surgical residency. That meant that the American College of Surgeons would occasionally come by and inspect to make sure the residents being trained there had some idea of what they were doing. How they got approved is more than I could have imagined but I guess at one point in time, it was necessary to turn out many "certified" surgeons. So every place would be approved for residency training. I guess this would be similar to pilots taking flight training on their computers using flight simulators. Actually, many of the "residents" who were "in training" there had been fully trained in Italy, so it was just to comply with New York State regulations that they were "being trained" again. Some of them were older than I was.

I began by making rounds and taking night call there. They gave me a surgical office in a building they owned across the street from the hospital. Ray had me cover his practice on nights and weekends and he also gave me a salary. With all that going for me at the time, thanks to Dr. Ray Laraja, I was golden.

The plan was to create an ambulance service and also train paramedics. Getting paramedics and an ambulance service would bring in patients and thereby bring in money. Coming from my residency at Bellevue, I was skilled at trauma surgery. I knew how to operate.

In contrast to my surgical skills, I didn't know how to run an office, charge for my services, generate private patients, or become known at the hospitals where I was granted operating privileges. You learned absolutely no economics, no business skills, no competitive skills, and few survival skills for surgical office practice during your residency. I guess the feeling was that since the older attendings had to struggle, it was appropriate to let you flounder, lest you become a competitor too quickly. In the early days of practice, the best way of doing all of the former requirements of practice building was a crucial Dr. Spencer "A", availability. I was ready and willing to come in day or night and take care of any patient in the Emergency Room or any referral that anyone might send me.

Ray Laraja was a surgeon who also worked part time for HIP in Manhattan. He allowed me to cover his practice and his HIP practice when he was away and on weekends. I would acquire patients. HIP (Health Insurance Plan) was created in 1947 for New York City employees, designed as a health maintenance organization. HIP took care of the police, firefighters, teachers, and other union employees. The premiums were paid as part of their union contracts and union leaders were on the Board of Directors of HIP.

The design of HIP was basically a nascent model for socialized medicine. Premiums were all encompassing and the patient could visit as often as necessary for free. Not even a co-payment was required. So if the patient had an ache or a pain or was bored or lonely, they'd go to the HIP Clinic for a "checkup." HIP doctors didn't get paid by the patient, by hospitalizing patients, or by office visits. They'd get a monthly salary based on the number of patients assigned to them. I began working part time for HIP, covering for Dr. Laraja, taking emergency night call and doing anything else that was available. I just worked as hard as I could. HIP even paid part of my malpractice insurance.

I was in practice a few months when my first major trial occurred. Dr. Laraja was out of town and I was covering. A teacher, a HIP patient, was admitted with severe abdominal pain of sudden onset. In those days there was no CT scan, no MRI. You would actually have to examine the patient and figure out the diagnosis without endless imaging studies.

So I went over and did an examination and took as complete a history as I could. Around noon, she experienced severe abdominal pain, with some radiation to her shoulders. It made her double up. It came on suddenly and was excruciatingly painful. Now it was a little less painful but it was still there and she suffered severe pain whenever she moved. It was now 3 p.m.

She had x-rays taken. They were non-diagnostic. Blood tests revealed a mildly elevated white blood count, indicating only an inflammatory process of some kind. When I pressed on her abdomen, it was quite rigid and she experienced severe pain when I gently let go. That's a diagnostic sign called rebound. I was convinced she had peritonitis and probably a perforated ulcer. I thought she should go to surgery.

She told me Gary, her son, was coming and she would wait for him. He arrived, dressed in a suit and tie and introduced himself. He questioned me about my findings and asked if her internist had been by to see her. A few minutes later her internist arrived. I had seen him around in the hospital. He was a full time HIP internist, not board certified. He had never impressed me with his clinical acumen.

He pushed hard on her abdomen. She obviously winced. There was never any doubt that she had pain in her belly. Pushing hard, it wasn't hard to elicit pain. He diagnosed gastroenteritis, which actually doesn't cause anywhere near as much pain as she had. He totally disagreed with the need for surgery and suggested we wait until the morning. Now came the dilemma. Her son asked me about her white blood cell count, which was only slightly elevated. He asked if her x-rays showed free air under the diaphragm. No they had not, but she had not had an upright chest x-ray. I agreed that free air under the diaphragm was diagnostic of a perforated ulcer, but I felt that his mom had been in so much pain, she couldn't tolerate sitting up for the x-ray. The absence of free air on the x-rays did not preclude the diagnosis of a perforated ulcer.

Her son asked why her white blood cell count wasn't elevated, and suggested I re-examine her with him watching. His knowledge of the medical diagnostic tests caused me to ask him if he was in medicine. No, it turned out that he was a lawyer with experience in malpractice cases. I examined her again. She was more rigid and exhibiting more signs of peritonitis. I told him that she was also running a fever of around 101. He corrected me saying that she had no fever according to the last recorded temperature. Bellevue training allowed you to be able to touch patients and discover fevers. I was sure she had a fever and we asked the nurse to take her temperature again. 101.5.

I took her son aside. Let's face it, I said, if she has a perforated ulcer, she seems to be continuing to grow worse and if we wait, she may develop abscesses or further complications from peritonitis. If I'm wrong, you'll sue me, but it's clear there's an acute process going on. He said he was impressed with my confidence and the fact that I could tell she had a fever. We went to surgery and needless to say she had a perforated ulcer that had not sealed itself and was continuing to leak gastric acid. I patched it as I had done multiple times in the past on other patients. She was home in less than a week.

Her son, the lawyer, then asked if I would be willing to review malpractice cases that he had and offer testimony regarding my opinions. And I would get paid. Sure. This was something new to learn.

It didn't take long for Gary to call me. He had been dealing with an unpleasant case for many months and really didn't know where to go with it. Would I be willing to look it over? It was against Cumberland Hospital in Brooklyn, which had an awful reputation.

A 27 year-old man who was a known drug addict had injected himself with a speedball, a combination of cocaine, heroin, and whatever else was mixed into the noxious batch. His family was large and most of his siblings were successful at their professions, so they had decided to talk him into going into the locked detoxification ward at Cumberland. Cooperating, he was admitted but complained of discomfort in his upper arm, at the site of his last self-injection. He told the admitting physicians that the area was red and tender.

He was admitted to the locked ward where each day his arm became more painful. The psychiatrists and detox experts who examined never bothered to look at his arm at all. All they did was document on the chart that he was asking for pain medication. Finally, when his temperature hit 105 and he was bed ridden and semi-comatose, they, psychiatrists on the detox ward, called a surgeon to evaluate him for an "abscess".

He didn't have an abscess. He had gas gangrene, diagnosed by the surgeon who examined him at the time, a life threatening infection of his entire arm. He was rushed to the operating room within two hours of being examined, where his arm was at first filleted open to relieve the pressure that had built up inside his tissues. Within six hours following the surgery, it was apparent that it was either his arm or his life. He had an amputation above his elbow. There is no doubt that had the infection been recognized and treated when he first complained of the soreness, it would have responded to appropriate antibiotic therapy and he would have still had his arm. Now all that remained was a six-inch stump below his shoulder.

He recovered. His family sought a lawyer and felt strongly that the hospital was significantly at fault. So did I. Although I never treated nor examined the patient, it was clear from the chart notes and the notes by the surgeons that he never needed to lose his arm. So this was what I told a reasonable jury in Brooklyn who awarded him over 1.5 million dollars. The money was placed in the trusteeship of his family who the young man agreed should supervise his future spending and help him regain what would be left of his life.

Such was my introduction to the courts. With that case and my successful testimony behind me, I became willing to review cases for what I considered egregious violations of the standards of care of medicine. Several lawyers would call me about cases, but generally I would only offer favorable opinions if I could see myself testifying and felt very strongly about the strength of my opinions. That didn't mean either I would always win or that they would. But at least there might be an appropriate outcome.

Another case in which I was strongly committed occurred in Yonkers. A 20 year-old Irish nanny working for a famous family in Westchester County had consulted a dermatologist about a bleeding mole. You can guess the outcome, although the events were even more outrageous than one could imagine. The dermatologist had scraped and removed part of it but didn't bother to send any sample for biopsy. Needless to say when it grew back six months later, it was a highly malignant melanoma that had spread to her liver. She was at death's door when the case went to trial. The jury awarded over four million dollars, at that time the highest award in Westchester County. Sadly, she died not long after the verdict.

I became the trauma surgeon at Cabrini. I was the surgeon for the ICU trauma patients and for Dr. LaRaja's patients, so I always had one or two patients in the ICU. During my residency and in the early days of my practice, no specific attending covered the ICU. Each attending would be responsible for his own patients in ICU and would be expected to supervise the residents taking care of those patients. Therefore most of the patients were usually in the care of only residents and experienced nurses who kept them out of trouble.

A construction worker, employed near Cabrini had fallen down an elevator shaft approximately 40 feet and was rushed to the hospital. With an expanding abdomen and discovered frank blood when we inserted a needle into his belly, we took him to the operating room to find a torn liver, torn spleen and other blood clots. In addition, he had fractured many of his ribs and also his pelvis. We repaired the liver injury, removed the spleen and closed his abdomen as tightly as we could to try to contain the bleeding. In subsequent years, his abdomen would have been left open as an alternative treatment. We weren't aware of that treatment in those days. Everyone thought he was going to die. Except me.

He received almost 50 units of blood and blood products. His lungs deteriorated. He swelled like the Michelin Man. No one had seen any patient like this at Cabrini handled so intensely. I spent hours a day taking care of him. I called all the shots for the residents who were inspired and proud to contribute to his care. He spent three months in the hospital and eventually went home. His mind remained intact.

As I was driving home one night, a patient with a gunshot wound of the chest was rushed into the Emergency Room. Normally, major traumas were transported by the ambulance service of the city to Bellevue, just up the street. Occasionally if it appeared the patient wouldn't live to make it a quarter of a mile away without dying, the ambulance would stop at Cabrini.

My beeper told me to come back and I made it back to Cabrini as soon as I could. In those days, the only communication from the hospital was via a beeper which would provide a simple beep which meant call the hospital. If a patient sustained a small heart wound, some of them might be stable with low blood pressure for a short period of time. The pericardium, a thick membrane-like sac which surrounds the heart, acts to prevent massive open bleeding in very discrete and small wounds of the heart. Taking the patient up to the operating room, it was clear that in order to resuscitate the patient, we had to open his chest.

There are two choices of exposure for the heart, either the left side of the chest or the middle of the sternum. I was facile with either but in a major trauma I preferred the midline approach so you could handle anything unexpected. It was this exposure, the year before that had given me hepatitis and might have saved John Lennon's life.

I asked two of the nurses for the sternal knife, an instrument that looks like a crowbar, is placed behind the breastbone and hit with a mallet. It splits the chest down the middle and does it quickly. Prior to doing this, however, I asked the nurses if they had sternal wire, thick stainless steel wire used to close and pull together the sternum after it was split. Both reassured me that they had wire.

Chest opened. Cardiac wound to the right atrium repaired, prepare to close. Sternal wire, please. They brought me wire used in years gone by to repair hernias. This was thin, spindly wire that would never close the sternum. That was the wire they had. Now what? I went out, placing some wet gauze over the beating heart and called the operating room at Bellevue where I had finished my training only a few months earlier. Sure, they had sternal wire. Yes, I could have some. It was six blocks away but I garnered a Cabrini ambulance and we went speeding with lights and siren and were back in less than 20 minutes. We closed the chest with Bellevue's sternal wire.

I was an ambitious, aggressive young surgeon, and anxious to work. Two blocks south of Cabrini was the New York Infirmary Hospital. Another one of my NYU attendings was chief of surgery there, a friendly, outgoing, loud, boisterous surgeon who when making rounds at NYU with the residents would refer to everyone as "dear boy." He loved to "hold court" sitting with residents and discussing just about everything, once in a while, even talking about surgery. You could not help but like him although rounds would often end outside in the street so that he could smoke a few cigarettes.

So I got a hold of the "dear boy" and got surgical privileges at his hospital too. I hoped that an occasional referral or coverage might be thrown my way. This happened rarely, but there was no downside to being "A" as in Available.

Part of my job at Cabrini was to round with the residents. Rounding with them I would see some of the results of surgery by the other attendings. Obviously it was quite a change coming from a major academic center to a full-blown community hospital only 10 blocks south. It was like going from a three-star Michelin Restaurant to a McDonalds and comparing lunches. I got to know the various surgical attendings, first by their patients and their outcomes. Then I would see the other surgeons at the weekly surgical grand rounds and conferences. They were quite a collection at the time.

Cabrini had a strange assortment of physicians, some of whom were older, foreign and essentially unable to obtain privileges to work at any other facility. I had come from NYU, a top notch, world-class facility where well-trained surgeons and internists had struggled for bed space and operating time. It was assumed that most of the young surgeons would not be given privileges to operate there after finishing since there was no room to accommodate them in the extremely busy operating rooms.

Cabrini was just the opposite. Anyone and everyone who wanted to work there would be allowed. Little attention to age or skills or even ability was given in considering who was allowed to work. It was quite a culture shock to me seeing the hodge-podge collection of surgeons who were working just down the street from where I had trained. Obviously, some of the surgeons at NYU were more skilled than others, but my NYU experience had little prepared me for what I would be encountering at a "community" hospital.

There was Dr. N, M.D., a flamboyant older thoracic surgeon who had been at Harlem Hospital when Martin Luther King was stabbed by a psycho patient in Manhattan. He had operated on Dr. King in 1958 and received an appropriate letter and thank you. He let everyone know it. This was 1979, but it still happened yesterday according to him. He was now 73 plus, but still fancied himself the ultimate trauma and thoracic surgeon. He would occasionally make rounds in the ICU and perform tracheostomies on patients whom he felt were intubated (had a breathing tube inserted via the mouth) too long. He occasionally did that without telling the attending physician who was in charge of the patient and would talk the family into signing some sort of consent.

A patient was rushed to Cabrini after sustaining a gunshot of the right atrium, a heart injury. I had taken him immediately to the O.R. and was quite proficient in repairing the injury. Looking up from the operating table, I witnessed Dr. N bare chested with street pants under his scrub pants assuring me that he was there. It was clear that his retirement was imminently necessary.

There was Dr. R, a thoracic surgeon who had invented a suction catheter that he named for himself. The big deal was that the catheter was appropriately shaped to be inserted into the windpipes of severely compromised emphysema and other chronic lung patients. He would prep the patients, take them to the O.R., and perform the suctioning, convincing himself and the patients that they had significantly improved. He would apparently bill for a specialty operative procedure. Or so everyone said.

There was Dr. L. He was a general and vascular surgeon in the twilight of his career. He had long tapered fingers and carried himself with the ultimate *Doctor* with a capital "D" demeanor, haughty and pompous. It was alleged that he stopped doing general surgery when he removed an ovary instead of an appendix.

There was Dr. G., who touted himself an orthopedist whose specialty was no fault. I guess you would have to call him a "no-fault-ologist." He would admit patient after patient with back pain for traction therapy. The patients would be placed in some sort of contraption pulling their legs or hips or neck. They would be given painkillers and some sort of sedation. Most of them were there because of car accidents or workers' compensation injuries covered by New York State or No Fault. Money for the hospital for the occupancy of beds, and money for the doctor who spent several seconds making rounds each day was unquestioned before the insurance carriers got wise and almost went broke with colossal payouts. I'm sure during his heyday he made a fortune.

The prominent vascular surgeon at Cabrini was Dr. Rossi. He was a small, quiet man who got superb results. He also worked at St. Vincent's across town, knew that he was talented, and spoke with a heavy Italian accent so he spoke very little and quietly. His talent was in the operating room where he spoke volumes, saving critically ill patients, fixing abdominal aneurysms, and resupplying compromised limbs with new blood flow. His modest approach, dignity, and skill were a ray of hope in a cadre of semi-skilled surgeons.

There was Dr. P and Dr. P,, a money-making combo of two physicians. They were considered surgeons although they ran a rehab facility in Brooklyn. This consisted of hot packs for strains and sprains, some bicycle and other exercise equipment, and mostly prescriptions for painkillers as well as notes to stay out of work. Accompanying these were large bills to insurance carriers, workers compensation, and other job-related injury places. At one point they had approached me with the idea of a partnership. Seeing their operation, I rapidly headed out of Brooklyn.

One of the more interesting surgeons was Dr. Joe Malejka. He was a surgeon, trained in Poland, and an older member of the staff. His brother was active in the Polish Solidarity Movement and, although Joe never much discussed what was happening in Poland, it was clear that his thoughts remained with the freedom movement in his homeland. He was always an interesting gentleman and, although his surgical skills were less than stellar, his patients were devoted to him. They came from a Polish community in Brooklyn and he could do no wrong by them. He also knew the limitations of his skills and would without hesitation call for assistance. I was honored to help him do his cases, as he would always offer fascinating discussions of the hardships of the Polish people and the optimistic outlook for their future.

I wouldn't want to give the impression that there were no skilled surgeons at Cabrini. There certainly were. As a community hospital, even though it was a training institution for young surgeons, it was not imperative that every participating surgeon be a teacher. Many would do their cases without sharing anything with the residents. Their results were as good as any I'd seen at NYU. They would do their work and their patients would go home without problems. I was the new young hotshot.

One of my assignments was to create a class of paramedics assigned to the ambulance service at Cabrini. At the time, the only paramedic classes belonged to Shelly Jacobson, M.D. at Jacoby Medical in the Bronx. Jacoby was part of the New York City Health and Hospitals Corporation; however, New York State Department of Health approved paramedic training. So the people at Cabrini armed themselves by hiring quality paramedics trained by Dr. Jacobson at Jacoby. As in the major leagues, sometimes the most effective way of achieving talent was to steal it from someplace. I was then given the curriculum and teaching assignments so we could request state approval.

With my Bellevue experience, my trauma training, and my support by the administrative and medical leadership at Cabrini, I went to the state meetings. Presenting our facilities, our ambulance capabilities, and the quality of our instructors, Cabrini, much to the chagrin of the Jacoby group, was approved for the first private hospital paramedic class. We trained some extremely dedicated and outstanding paramedics. I became very familiar with the early curriculum of paramedic training and was the only surgeon who was a member of the committees in New York City, which organized Emergency Services. I helped set the standards for the various levels of surgical care required for hospitals that would receive ambulance cases. I also had the unique opportunity to ride with the ambulance EMTs (Emergency Medical Technicians).

In those days, EMS (Emergency Medical Service) was a separate branch of New York City services. They ran the ambulances for the city. Their patients were taken to city hospitals but, in the struggle to remain viable, many of the private hospitals had created their own ambulance services, basically competing with the city system for patients. Ambulances were dispatched by a central EMS service in Queens but it was often a free for all for patients, with some hospitals actually offering incentives to ambulance crews to bring patients to their private facilities.

In those days, the specialty of Emergency Room Physicians had not been clearly established. Many Emergency Departments were supervised by retired or retiring general surgeons. Old surgeons never died; they just ended up running Emergency Rooms. This was the situation at Cabrini and Bellevue. The ER physician would examine the patient, determining only if there was a need for admission or perhaps a referral to a specialist such as a gastroenterologist or cardiologist, and act accordingly. Little treatment was performed in the Emergency Department and admissions were numerous, sometimes without any diagnosis and generally unrestricted.

Credibility in surgery and the possibility for me to somehow get a job as a police surgeon meant taking the certification boards in Surgery. Board certification in Surgery was a two-year process. The first year was the "qualifying examination," a series of short answer questions to test general knowledge of surgery. As usual, the questions were less pertinent to the specific practice of surgery and more designed to have the candidate spew back memorized facts, although they had recently introduced clinical scenarios that actually described patients. Coming fresh out of Dr. Spencer's residency, I passed on the first try without too much trouble, although the exam was something for which you had to study the entire curriculum.

The second part of the boards occurred about a year later and was an oral exam. The exam was designed to determine that you were going to be a "safe surgeon". The exam was given by three sets of two examiners. Each pair consisted of a local doctor paired with a high-powered member of the American College of Surgeons. The examiners were not supposed to know what program you had come from or your specific background, but somehow I was paired with Doctors Shires, Sabiston, and Schwartz, the highest-powered players in the country in surgery. Each of them was responsible for a text in surgery and personal friends of Dr. Spencer. I passed. I knew the answers. I could answer short answer questions on the "qualifying exam" the year before by filling in the dots and answered correctly during the cross-examination on my oral exam by the "important surgeons." I guess being Board Certified made my surgical skills so much better. Like the scarecrow in Oz, I had the diploma. I was a "safe surgeon". I should be since I had finished one of the best residencies in the country.

It was soon going to be time to go back to the Police Academy and see Dr. Robinson who had told me to return when I was certified. I was a Board Certified surgeon, practicing a few blocks from the Police Academy. I was still friendly with the police officers in the

13th Precinct that covered Bellevue. Times were changing in the city. Mayor Beame had given way to Ed Koch and the budget that had caused the hiring freeze and the police layoffs was over. More money was available and it looked like there might be a police surgeon job opening. There was no reason not to go back and ask again.

Baby Boomer

High School Class of '64

Cornell Class of '68

Medical School...Class of '72

23rd Street, 1973 NYC

Surgery Resident 5:30 a.m. 1977

1980 Sworn in by Police
Commissioner Robert McGuire

Promotion by Police
Commissioner Ben Ward

Mayor Ed Koch 1987

With Stephen McDonald at Bellevue

Cardinal O'Connor

Commissioner Lee Brown, Mayor Dinkins, First Deputy Ray Kelly

With Governor Mario Cuomo when he signed COPS Legislation

It's not everyone who gets a horse named after him

May 16, 1992

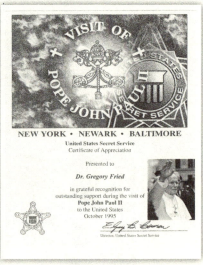
Commemorating the Pope's Visit

St. Patrick's Day, in City Hall with Anne and Commissioner Bratton

Working for HIP in my Manhattan Office

Introduction to President Clinton

Commissioner Howard Safir and Mayor Giuliani

Times Square Y2K

Press Conference Encouraging use of Vests

Press Conference, Officer Killed

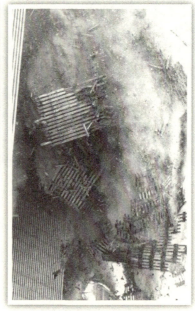
What I saw on 9/11

Police Rescue Boat...How I Survived on 9/11

Commissioner Bernard Kerik at my Retirement Party

Medal for Valor from 9/11 with Mayor Bloomberg

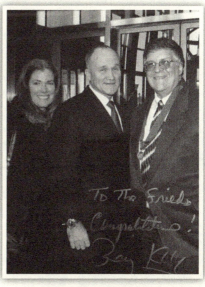

Commissioner Raymond Kelly on Medal Day

CHAPTER 9
POLICE SURGEON

Looking back, I never realized what a profound impact the job of Police Surgeon would have on my life and my future. I thought of it as another opportunity to earn some money, perform some interesting work, and advance my career. Never at the time did I think it would be a life-changing job that would afford me so many extraordinary experiences. Nor did I think the job would nearly cost me my life.

I figured it was time to get an additional job since I was board certified. I called Dr. Robinson and told him that I was boarded and would like to sit down with him again. Always a gentleman, he was willing to see me. My credentials were in order. He was favorably impressed but had not gotten the word to hire new people, although he thought the authorization would be coming any day. When he got approval, he would be hiring new surgeons to fill in the vacuum created by the city job freeze.

I guess it was time to inquire what exactly a police surgeon was expected to do. I knew that they didn't operate on police officers. He explained that according to the union contract, police officers had unlimited sick leave. That meant whenever they went sick, they could stay out of work forever, but they had to see the police surgeon who would decide if they really needed to stay out sick. In those days, cops would report to the private offices of the police surgeons.

The officers were divided up among the various surgeons based on zip codes. The police surgeon offices were scattered throughout New York City and Long Island. Some of the surgeons were pleasant enough to the officers but in general treated them like scammers and sick-leave abusers. One of the surgeons located on Long Island refused to allow the officers into his private office and made them wait in the street.

Dr. Robinson set up an interview and an office visit pending approval to hire new surgeons. Leo Lenardo, a sergeant who worked directly for Dr. Robinson would visit my private office to check it out. Leo had been a hero-cop who had been involved in a shootout in Brooklyn. A perpetrator had robbed a grocery store and when confronted by Leo had opened fire. Leo was hit in the spine but returned fire, although the shooter got away. Leo was supposed to be paralyzed but recovered sufficiently to walk with leg braces. He didn't want to retire. He became special assistant to Chief Surgeon Robinson. The perp's body was found several days later. He had tried to escape but had bled to death apparently avoiding going to a hospital for fear of being caught.

Leo was a first-class gentleman. He approved of the office, and had heard about my interest in actually helping police officers. He knew my supporters in the 13th Precinct. He would be delighted if I came on board. But there was one problem: I shared the office with three other physicians and the office was always crowded. I was the junior person in the office and, although I had my own secretary, the others in the office were concerned about crowds of cops coming and going.

I called Dr. Robinson and told him I was concerned that crowds of officers might interfere with the other doctors in the office. He said he would get back to me as soon as he got approval to do hiring.

A few weeks went by. It was late on a Thursday afternoon in July that I got the call. The situation had changed completely. They were no longer hiring physicians to see officers in their offices. In response to the complaints of officers being mistreated by some of the doctors, the plan was to centralize the health facilities and to supervise what was going on in the outside offices by bringing the doctors to a police facility. In addition, a new hire has been approved so the need was to begin doing physical exams on potential candidates. The physicals had to be done ASAP and at the Police Academy and "could you start on Monday?" Sure. Oh, yes, I could come in tomorrow to fill out the appropriate papers.

I reported to the sixth Floor of the old Police Academy on Friday, August 1, 1980. That became the day I was sworn in as a provisional police surgeon. The police surgeon job was on the civil-service list so the job had to be advertised, an examination given, and a formal appointment tendered. That would happen someday but now I was appointed. Monday would begin the new physicals. Could I do around 100 a day? In two to three hours? No problem.

Because there had been no scheduled hirings for quite a number of years, the pool of candidates was large. The plan was for three classes running eight hours times three per day with more than 1,000 candidates in each class, running for approximately nine months. The purpose of the physical was to weed out those with potentially disabling conditions prior to being hired. Even if someone slipped through, there was a year's probation during which they could be terminated for any medical or other situation that might have been uncovered.

The exams took all day. They included a history form, releases to obtain all medical records of everything that ever happened to someone, assignment to a psychologist for an interview, and an investigator who would be charged with finding out any past problems, legal, drug or otherwise that might prevent candidate from being a police officer. My part was about a 15-minute once-over to make sure they could walk and chew gum at the same time. Mike R, a hard-boiled old-timer cop was assigned to the candidate testing, had them line up in rows, wearing only underwear. Screaming, he would yell at the candidates referring to them as "skippy" and "skippettes." Get rid of the gum, stand up, pay attention, shut up. He spent many years in candidate testing and was well remembered by all those who were hired in those days. When, the department decided that needless hazing needed to be replaced with respect, he was out of there.

By the afternoon, all the medical histories were available and the candidates would be marched into a large open room. Mike R. and his henchmen had screened the forms and pointed out the potential problems. I would read them and then bring the candidate forward for an interview. Many of them had served in the armed forces. Some were on disability. They were disqualified. Others had significant orthopedic injuries, some requiring surgical repair. Those were placed on "review" to be examined by a department orthopedic surgeon after providing medical records from their private physicians.

The actual physical examination consisted of a nurse taking vital signs including blood pressures and pulses and checking weights (too fat or too thin meant come back when you could make the weight). I would then walk up and down the rows listening to their breathing and their hearts. Important to be sure they were alive, but actually walking up and down the rows allowed you to inspect the potential applicants.

Originally I performed hernia checks, telling anyone with a hernia to get it repaired, and they even had me originally doing checks for hemorrhoids. Because they would be sitting in police cars for long durations, it was felt that if they started their careers with hemorrhoids, they would only get worse when hired. So originally everyone in the group would individually moon me. I finally put an end to those examinations, stressing that neither hernias nor hemorrhoids were conditions that could lead to retirement. So, turn your head and cough and turn around and spread your cheeks were thankfully eliminated from my once over.

All candidates got hearing checks and vision checks. One had to be 20/40 without glasses to pass, although once again, this made no sense since if someone was hired and the next day needed glasses, they weren't terminated. Poor vision also did not lead to disability or retirement. They were also checked for color vision. I guess it was for descriptions of perps like, man with a green shirt in a red car.

Females were examined slightly differently but with a female nurse in attendance were also to be checked for hemorrhoids. It certainly didn't take me very long to end that degrading and useless practice. Another useless practice was x-rays. The department had an old-fashioned X-ray machine and each candidate had a back and a chest X-ray performed. It took me much longer to convince the powers that be that this, too, was wasteful, useless, and should be eliminated. I demonstrated by statistics that of the thousands of X-rays done, the number diagnosed with any potentially disqualifying condition was so minimal, that the waste of time and money was totally unnecessary.

Clearly, as in most of the activities with which I was involved, both in the police department and in surgery, the way things were done was the way things were *always* done. It's worked for so many years, so why change? The fact that times change, technology changes, and that assumptions like the need for chest x-rays, hemorrhoid examinations or in-patient surgery was long obsolete made no difference. I knew each battle would be uphill, but I was still young and energetic.

Five days a week, two to three hours a day. I became quite proficient at processing large numbers of willing young men and women. I also became very friendly with Dr. Robinson who worked at the Academy. Naturally, the assignment became increasingly boring and rather than allowing me to burn out, he began the process of consolidating the police physicians into police facilities. The first move was into the Police Training Academy and I was relieved of perpetual physical exam duty and assigned to a district. That meant police officers who went sick for any reason would be expected to report to the Police Academy and see me with the thought of being returned to duty in full or limited capacity, kept out on sick leave, or, if a line of duty injury, given authorization to see workers' comp doctors for treatment.

The police surgeon role, Dr. Robinson explained, was a mixed role. You were a physician, expected to behave appropriately and offer help, but also an adversary because you were often compelling someone to return to duty when they either felt too ill to do it, or just didn't want to go back. I had a three-day orientation to the ins and outs of the job by observing the "Special Medical District" run by Dr. C.

Dr. C. was a mean old codger who had become jaded and grizzled in running that group. In 1978, there were more than 1,000 officers on long-term "restricted duty." That meant desk jobs, no patrol, and essentially clerical work for police pay. Mayor Koch had issued Mayoral Directive 78-14 stating that no officer will remain on restricted duty for more than one year without being evaluated for retirement. In order to address the problem of long-term restricted duty, the NYPD supervisors in conference with the unions created the "Special Medical District" (SMD). Anyone who was out sick four times and a total of 40 days for non-line-of-duty injuries or 60 days in a year would be in SMD.

SMD was the punishment district. Officers could come to your home and see if you were at home. If you were out without permission, you could be suspended. You were restricted to residence unless you obtained a specific pass from your surgeon or called the Sick Desk to tell them you were going to the doctor, pharmacy or church. This was supposed to be a cluster of phonies, but obviously some of them were clearly sick or injured. But that didn't make a great deal of difference to Dr. C.

Many in SMD had back and other orthopedic injuries. Dr. C. would do a cursory examination and then say the officer can go back to work. *"See he can touch his knees. See, he can stand up from the chair. Back to work."* Some of those in SMD would come in using canes, some crutches. The first examination was the rubber tips of the canes or crutches to see if they were worn from use. Sometimes, you would see them carrying the items down the hall and only using them in the office.

Every so often Dr. C. would get into shouting matches or shoving matches with the officers. Once in a while, these were either so loud or so intense that a supervising police officer assigned to the office would actually intercede. He did what he was assigned to do, however, reducing SMD from more than 1,000 to slightly more than 200. I went on to a normal district, however, seeing officers who lived far away in Suffolk County, travelling 50 or more miles sometimes to get to work or report to the academy. This clearly reduced the likelihood of the officers going sick, knowing that they'd spend half the day driving.

Sometimes, based on the sick records of the officers, they'd be allowed to return to work and not report to the surgeon. Other times at the discretion of the surgeon's office the officers would be asked to report to the office regardless of how far they lived. The reporting could be daily, every few days or less often depending on the diagnosis. Only those in SMD would be tortured and forced to report almost daily.

Although it has been proposed many times that NYPD officers should live in the city, the numbers are too large to restrict it that way, so they are permitted to live in the five boroughs outside of New York City, Nassau, Suffolk, Orange, Rockland, and Westchester counties. But it was understood that your assignment as an officer would generally not be made to accommodate your geographical choice of location. In addition, you could not live in the precinct to which you were assigned. Geography was often considered, but not always. Staten Island presented the problem of the residents having to cross the expensive Verrazano Bridge to get to Brooklyn.

So I did my district. The bulk of officers neither abused sick leave nor did they have much guidance or experience in what constituted proper medical care. I thought that if I established rapport or could establish myself in the officers' minds that I was a physician first and the truant officer later, I could accomplish what I needed to do. So I approached things by giving them the benefit of the doubt. Dr. Al C. had set a model for me to avoid. I didn't want to be him nor did I want to approach every officer with suspicion. I didn't think the officers were all liars.

Dr. C. worked down the hall from me. We would occasionally overlap district times. One afternoon there was shouting. Aparently some officer had taken a swing at him. Dr. Robinson had me see him the next day. He had decided that it was time to give Dr. C and the officers in his SMD group a break. So I was going to get the pleasure of SMD. I would start seeing the chronic sick and chronic abusers the following week.

This was the most amazing group of people you'd ever seen. Some had gone sick 400 plus times in the eight or 10 years they had on the job. Most had applied for an Article II disability pension multiple times. Article II would give you three-quarters pay for the rest of your life tax-free if the disability was line-of-duty related. The majority of SMD people had back injuries or back pain. Some of them were burned out and didn't want to work. Others were scammers or those who felt they could manipulate the system. Once you hit SMD, there was nothing to lose by going sick. Some felt if you went sick enough times, you would show the department that you were disabled.

When I took over SMD, there was another group of chronic sick officers: pregnant women. Detective Lillian Braxton, a bright, assertive officer was president of the Policewomen's Endowment Association and the appropriate person to agitate for women's' rights in the department. I had met her a couple of times. Now that I was in charge of SMD, we became allies. I insisted that policewomen who went sick with pregnancy-related illnesses should be excluded from SMD. I insisted that pregnant policewomen not be allowed to be on full duty but be placed on restricted, desk duty.

SMD was quite an experience. I guess by the time I was done, I had heard every story and seen every possible manipulation regarding injury and illness. I had seen officers who had applied for disability pensions scores of times only to be denied and reapply. I had seen officers who, while out sick, were photographed tarring the roofs in their houses, working second jobs, doing construction. I occasionally saw officers who, while out sick were involved in bar fights and claiming line-of-duty injuries. I saw people with no discernible injury report to the range for yearly firearm testing and fail. Surrendering their guns, they were automatically placed on restricted duty for no apparent medical condition except that they didn't want to shoot. I saw failed back surgery for minimal findings by third-rate orthopedists in fourth-rate hospitals.

When I was in charge of SMD, Captain Tony was commanding officer of what was at that time known as Health Services. Tony was a strange guy, to say the least. Rumor had it that he had a previous incident in Brooklyn after a fight, firing shots in the air. He allegedly had been placed under supervision via psych services and had his firearms removed until he was found to be "recovered." No one could verify any of this information since for some strange reason all of his medical records were somehow missing from Health Services, of which by coincidence he was in charge.

He was old-time Brooklyn, bossy and somewhat resentful of physicians and certainly of the fact that I carried the assimilated rank of inspector while he was only a Captain. Old-time cops exhibited old-time cop mentalities. He was well educated but exhibited the macho pseudo-toughness that one often sees in the movies.

When doctors were seeing cops in their offices for duty status determinations, it was obvious that they didn't work by the clock. They saw everyone they needed to see usually separated from their private patients. They would then have their office staff send the information into the "Sick Desk," the area where all the information would be compiled.

As we moved to central police locations, there was a debate about how many hours per day constituted the physicians' work schedule. The police surgeon job was always constituted in the civil-service roster as a "half-time" position. Although the surgeons were considered uniformed members of the service, had the "assimilated" rank of Inspector, and theoretically could wear uniforms, the surgeons were not cops. We received the medical, pension, and other benefits including vacation time and retirement benefits, including the "Heart Bill." But nowhere was it ever defined exactly how many hours the surgeons should work per day and per week.

Dr. Robinson was a true gentleman. Tony was a bully. Robinson felt that when you finished your work, you were free to leave. See the cops, do what you needed to do, and go. Tony, always had a hard time relating to the doctors, decided that half time was half of the 40-Hhour work week, so regardless of whether you had finished, you had to put in four hours a day, five days a week. Until the Captain Tony fiat, most of the surgeons had been working between two to two and a half hours a day. Tony demanded four a day. Naturally this played havoc with physicians' schedules and lives. Private office hours were impinged upon, my operating schedule was impacted but, fortunately for all, as police surgeons we were in the Captains' Endowment Association, (the CEA) a union of the highest-ranking officers. Everyone, Captain and above, was a member except for commissioners, who were civilians.

The CEA was protective of its members and had attorneys on retainer to handle labor disputes. This was one. Naturally, most of the police surgeons were severely impacted by the Tony decree of 20 hours a week. But with union encouragement we were able to accommodate the new schedule pending a decision. The union went to arbitration regarding the hours and Tony's new rules. Since the time precedent was at first office based, and ill defined, his arbitrary new decision was inappropriate.

Tony lost big time. After months of meetings and arbitration, it was officially decided that surgeons would work two and a half hours a day five days a week, at times and locations usually decided by the needs of the department. They would also have a two and a half hour a week reserve time which might encompass responding to a hospital, working a slightly longer time in a district, or performing duty on weekends or nights. Anything more than a 15-hour week was overtime.

Tony never anticipated losing. This decision was not only binding on both sides, but all of the district surgeons who had worked 20 hours a week for months were getting five hours a week of overtime per week and Tony was singularly at fault. So he was not very pleased with the physicians or the outcome. However, we were.

We moved out of the Police Academy to a location in Jamaica, Queens. Down the block was a house of prostitution. In the empty lobby of a nearly empty 10-story building, you could buy narcotics. Moving the police there was a good idea, I guess. The idea was to put a police presence in a bad neighborhood. I don't think any cop who reported to the Jamaica Clinic ever made an arrest, however. I was finished with SMD. I had a district with cops from Long Island.

Donald Manes, the former Borough President of Queens was rumored to have a financial interest in the building, although that was never confirmed. After having served as Borough President, he faced investigations of corruption and committed suicide by stabbing himself in his heart. The police officers called to the scene were shocked that he had stabbed himself and his wife pulled out the knife.

Then it was decided that the entire medical facility should move from the Academy to Lefrak City, a major apartment complex in the heart of Queens. The location was near mass transit but was a terrible trip by car because it was at the intersection of three major highways: the Grand Central, Long Island Expressway, and Van Wyck Expressway. There was traffic in both directions, almost all the time. In addition, there was absolutely no place to park a car. Naturally, it was a bureaucratic triumph. It made everyone universally miserable.

Dr. Robinson, the Chief Surgeon, did not want to travel to Lefrak. He announced his retirement. Ben Ward, Police Commissioner was given the task of appointing a new full- time Chief Surgeon. In my time spent with Dr. Robinson at the Police Academy, I had learned much of what the job of Chief Surgeon entailed. The problem was that the Chief Surgeon's job was supposed to be a "full-time" position, 40 hours a week with little room for outside work. Robinson encouraged me to take the job, but I was not about to take a major pay cut, curtail my career, and become a full-time employee of the NYPD. Police surgeon was a half-time job allowing for a full practice.

Dr.T, M.D., had known Ben Ward at Brooklyn College and was serving as a district surgeon was appointed. He had been working as a family physician in Bedford Stuyvesant, Brooklyn and was willing to come on as Chief Surgeon full-time. Unfortunately, Dr. T. had not really become acquainted with the cast of characters he would be facing as Chief. Robinson had worked with them for years, but he had never been exposed to them because district surgeons had little contact with each other. In addition, the district surgeons, working only two and a half hours a day never really met those in charge of the other clinics.

The cast of characters on the police side included some cops who couldn't or didn't want to fit anywhere else. Many of those assigned to Health Services were awaiting retirement and many had been on long-term restricted duty. Some actually worked, but not as cops. Health Services was a good place to study, so Sergeant TM, a trained nurse got assigned there. He worked to help those cops who were out sick but he could also study for the Lieutenant's Exam and practice playing the bagpipe.

Sergeant JC an unhappy and older cop became the boss of "absence control." He became a bounty hunter and tracked down those he felt were scammers and sick-leave abusers. He was a bulldog and would sit outside people's houses waiting for them to violate some regulation about being outside when on sick leave or working while on sick leave so he could give them charges.

Mike R., from candidate testing, smoked so much that his yellow fingers matched his yellow teeth. He could barely go out in the summer because of his end-stage lung disease and eventually died of emphysema. Charlie F, a chipper dude that you would love to go to a bar with was such a regular in alcohol detox that he held the record for the number of trips to the "farm", Camp Smith, in upstate New York. Somehow, he remained on the job, his firearms a distant memory.

The cast on the doctor side also included a few oddities. Dr. C, as I mentioned had been destroyed by being placed in charge of SMD, the group of some long-term sick abusers. He could no longer recognize the fact that some of the officers actually had real injuries, but his mission in the job became the truant officer, putting as many as he could back to work. He was the doctor who supposedly trained me.

Dr. HR, a colonel in the military reserve, saw himself as General Patton. He smoked incessantly, sharing second-hand smoke with anyone who came near him. He was according to him double boarded in Surgery and Critical Care. His attitude was that he knew everything, that anything he said was correct, and that he could tell within seconds whether an officer was a faker or legit. Needless to say, this led to a few conflicts.

Dr. T. had trained years before in Belgium. Now appointed Supervising Chief Surgeon, he occasionally would have to appear in legal testimony about the decisions made in Health Services. Asked about his specialty, he described himself as a "running doctor." He had been boarded in Medicine years before and had been grandfathered so as to not need to retake boards at 10-year intervals. Each summer he would take a trip to Harvard for a review course for family doctors and return with stacks of paper to demonstrate how much he had learned.

Dr. TR, M.D., was supposedly a surgeon at NYU although during my nine years there I never once encountered him. He had been designated Deputy Chief Surgeon by Dr. Robinson and originally assigned to reviewing fees submitted by outside consulting physicians for medical services performed on officers. The NYPD was unique in that the City self-insured cops so the Workers' Compensation fee schedule was only a guideline. Dr. TR would ponder bills all day and decide what he thought the doctors should charge. He kept a going record of how much money he had supposedly saved the city by disputing the charges. TR seemed to be old when I got there. He's still there to this day doing the same stuff. In spite of the fact that police officers are retired by statute at age 63, there is no retirement age set forth for police surgeons. He finished medical school in 1951.

I was quite satisfied to be a district surgeon doing my own district a few hours a day. Robinson was dissatisfied with the way things were being handled and although retired would occasionally show up at the office and attempt to coach his replacement. Dr. T. had difficulty adapting to the role and started to lag behind in candidate processing and other important things that had to be attended to. He had some difficulty organizing things and seemed a bit overwhelmed by the new position. I did my district in Lefrak and continued my private practice. I was still a very busy general surgeon.

Richard Kohler was Chief of Personnel for the NYPD. He and I had interacted several times in the past, including when I was asked to become Chief Surgeon, a designated full- time position. I didn't consider applying for the position, unwilling to stop doing surgery or seeing patients. I was never attracted to a full bureaucratic role and abandoning all my training and surgical skills. Half time for the NYPD was enough for me with defined hours and specific duties.

Kohler invited me down to his office after Dr. T's appointment and asked if I would informally assist Dr. T in adapting to the new role since I had been so helpful to Dr. Robinson. No problem, I'd do my best, but it was also important to tread as lightly as I could, so as not to insult the new chief. It was hard for a guy as pushy and aggressive as I am to tread lightly.

I'm afraid it didn't take very long for me to tread fairly heavily. I was in the office at HIP on 23rd Street in Manhattan when I got a call from Chief Koehler. The "PC" (as the Police Commissioner is called if you're a member of the department) had a serious problem that needed immediate attention. Dr. T. had told the chief and the PC that he needed a surgeon.

The problem was that over the previous weekend the PC was in his summer house upstate and was chopping wood. A large splinter was lodged under his thumbnail and was festering and now causing him severe pain. He also had a press conference about something or other coming up in the next two hours. Gathering the supplies

I thought I'd need, I headed to Police Headquarters, about a mile and a half downtown. I got there and was escorted into the super-duper secured parking garage under the building. This was actually long before 9/11 but the security of Headquarters had been a serious issue since the F.A.L.N., a Puerto Rican terrorist group had bombed the parking lot at Headquarters on New Years in 1983. It took about 20 minutes to get up to the PC's office on the 14th Floor using the slow and crowded elevators.

The PC (Ben Ward) was waiting for me. He asked why it had taken me so long to get to his office, since he was aware that I had arrived in the building at least 20 minutes earlier. Explaining that Headquarters was crowded and the elevators slow, he turned to his head bodyguard and screamed that I must be given the elevator key. Apparently there was an elevator that was private and restricted to the top brass alone. Getting this key was a triumph and a major coup. This was the greatest gift and one of the highest honors one could get in police headquarters. Over the years, the key went from a round Chapman lock key to a magnetic card to a card with an embedded chip that was inserted. Every time the PC changed, the card was changed. Every PC from that time forward made sure I had the key. It's always the small stuff that makes the difference.

I proceeded to give him local anesthesia in his thumb. He was less than pleased with the injection. I carefully split the nail to remove the wood. He was quite relieved and asked me to hang around for the press conference, which went quite well. After the conference, I met Richard Condon, the First Deputy Police Commissioner, and Alice McGillion, the PC's press secretary. When Ward retired, Condon became Police Commissioner and McGillion was promoted to First Deputy Police Commissioner. She was the first and to date only female to have the role of First Deputy. Their tenure in the offices only lasted for three months, after Koch lost the attempt at a fourth term as Mayor and David Dinkins appointed Lee Brown.

CHAPTER 10

BETH ISRAEL

Surgeons need to perform surgery. Working for the NYPD was interesting, allowing me to do things and go places that most other people don't have the opportunity to experience. Growing my surgical practice, however, was still my higher priority. In order to maintain my skills, earn a decent living, and keep current, it was clear that I had to perform the surgery that defines a general surgeon.

I was still in practice, although now I was entrenched in the police department as a district surgeon. First assigned to the Police Academy in Manhattan and working for HIP part-time, I would walk back and forth between Cabrini, the Academy, and the New York Infirmary. A five-block radius.

Occasionally I would get a patient at the New York Infirmary and would walk the two blocks between the two competing hospitals to make rounds. Situated between these two hospitals was a huge 13-story edifice, Beth Israel Hospital. Founded at the beginning of the 20th century to serve the Lower East Side Jewish immigrant population, it provided service to the newcomer population of Jews and an environment where Jewish physicians could practice, admit patients, and perform surgery. Beth Israel ignored its two neighboring hospitals, Cabrini and the New York Infirmary, which happened to be directly across 16th Street and next to Stuyvesant

High School. During the day as you walked by Stuyvesant, you'd be enchanted by the sounds of the high-school band practicing their music.

Walking past Beth Israel Hospital sometime in 1979 as often as I did but knowing no one who worked there, I realized that there was nothing to lose in trying to get an appointment with the chief of surgery. I called for an appointment with him. Charles McSherry had recently been appointed chief of surgery there, although I couldn't understand how an Irishman was chief surgeon at this major Jewish institution. (I learned later that William Wolff, a Jewish surgeon had resigned from the chief position in 1977.)

McSherry came from New York Hospital and fancied himself a bile duct, liver, and gall bladder surgical expert. I did my homework before meeting him and discovered that he had published articles on biliary surgery.

Confident and cocky regarding my credentials and Board Certified, I told McSherry that I wanted privileges in Beth Israel. He pointed out that no one had been given general surgical privileges at Beth Israel in years and that they were busy, but perhaps it was time to open the place to new blood. "What can you do for us?" "What do you need?" Beth Israel had a free-standing residency program certified by the American College of Surgeons, as did Cabrini.

Amazing as it sounds, neither program interacted in any way. His residents needed trauma experience. I told him I was running the paramedic program at Cabrini and that they had sufficient numbers of trauma patients to share some of them. I would discuss the possibility with the paramedics and the ambulance service and bring some of the less serious ones into Beth Israel, on the condition that the medics could also accompany me to the operating room. Bringing the medics into the operating room gave them a chance to see anatomy and get a feeling for what resuscitation of trauma patients required. It actually gave them a great adrenalin rush to see surgery performed, and brought them into the inner circle of the medical team. There is something mystical about the operating room for those who've never been there before.

McSherry also needed resident supervision and resident teaching. I was by far the youngest attending; the next youngest, trained at Beth Israel, was eight years older than I was. I would therefore be willing to cover the Emergency Room for those older attendings, who, although assigned to occasional night call, really had no interest in coming in at night to operate on uninsured or Medicaid patients. I would be willing to do anything they wanted. And I did.

I got my surgical privileges. He got his patients. I went to the O.R. two nights a week with patients admitted from the Emergency Room. I taught the residents. I became the busiest surgeon at Beth Israel. Still having an office at Cabrini, only four blocks away, I would see postoperative patients in my office. I hired one of my nurse friends, Susan Callaghan, a Bellevue Emergency Room nurse, to staff the office when convenient. I had few patients and didn't need much help when I began.

No one told the young surgeons anything about practice. You weren't instructed about charges, insurance or compliance with rules governing practices. You weren't told how to enroll or participate in the various insurance plans. Two of the most important insurance enrollments were Medicaid and Medicare although the list was extensive, including no-fault, Workers' Compensation, Blue Cross/Blue Shield, Aetna and so on. Medicaid was important if you worked for the hospital since the hospital office would collect the fees and give you a portion. Medicare was Uncle Sam's Insurance Plan for patients over 65 and would pay consistently.

I enrolled. Medicaid set the fees ridiculously low. I would get checks as small as nine cents. I, as did everyone else, pretty much stopped billing Medicaid at all. Medicare required you to set a fee at the time. I asked the senior surgeons how much to bill. At that time whatever you billed, as long as it was similar to others, became your "profile." Medicare would pay 80%. So the surgeons in practice advised me to set your fees as high as possible since once you did set your fees, you were locked into that profile. "We bill $850 for a hernia, you should go for $1500."

I was on a roll. I was operating several days a week, frequently at night. I would be called in at Cabrini but more often at Beth Israel. I mentioned that I was the new, young energetic guy there and the residents loved having me help them. I hadn't burned out yet nor was I concerned about the type of insurance the patient carried, so I was always willing to come in. The Spencer "A" availability.

I also brought a different experience to Beth Israel. In spite of the proximity to NYU, there was absolutely no interaction between the surgeons. There was no cross fertilization of ideas, techniques or approaches to surgical diseases. Leon Ginsberg, M.D. was the major surgeon at Beth Israel. He had worked and trained years before at Mt. Sinai in upper Manhattan. He worked closely with Dr. Crohn, who was a pathologist at Mt. Sinai, after whom Crohn's Disease of the bowel was named because he and supposedly Dr. Ginsberg had described the disease. Dr. Ginsberg insisted that it be referred to as Crohn-Ginsberg disease and felt a bit deprived because he was only a resident at the time when the paper was published and the disease was described.

Ginsberg, only approximately five foot five, was the big man at Beth Israel. He had the largest practice, performed the most cases, and headed the major group of surgeons. He was old at the time I met him and only peeked into the operating room so that he could tell the patients he would keep an eye on them. He had stopped smoking years before but used a plastic smoking simulator to suck on which always hung out of his mouth.

Dr. Wolff had been chief of surgery for years until 1977. He had been accused of using service case funds, sort of assuming that as Chief of Surgery you could use money generated from service cases, that is, patients with no private surgeons but with some sort of insurance, for your own department. There were actually no written guidelines at the time about funding allocation and rather than sharing this money with the hospital general fund, Dr. Wolff had apparently spent the money on advancing the surgical service rather than sending it into the netherworld of hospital general coffers. Dr. Wolff, however, as Chief of Surgery was also wise enough to see the future in a resident who came from Japan.

Hiromi Shinya, M.D. was a resident at Beth Israel when Dr. Wolff had been chief. Shinya had brought colonoscopes and endoscopes from Japan from the Olympus Corporation and began doing procedures under the auspices of Dr. Wolff. Shinya was responsible for demonstrating the ability to visualize the entire colon from the inside, had perfected the cautery-snare, and performed thousands of colonoscopies. Together, Dr. Wolff and Shinya had brought colonoscopy, a procedure that detected early colon cancer to the fore in the U.S. Dr. Wolff resigned in 1977. Shinya and Wolff had made a fortune. So much so that Shinya was rumored to have purchased a mountain to build a home on in Japan. If anyone could be credited with popularizing and perfecting colonoscopy as a part of mainstream medicine in the United States, both of them should be. They were true visionaries and pioneers. With Dr. Wolff resigning, a search committee brought in Charles McSherry M.D., who had made a name for himself academically at New York Hospital

Night call at Beth Israel was rotated among all the non-senior attendings, most of whom were delighted to hand the cases over to me. Only occasionally would a patient have "good" insurance, i.e. Blue Cross or Medicare, allowing the surgeon to anticipate some sort of payment. Many patients were categorized as "self-pay" meaning absolutely no insurance, and generally no chance of getting any payment. I still was ambitious, eager and willing to come in at night. I became one of the busiest surgeons at Beth Israel. Bad idea.

No one ever warns you to stay under the radar if you're a young or new surgeon. One would expect that staying up all night a few nights a week taking care of non-paying patients would be gratifying to the powers that be, who would be relieved of that burden. For some of the senior surgeons that was fine. Others, not so fine. McSherry was a not-so -fine. He was always aware of the fact that I was covering other surgeons' night call and doing cases that none of them wanted to do. On the contrary, however, he saw how busy I was and it bothered him.

So he would make a passing comment about how he couldn't understand how a young guy like me was so busy. Then he would ask where a particular patient was referred. He asked the residents to check my charts to be sure I was doing appropriate surgery. This came to a head on a night when another surgeon on call asked me to admit an elderly gentleman with a strangulated hernia. I operated on the patient that night and the next morning McSherry had me in his office. He accused me of bribing the residents to send me patients.

First of all, I wouldn't have considered anything like that because it would have potentially compromised either the residents or myself and, secondly, I didn't need more patients. So in my usual manner, I let him know that he was totally off base with the accusation and suggested that he either bring formal charges and prepare for a major fight or leave me alone. He told me he would investigate the matter so for weeks he and I hissed at each other as he audited my active and older charts. I got tired of being harassed and decided to bring it to a head, demanding a hearing before the Medical Board of Beth Israel. Clearly, the old male doctors who comprised the board in no way wanted to get involved in an altercation between a young busy surgeon and the chief of surgery. They postponed the hearing, writing me letters, and apparently negotiating with him.

He finally stopped because he obviously found nothing. I know he interviewed the senior residents several times and was quite displeased since they assured him that I was one of the only available attendings willing to come in at night for indigent "self-pay" patients. And I did it as often as necessary.

Meanwhile, at Cabrini, I was covering HIP part-time for Dr. LaRaja. I became a part-time employee and received an appropriate salary, part of my malpractice coverage, and the use of a HIP office to see patients. Not long after the altercation with McSherry, the medical director of my HIP group, Irwin Weiner, a gynecologist presented me with the ultimatum of either going full-time into the group or leaving. I decided to go full-time for HIP.

I was expected to do any and all appropriate surgery on patients I would see. I was expected to cover night call several times a month. I would get no extra salary for any or all the surgery I performed. Surgeons were scheduled for 18 hours a week in the HIP offices. I could set my own schedule. I would dovetail it with my days that I operated and also with my job as a police surgeon. I created a fairly rigid schedule that worked for me, got me to the police office as needed, and when the HIP schedule wasn't full, got me home in the afternoons.

I knew that all this activity, all the time spent away had impacted negatively on my marriage. Linda and I had drifted apart and gone in separate directions. We tried to work things out. We had a son, Eric, who was born January 7, 1982. Once again, when Linda went in to labor, we drove in from Queens, this time at 2 a.m. I called Dr. Zinberg, the obstetrician to tell him we were coming. This time he overslept and Dr. Q, a resident, and I delivered Eric.

Everyone tells you kids don't save your marriage. They do, however, make it tolerable and can mitigate marital tensions. You can always talk to kids, play with them, and even put them between you and your wife so you don't even have to hold hands. Every summer we vacationed at Disneyworld® in Florida, good for the kids, easy for me. Life went on and my marriage moldered along.

HIP also gave me the ability to schedule my life and activities better. I needed to integrate a surgical schedule, a police schedule, and office hours. The police job was far too good to give up, and HIP required around 18 hours a week for seeing surgical patients in the office. Around all that, I had to perform all the surgery HIP generated in those office hours every week.

Fortunately, I was an efficient and skilled surgeon, thanks to the training I had received. I could perform three hernias in a morning, perform a colon resection in a few hours, or remove a stomach in a similar amount of time. I knew how long I would expect things to take and could schedule things far enough in advance to get first case time in the morning. This meant that the amount of time you took depended only on you, as opposed to the "TF" (to follow) situation where it was necessary for the surgeon operating before you to finish, have the room cleaned, and bring your patient to the operating room.

This plan usually worked but there were exceptions. The most significant exception was the day Eric was born. I had two major cases scheduled for first case and to follow myself on Thursday, January 7, 1982. Eric had come a few weeks earlier than expected. One of our neighbors was on call to watch our daughter Sandra if Linda was going to deliver at night. Sure enough, at 2 a.m. we called our neighbor. She came and took over baby-sitting duty. It was off to the hospital and in the morning Sandra was off to day care. I was ready and headed for the hospital because both of my scheduled cases were major and would be done by early afternoon. Then I would take over from our babysitter when Sandra returned in the afternoon.

Since I was down the block at NYU where Eric was born, Beth Israel was an easy commute. I arrived early to begin my 8 a.m. case only to discover that Murphy's Law had taken over: Anything that could go wrong would go wrong. Dr. L, a vascular surgeon, had done some sort of lengthy procedure over the course of the night. He was one of the less skilled vascular surgeons, whose operations more often than not resulted in serious complications owing to his own technical limitations or poor decisions at surgery. Sure enough, the patient had clotted all the grafts he had placed and the patient was in danger of losing his legs. He had to go back into surgery to attempt to salvage the disaster.

Beth Israel had 25 operating rooms. Dr. L was also trained at Beth Israel and had been there for many years. He was a prima donna and insisted that he alone could use the operating room I was scheduled to use. I would be delayed until he finished his case. His patient was going back to the operating room as we spoke.

I called him and asked him to please use another room. I told him that I literally had a child several hours before and that I really needed to get home to watch the older one. Impossible. He wouldn't consider another room. This was his room and the only room that he felt comfortable using. I guessed that it would be useless to point out that this was the room in which he created the disaster that required him to go back to surgery as he had done so many times before. Maybe he should have considered that the room might carry a jinx and that a dark cloud hovered over him.

I sucked it up. I explained to my friends in the scheduling office what the situation was and asked them if they could help me out. Another surgeon allowed me to move to his room after he finished a hernia. I finished my surgeries only a few hours later than I had anticipated so our neighbor only had to babysit for an extra hour or two.

I was home before Dr. L finished his attempted salvage. A week later his patient died. This seemed to have shaken him to the core and he took a significant hiatus from performing any major surgery for months. We never spoke again. Two years later, Dr. L succumbed to lung cancer, the result of years of heavy smoking. In those days, patient outcomes, surgical statistics and performance, time spent under anesthesia for the patient were not tracked or trended. Today surgical performance and skill is tracked and a surgeon who is a constant disaster can be curtailed. In those days, surgery was truly "practice." Consistently bad results by a surgeon were blamed on patients or external factors, never poor performance.

With McSherry off my back, I continued to work at Beth Israel, the New York Infirmary, HIP, and the Police Department. Once again, I must emphasize that no one warns you during residency about the pitfalls of being a new surgeon. One night a younger patient rolled into Beth Israel with obvious signs of peritonitis. CT's showed an abdominal catastrophe relating to his colon. It was quite likely that there was a perforation of the colon probably related to diverticulitis.

There's an important adage in medicine: Never be the first or the last one to perform a surgical procedure. Perforated diverticulitis is a serious illness in which a diverticulum, a small out-pouching of the colon, sometimes congenital, more often related to low-fiber diets, gets clogged and spontaneously bursts. This allows small amounts of intestinal matter to soil the abdomen, i.e. peritonitis, and cause a fever and infection. Untreated, perforated diverticulitis sometimes leads to abscesses but sometimes it closes by itself.

Before antibiotics and improved anesthesia, this was traditionally treated in three steps requiring three separate operations. The first step was the performance of a colostomy, putting a hole in the bowel proximal to where the perforation occurred with the hope of diverting the intestinal contents. Weeks later, the next step was to re-operate, leave the colostomy intact, and remove the perforated, offending \ colon. Months later, the third step, was to operate yet again and close the colostomy, reattaching the remaining good portions of the intestine and removing the colostomy.

When I trained at NYU, this was a two-step procedure. Skilled surgeons would do the colostomy and remove the perforated colon at the same time. This saved the patient a surgery and made the time between operations shorter and the colostomy closure even easier. So this is what I did. I worked with Dr. Greif, the senior resident who confessed he had never seen this done before, but couldn't imagine why everyone didn't do it that way. He had seen the former three step procedure performed and this procedure seemed less difficult, avoided a major operation for the patient and seemed to make sense.

The next morning I got a frantic call. Dr. Ginsberg, who was at the time about 82 years old, needed me to come to his office. *"Fried, WE don't do two-stage resections at Beth Israel!!!"* He wasn't interested in explanations or statistics or my experiences or my training. *"**WE**"* didn't do it that way. Smiling, I simply thanked him for his input and decided to clue Dr. Greif to prepare for criticism at the Morbidity and Mortality Conference to be held in the near future.

An extremely bright resident, Dr. Greif researched the literature. He cited many studies and compiled statistics showing that our approach was not only preferable, but had a considerably lower morbidity, lower complication rate, and lower mortality than the classic, Ginsberg sanctioned operation. Our patient did well (or I wouldn't be narrating this) and Dr. Greif presented the statistics at conference. I would find myself consulted frequently for this approach to perforated diverticulitis by other residents.

So, in unknowing violation of the first-and-last adage I mentioned, I was the first at Beth Israel and Ginsberg was among the last to give up the three-step procedure. But it was most assuredly time for him to consider retirement. Grace Hopper, an early computer learning pioneer, once said "The most dangerous phrase in our language is, 'We've always done it this way." Old habits and old procedures die very slowly.

Meanwhile, McSherry, the new Chief of Surgery fancied himself a major biliary tract surgeon. Indeed, he had contributed countless articles and book chapters, researched gallbladder disease, gallstones and their treatment, and worked with Dr. Glenn at New York Hospital. This, however, didn't make him a talented surgeon. Believing his own hype, he would tediously operate on patients with gallstones. McSherry used to criticize me because I used the cautery to remove the gall bladder from the liver bed. This was a simpler, less bloody and more efficient means of doing the surgery that I learned at NYU. Without this technique, gall bladders could not be removed laparoscopically, but that was for him to learn in the future.

McSherry also embarked on numerous research protocols regarding biliary tract disease. He studied and worked on major dietary changes in hope of dissolving gallstones. His principal studies were conducted on baboons at Sterling Forest Research Lab in upstate New York. This required ingestion of industrial strength bile acids and was totally intolerable to humans, although he apparently had enlisted several patients to get them to try this diet. Eventually, he finally gave this up. I don't think the baboons were particularly thrilled with the diet either.

He convinced the administration at Beth Israel, which owned Doctors' Hospital uptown, to invest in the "next big thing:" This was an ultrasonic machine that was supposed to fracture gallstones in the way kidney stones are fractured. This was a multimillion-dollar machine imported from Germany and installed at Doctors' Hospital. It was the first one of its kind in the U.S. It was also the last one because it failed to do what it was supposed to do. Instead it fractured the liver and sometimes the kidney in the few patients upon whom it was used.

McSherry also worked for the New York City Fire Department as a fire surgeon. Their role was slightly different than police surgeons in that they were on call a full day a few days a month and were expected to respond to NYC fires in cases there were injuries at the scene. Part of the requirements as full-time Chief of Surgery at Beth Israel, where he was quite generously paid—and rumor had it that they even paid for his daughter's college tuition—required that all other monies earned would be turned over to the hospital with only a percentage returned to him. When the hospital enforced this part of his contract, he quit the fire department.

McSherry finally hit pay dirt with the introduction of laparoscopic surgery. He actually brought in one of the pioneers of this technique wherein only a few small holes were made rather than a large incision to remove the gall-bladder. The French physician did a remarkable presentation at Grand Rounds, a weekly conference for the surgical staff to discuss surgical topics, under the gaze of the beaming McSherry. McSherry was tutored in the technique and introduced it at Beth Israel. He would be the sole instructor. He bought the instruments. He owned them. He worked full-time for Beth Israel, however, so his fees were supposed to revert to the hospital. Allegedly they ended up in the surgical department to be used by the chairman. The questionable billing practices by McSherry were discovered by the hospital. Soon he was history.

When McSherry resigned in 1991, I had already been promoted to Deputy Chief Surgeon for the NYPD by Commissioner Ward. This was more a title than a reflection on the fact that I was indeed a real surgeon. All physicians, regardless of specialty who worked for the NYPD were designated as "surgeon." A more appropriate designation for the doctors was used by the Fire Department, whose doctors were designated as medical officers. But NYPD docs were "surgeons." I was one of the few who were in fact a real surgeon.

I must admit that I gloated when McSherry, who had given me such a hard time to first get privileges at Beth Israel and then had bothered me about my activity, called me to ask if there was a position available as a police surgeon for the NYPD. We all know the cliché "Be nice to those you meet on the way up because you will meet them on the way down." In the end, he finished his career back at New York Hospital as a consultant and biliary "expert." He never did get that job with the police department.

CHAPTER 11

TALES FROM THE NYPD

My position in the NYPD combined with my aggressive self-confidence put me in a unique situation. From the time of my promotion to Deputy Chief Surgeon, with the expectation that I respond to the hospitals when officers were shot or seriously injured, I immediately became a more or less integrated part of police brass in the inner circle of what is known as the "bosses." It was here that I became involved in several important episodes in the history of the NYPD, two of which are of special significance to me.

Bullet Proof Vests

We all hope to leave something behind, a legacy. Surgeons, one life at a time, often make a permanent difference in people's lives. Sometimes it's good, sometimes bad, but many times it is routine and forgotten by both the surgeon and perhaps the patient. Even when surgery goes well, over time the name of the surgeon, the date, and even the type of surgery is forgotten. When complications ensue, the legacy of the surgery and the surgeon are more likely to linger and patients vaguely remember the heroic efforts of teams of physicians who saved their lives.

Similarly, as Deputy Chief Surgeon and then Executive Chief Surgeon for the NYPD, I know I too made a difference in the lives of some individuals, sometimes good and sometimes bad but usually of no great consequence. One event made a difference for many lives and changed the department.

In the late 80s in New York City suffered from a crack epidemic, the AIDS epidemic, and general unrest throughout the city. Cops were being shot far too frequently. On the dreary night of October 18, 1988, the call came in that a cop in an undercover operation was shot and taken to St. Luke's Hospital in upper Manhattan. In those days, the police operation was known as buy and bust and was felt to be a strategic way of taking drugs off the street. Undercover cops in plain clothes would set up sting operations and attempt to buy drugs in known drug locations or from known dealers. Once the action went down they would arrest the bad guys.

Christopher Hoban was a young, clean-cut college-looking type. He was in fact an undercover buying drugs in Harlem. Apparently something went wrong and the sellers became suspicious that this was a buy and bust. His partner, Jermyn, stood next to him. Chris apparently thought fast, having been accused of being a cop, lifted his shirt and said he wasn't. No gun. Someone turned to Jermyn, however, grabbed his concealed gun and shot Chris in the head. He was rushed to St. Luke's Hospital in Upper Manhattan.

Arriving at St. Luke's, I was ushered into the trauma room. It was clear that Chris was near death, head deformed, no pupillary reaction, and almost no vital signs. David Scott, the borough commander of Manhattan North, had responded first to the scene and then to the hospital. We both knew what was going to be the outcome. Before the neurosurgeon was able to take Chris to the operating room, he died. Mayor Koch, Commissioner Ward, the next of kin, the PBA brass, and the union officers were all responding. They did the press conference after Chris's mother and father received the awful news.

Then the police radio reported more bad news. David Scott approached me and told me that there was a report coming over the air of a cop shot. We thought and then hoped it was somehow a mix-up at the time, that it was a report about Chris. Police operations seldom makes mistakes with that kind of report so both of us were obviously concerned.

Then we got the word that another cop was going to Columbia Presbyterian Hospital 50 blocks north of where we were. David and I peeled off and headed up to Columbia. He drove my police car, lights flashing and siren wailing. Arriving at the Emergency Room, it was clear another cop had been shot and also mortally wounded. All attempts to resuscitate including open chest failed. Michael Buczek lay dead on the gurney.

In the months before these events, the unions had been advocating to allow the police to carry 9-mm, 15-round clips instead of their service six-shot .38 caliber revolvers. Some argued that the revolver, the more reliable weapon, requiring less maintenance. Others said the revolver was less powerful and limited to only six rounds. Further, the "speed loaders" associated with the revolvers weren't particularly speedy in a life-threatening situation. Indeed, officer Scott Gadell had been killed in Far Rockaway when his six-shot revolver ran out of bullets several months earlier.

Word was sent to the group still at St. Luke's that another officer had died. After a delay which included a press conference, the arrangements for the transport of Chris Hoban to the Medical Examiner's Office and the reopening of the streets near St. Luke's, the entire entourage made its way north. Trenchcoat (see Chapter

1), the detective who could get things done, was again quite remarkable in his ability to assist and coordinate the situation. First Deputy Commissioner Condon was present; Commissioner Ward was still downtown at St. Luke's. Pat Burns, the PBA vice-president was present; Phil Caruso, the PBA president was still at St. Luke's.

The department chaplain had remained at St. Luke's, so Father Mychal Judge, the fire department chaplain, came to Columbia. He had heard that a police officer had been shot and brought to Columbia and Fr. Judge was nearby. Because Michael Buczek lived a long distance away in Rockland County with his new wife, it was decided to dispatch people from employee relations, and Father Judge to the home by helicopter and give the news to his wife. The police brass at the hospital decided that there would be little reason to tell her that he was injured and to bring her down simply to learn that indeed he was in fact killed.

When the group arrived at her home, they convinced her in the heat and anguish of that moment not to travel down to the hospital to see Michael. Some time later, however, she confided in me that she felt robbed of her ability to properly grieve or come to grips with the situation. Over time I came to learn what mattered to the wives of murdered cops was far different from the impressions of the police brass. Those concerns and the insights I received from the widows of murdered cops will come in a later chapter.

It was 3 a.m. at a private area in the Columbia Presbyterian Emergency Room. Having recently arrived, Mayor Koch was silent, crushed. Two cops were killed in separate unrelated incidents in one night. It didn't get much worse than that. He turned to Deputy Commissioner Condon and suggested that maybe the cops ought to be allowed to carry the bigger, more powerful guns.

I told him, "Sorry Mr. Mayor, that wouldn't have mattered. If Michael was wearing a bullet proof vest he might have survived." The Mayor was shocked that cops didn't wear bulletproof vests. "Sorry sir, but you don't supply them. They're not required and not part of the uniform." Condon totally agreed. So did the PBA vice president, Pat Burns. We'd wait for the top brass and PBA president to arrive, discuss it further, and figure out how to implement the major change. The next morning, October 19, 1988, the order went into effect that all uniform police were obligated to wear vests and the city would provide them. Koch would get money in the budget to issue them to all officers.

The question then arose as to how you change the generations-old perception that vests were for weaklings, that they were hot, uncomfortable and that they were unnecessary in certain kinds of work the police did. *My precinct is safe. I don't need one.* Or so the argument went. Cops don't handle change very well. I offered another suggestion: "If a cop turned out without his pants, you'd send him back and tell him to put pants on. All you need do is pat them on the back to find out whether they're wearing their vests." It took a while, first to distribute vests and then to get the officers used to wearing them. Dick Condon and I would phone each other on every occasion when an officer was saved by his vest, proudly sharing one of the greater contributions to officer safety.

Ironically, Christine Buczek, Michael's wife had bought Michael a state of the art vest upon his graduation from the Academy. She would ask if indeed he was wearing his vest at the time he was killed. I could honestly say that I didn't know for sure and that he was undressed when I responded to the hospital. Whether he was at the time or not, this was the opportunity to put the department in mandatory vests. Sure, vests are not foolproof, but they certainly have made a major difference. Sometimes they fail. Sometimes they ride up and sometimes officers have been killed wearing them when bullets have penetrated through the sides or armholes. But they have saved many police officers' lives.

The Secret Service, The Pope and I

In October 1995, big time events were going to occur in New York City. Pope John Paul II would arrive and conduct mass in Aqueduct Racetrack in Queens and then say the Rosary at St. Patrick's Cathedral.

Dr. RS was an interesting character who was a dentist in the Bronx but was a police and fire buff. Although not serving in any official capacity, somehow he was an honorary fire surgeon, who had purchased a black Crown Victoria car, the same car the police chiefs drove. He had managed to outfit his car with lights and siren, and carried a shield from the Fire Department which kind of allowed him to act "officially". He was your typical wannabe. He was a bit strange and a bit mysterious but typical of people who somehow want some kind of position without actually earning it but hang around enough to somehow become integrated. They're in the great imposter category: They are familiar and friendly to everyone but no one really knows how they got there or what their purpose is.

He owned a dental practice in the Bronx, having multiple employees, although he himself had supposedly broken his arm and no longer practiced dentistry. He was quite wealthy and via numerous contributions to marginal police support organizations, had become familiar to police, FBI and Secret Service folks in the city. Dr. RS, at one time ingratiated himself to the department as a volunteer instructor in the NYPD Cadet Corps, groups of high school students who were considering a career in the NYPD.

I forget where I first met Dr. RS, but I'm sure it was at a dinner sponsored by one or another civilian police support organizations of wannabes. These groups, usually organized by wealthy civilians, hold fund raising events and award grants and money to individuals or the NYPD for various reasons. They go by various names such as, to name but two, the Centurion Foundation and New York Law Enforcement Foundation. Their varied memberships often include police supporters and "buffs" in New York. As a result, they find themselves with shields and ID cards naming them "honorary" police commissioners.

Dr. RS somehow became friendly with the Special Agent-in-Charge (the SAIC) of the Secret Service in Manhattan. Through Dr. RS, the SAIC contacted me, asking me to come to the Secret Service Office at 7 World Trade Center, later destroyed during 9/11. Dr. RS and I appeared at the lobby. The security desk announced our arrival. The 20th floor sported a steel door with a touch pad outside to restrict entry. There was even a secret sign which said "U S S S." No one would ever suspect the Secret Service was there.

It was almost a flashback to Maxwell Smart television series. Entering behind the steel door, one saw lavish mahogany furniture. A quick tour of the facilities showed that the main focus of this office dealt with counterfeit money, although the office was also concerned with other things, including security for the United Nations, preparations for any presidential visits to New York and secret stuff that they didn't tell me about. You know, the old "if we tell you we'd have to kill you..."

Anyway, the UN 50th Anniversary was approaching as was the Pope's New York visit. The Secret Service would be importing a large number of agents for protection. The SAIC heard that the Medical Division of the NYPD had a large number of doctors working for them. "Would we be willing to be on call for the

Secret Service in the event any of their members were injured or became sick?"

I told him that I'd have to clear it with Commissioner Bratton, but I didn't anticipate a problem. Asking me what it would cost him, I smiled and told him that my mother-in-law and wife were both active Catholics and that I'd require access to the Mass at Aqueduct and maybe even an admission to the Rosary at St. Patrick's Cathedral for them. I personally didn't need access and didn't need to take up space.

Commissioner Bratton approved. We would provide backup only to the Secret Service agents but not the Diplomats who would be obligated to obtain their own doctors if they were needed. After clearing it with Bratton, I revisited the Secret Service and told them that indeed we would assist them with care for their agents, stressing that the surgeons would be indemnified if there were any extraordinary events. I suggested that some sort of ID for myself would be appropriate.

"We don't have shields for non-agents," I was told. I didn't really need another shield. "We don't have the ability to photograph you. But downstairs is a Duane Reid, which has a photo booth. So if you go there and bring up a picture, we'll take care of getting you an ID." So for 10 dollars, I got four passport photos and gave them two.

The Secret Service got what they needed. Anne, her mother and got into the Mass at Aqueduct, where we sat next to Rudy Giuliani, and they both got into the Rosary at St. Pat's. I was one of the honor guards on the steps of the Cathedral and I got incredible pictures as the Pope walked by. I even got his blessing. Never hurts.

The Secret Service officers were interesting. Supposedly they had medical exam each year except there were some who didn't. Early in the week, I was called to attend to an agent who was admitted to the hospital for a possible heart attack. I responded to find a two pack-a-day smoking, overweight veteran agent with extensive coronary artery disease. Obviously, he was much too big to slip through the cracks, but as in most uniformed services, sometimes they take care of their own by looking the other way. He underwent successful bypass surgery in Manhattan.

Another agent tripped and fell as he exited the transport van. His ankle was shattered. I met him at the hospital where he would need surgery. The SAIC called to ask what I thought, so I told him to pack him up and send him home. They did.

One night during the UN session, I received a call from an agent assigned to the Waldorf Astoria Hotel on duty for the Ukraine delegation. Apparently the wife of one of the diplomats had overeaten and had a bellyache and demanded that we send a physician, preferably a Russian female, to the Waldorf to examine her. Her imperious demands meant nothing to me. The best part of being a non-employee was the ability to tell her no.

Explaining that we were only to assist the agents in the event of serious problems, I pointed out that we did not make house calls, that there were plenty of available physicians in Manhattan, and that they should consider calling their own physicians. It took three more phone calls including one to the SAIC to make it clear what our role was and avoid any international incident. No good deed goes unpunished.

I continued to help out the Secret Service on an informal basis after the big events ended. I had the opportunity to do a "photo op" with President Clinton in the basement of the Waldorf. He greeted me, shook my hand with two of his and informed me that "It was a pleasure to meet you, Dr. Fried." Assured that the White House would forward the photos from the event, I'm still waiting for the official photographs from the White House. Fortunately, the NYPD had its own photographers at the event.

While I never worked directly for the Secret Service, I was involved with some of the inner workings and strategic planning that they had engaged in regarding New York City. I was told that, whenever the president came to New York, the advance team would sit down with maps and information regarding possible evacuation to medical facilities in the event of an unfortunate incident. The agents would map out exactly where the president was travelling and locate the nearest hospitals and possible trauma-designated facilities.

I must admit that I found it peculiar that they never interacted with local physicians, including me, to really discern which facilities on their maps were adequate to treat an injured president. They mostly relied on bureaucratic published information, often either dated or out of touch with reality. One of the major problems with their planning was that high-quality "private" hospitals have no interest in treating trauma patients and thus they aren't qualified as trauma-designated centers. Often trauma patients may be victims of car accidents or the like. More commonly, however, during times when crime is higher, they are victims of stabbings and gunshots. Sometimes they are gang members or low-level criminals, drug addicts or other unsavory characters who provide excessive disruption to facilities. They are often uninsured. To tell the truth, the best places don't want the gunshot wounds or the stabbings. Fortunately, to date there has been no need for a trauma facility for an injured president in New York City.

CHAPTER 12

THE PC: (IT'S GOOD TO BE KING)

After the Mayor of the City of New York, the most visible public figure is the Police Commissioner. As a first responder and later as Executive Chief Surgeon, I got to spend time with the commissioners, beginning with Benjamin Ward and lastly with Bernard Kerik. I became part of that inner circle of police brass that sat in the hospital conference rooms after officers were shot or killed. My status was unique because, although I was considered a member of the uniformed service, I was not a police officer. Remaining part-time, my position was one of advisor, observer, and medical officer. Meanwhile, however, I got to see the inner workings of one of the largest police departments in the world.

The New York City Police Commissioner, commands a large standing army of armed troops thrust into innumerable ambivalent and conflicting roles. They carry guns but are supposed to protect and serve rather than fire first. They are expected to maintain order and are supposed to be a "team" or a "family" but are generally alone when it comes to trouble. They wear the uniform and the enemy doesn't. They can be attacked and shot at but are expected to respond with restraint and wisdom. Aggression is the last resort. Most cops are self-disciplined, motivated public servants. Unfortunately, it is the worst of them, an extremely small number in my experience, who make the headlines and who set the bad example by which the rest of the police force is too often judged.

When I was sworn in as a district surgeon in 1980, Ed Koch was Mayor and Robert McGuire was Police Commissioner. McGuire was a lawyer without a police background. He was a very dignified and classy guy, with whom I stayed in touch long after he retired. As a district surgeon, one of many, I had little interaction with the police commissioner in my early days.

That changed when Mayor Koch appointed Ben Ward. I got to know Commissioner Ward personally after our repeated interactions in the various hospitals when officers were shot. He trusted my judgment and would occasionally call on me for advice or medical information. Sometimes Ben was reticent about information concerning himself and on one occasion it nearly got him killed.

He had struggled with his drinking. He knew the dangers it posed and fastidiously avoided it. To ensure that his problem would not impair his ability to discharge his office, he voluntarily saw a physician who put him on Antabuse, a highly effective medication that causes a violent physical reaction if the patient consumes alcohol.

One day in 1987, however, he found himself coughing. He summoned Dr. T., Supervising Chief Surgeon to his office. Either Dr. T. never asked or Ben failed to reveal that he was taking Antabuse. Dr. T., to suppress a routine cough, prescribed an elixir cough medicine that happened to contain a reasonable amount of alcohol. Ben had a previous history of asthma. To suppress the cough, and never one to do things in moderation, he apparently swigged the cough medicine, unaware of its alcohol content. Ben was unable to breathe. 911 was called. He was rushed by ambulance to Booth Memorial Hospital with an extreme asthmatic attack and was nearly suffocating because of its severity.

I was quickly notified by Police Operations of the Commissioner's condition. I went to the hospital but was suspicious that something unrecognized was going on. I watched as I saw the skilled physicians save his life. Ben later asked me what I thought. I suggested to Ben that perhaps he ought not to rely solely on the treatment provided by the supervising chief surgeon, but instead obtain care from a pulmonary specialist at the hospital who was also a district surgeon. This worked for the remainder of the time while Ben Ward was police commissioner. Clearly it wasn't a good idea to risk the life of the commissioner with piecemeal medical care.

A few years later, AIDS was a major concern in New York City, taking the lives of far too many people. ACT-UP (AIDS Coalition to Unleash Power) was a protest organization that had begun in 1987 to protest the lack of progress and treatment for the victims of this dreaded disease. They had demonstrated during Sunday Mass at St. Patrick's Cathedral to call attention to their plight. Group spokesmen had threatened to bring tubes of their blood and throw it at people. The police needed to create an effective response.

There was a plan to arrest those trespassers who would invade St. Pat's, but a strategy had to be implemented to protect those police officers who would be involved. Meeting at Headquarters, the police brass decided that they would have the officers wear large yellow slickers with thick gloves, surgical masks and hats to invade and arrest the protesters. No one at the meeting had medical information regarding AIDS or its potential for spread.

Invited to the second meeting at Headquarters, I was informed of the plan. Practicing on the East Side of Manhattan, I had quite a few patients with full-blown AIDS and had become very familiar with the disease. I instructed that contagion was caused by direct blood-to-blood contact. I told the group that the slickers and masks were excessive. A much less aggressive and more reasonable response would be in order. Ben immediately countered with the comments that when doctors go into an AIDS patient's room, they wear slickers and masks and protective hats and gloves. I informed him that, because the patients' immune systems were severely compromised, the garb was worn to prevent the patient from catching anything from the doctor, not vice versa. The slicker plan was abandoned.

Ben Ward retired before the end of Mayor Koch's term and Richard Condon next served as Police Commissioner. David Dinkins became Mayor, defeating Koch who was attempting to win a fourth term. Condon left three months after the new Mayor took office. In spite of the tradition of appointing New Yorkers as police commissioner, Dinkins chose African-American Lee P. Brown, Police Commissioner of Houston as New York's new Police Commissioner. Lee Brown was a quiet, dignified gentleman, who knew little about New York City. He chose Ray Kelly as First Deputy Commissioner.

I had only limited contact with Lee Brown, seeing him at hospitals when officers were seriously injured or killed. He only served two years and, although the Dinkins years as Mayor were filled with homicides related to the crack epidemic, those two years were quiet with regard to trauma to police officers. That is, until August 19, 1991, the Crown Heights Riots.

A car driven by a Hasidic man had careened onto the sidewalk and killed a seven-year-old African American child. As a result, bands of African American youths to begin to roam the streets in that neighborhood of Brooklyn and attack Jewish residents. Police officers were under orders not to take action in the hope that the riot would burn itself out. It didn't. Many officers sustained minor injuries, cuts and bruises. Most injuries didn't require hospitalization or me responding, but large numbers of officers ended up in hospital emergency wards for treatment. Although I was informed of the ongoing situation, I had no intention of responding into the midst of a race riot alone.

Most of the officers were brought to Kings County Hospital. A 29-year-old Hasidic scholar, Yankel Rosenbaum, was visiting from Australia and was stabbed on the street. He was also taken to Kings County. Unfortunately, Yankel was not fully evaluated for his stab wounds. He had a chest X-ray performed but was never sat forward and a major stab wound of his back was thus never noticed. The radiologist reading the X-ray saw a chest full of blood and immediately sounded the alarm.

Yankel died, bleeding to death from the stab wound which went unrecognized until it was too late. The disorder in the streets accelerated and became more violent until finally 1,800 cops were dispatched and stopped the rioting. In August 1992 Lee Brown resigned and returned to Houston. I doubt if anyone noticed his departure. Except for Ray Kelly who became police commissioner.

I had known Ray Kelly for years. He often asked for my medical opinions regarding injuries to officers. Late one afternoon I got a call from him. He was in Brooklyn with an officer who was shot in the leg. The Supervising Chief Surgeon had responded to the shooting. I was seeing patients in my office in Manhattan and was totally unaware of the incident. It was thought that the officer could receive better care at Bellevue. Kelly had asked if it was safe to transport the officer. Dr. T. answered, "I guess so." Kelly had a fit.

I got a frantic phone call because "guessing so" was obviously not good enough. Summoned to "get your ass down here," I was told that nothing would be done until I personally came down to Brooklyn and assessed the officer's injuries and made a decision regarding the safety of his being transported from Brooklyn to Manhattan. Arriving after cancelling office hours, I determined that there was no major blood vessel injury and that the wound would require an angiogram performed by a skilled radiologist. If that turned out to be negative, the wound would require some cleaning and debridement of injured tissue. As I often did, I rode in the ambulance to Bellevue, having an officer follow in my car. Kelly was happy that I didn't "guess."

Ray Kelly was a tough, no-nonsense former U.S. Marine. He was definitive and expected the same from people who worked for him. He didn't delegate many responsibilities and in marked contrast to his predecessor, Lee Brown, and was a fully hands-on leader. For example, when he was First Deputy Commissioner, the first group of portable cell phones were issued to the PD and he was in charge. Seeing a stack of cell phones, I obviously wanted one to avoid having to search for a pay phone to answer my beeper. None for me. Not yet.

With the election of Mayor Rudolph Giuliani, however, it was obvious that Giuliani wasn't keeping anyone that Dinkins had appointed. Kelly's days were clearly numbered. Finding out that Bratton was the choice for the next PC, Kelly had summoned me to his office to discuss the possibility of a medical condition that might exist after his retirement. Seeing another stack of cell phones, I naturally asked for one. "Take as many as you'd like." I only needed one. Sometimes it's good to be around when they're packing up to leave.

I advised Ray Kelly to take a stress test to check for any potential heart disease. This is routine prior to retirement since the "Heart Bill" states that coronary artery disease, i.e. heart disease, is considered job related and heart disease that impairs is eligible for line of duty, a three quarters retirement pension. If one retired on a line-of-duty injury, including the "Heart Bill", the officer is eligible for a tax-free pension equal to three quarters of the previous three years' salary. This has changed in recent years. Kelly went for the stress test and failed. I suggested that he do two things that I considered important. First, he should follow up the positive stress test with a cardiac catheterization to see how severe his coronary artery disease was because coronary artery disease can lead to a heart attack. Second, he should apply for the "Heart Bill" if he was indeed planning to retire just to be sure he would get an appropriate pension if he had a severe heart condition.

He did the second and didn't do the first. The papers jumped all over it. They implied that he was trying to "steal" a pension. After several months, he reversed his application and withdrew it. He was looking forward to a further career without encumbrances like a disability pension. He absolutely qualified under the Heart Bill and would have retired on a disability pension. He clearly didn't want that and I couldn't disagree with his decision, although I also felt that failing to follow-up might significantly impair his health.

But not doing the first didn't make the coronary artery disease disappear. While serving as Director of Police under the United Nations Mission in Haiti, he was returned to the states for urgent open-heart surgery. Commissioner Kelly returned to a 12-year term as PC under Mayor Michael Bloomberg. I had multiple favorable interactions with him, although I retired long before he left the office for the second time.

When Mayor Giuliani took office, William Bratton succeeded Raymond Kelly as Police Commissioner. My first major interaction with the new administration was on March 15, 1994 at Columbia Presbyterian Hospital. The first officer murdered after Giuliani became Mayor was Sean McDonald, killed in a clothing shop in the Bronx. He was taken to Columbia Presbyterian Hospital in upper Manhattan, and pronounced dead. His wife was brought to the hospital. It was my job to tell both Giuliani and Bratton that the officer was killed.

"What happens now?" asked the Mayor.

"The wife will arrive, see the both of you, and immediately break down. She'll guess that he is dead because of your expressions and because she isn't being taken directly to see him."

"We can't let her see him like that, can we?" asked the Mayor.

"He belongs to her first, so of course we will." I told them.

And we did.

These events are terribly stressful; they require tact and finesse. As the one with the most senior experience, I was the one the leaders looked to for guidance. I'd obviously been there far too many times before. From that event forward, the Mayor would occasionally look to me for guidance and medical advice.

Bratton's inner circle of Chiefs included Mike Julian, Chief of Personnel, John Timoney, First Deputy Police Commissioner, John Miller, Deputy Commissioner of Public Information and Jack Maple, Deputy Police Commissioner for Crime Control Strategies. This was a young, energetic and focused group with whom I was both comfortable and informal. They would often call me regarding job-related and personal medical issues.

I generally was their "go to" doctor, and would make appropriate referrals to physicians I respected for the medical problems that would arise. I was a surgeon and didn't find it appropriate to attempt to be all things to all people. I was much more comfortable referring out problems that I generally didn't handle or that I considered beyond my scope of practice. By this time, I knew large numbers of specialist physicians in New York City who were honored to care for police officers.

Jack Maple was a larger-than-life figure who in conjunction with Bratton clearly changed the way policing was done first in New York City and then across the country. He was the architect of a new way of policing. He actually felt that statistics and tracking crime would lead to more effective policing. They called it CompStat and Bratton believed in it and promoted it. It definitely worked and has spread across the country. Using computer technology, maps, and crime statistics, everyone at the CompStat meetings could see where the crimes were being committed and how to best combat them.

Jack started as a cop in the Transit Police, which eventually became part of the NYPD. Bratton was originally the commissioner of the Transit Police. Dressed to the nines, Homberg hat, 3 piece suit, spats, Jack was unique. He was also very smart. He wrote a book on crime fighting and was a consultant for television. How could you not like working with someone like that?

I remember seeing him in his office: A desk, a chair, no pictures and a large punching bag which he would hit until his knuckles were raw. He would ask me medical questions pertaining to the officers. What about exposures to noxious chemicals? What about hearing loss? Why did cops get fat? How do we get more of them to interact with the community? Why were there suicides in clusters and was there anything we should be doing to prevent it?

In the scheme of things, Bratton's group didn't last very long in spite of a paradigm shift in policing that had sweeping importance for departments across the country. Sometimes politics and egos get in the way and may overshadow actual achievement. First, John Miller, perhaps too good at his job promoting the police over the Mayor, had his Public Information Office stripped of 28 staffers. He left. Bratton followed not long afterward.

After Bratton's unceremonious departure, Jack Maple became a sought-after consultant. He ended up in New Orleans, brought there by an administration hoping to staunch the murder rate. While there he experienced some rectal bleeding. He saw a local physician who, without examining him, diagnosed hemorrhoids. Unfortunately, the bleeding continued slowly for months. He came back to New York to see his old friends. On a Sunday evening John Miller called me. Jack had a problem. Would I see him? Of course, I said. First thing in the morning, it was my painful duty to inform him that he had a large rectal cancer. Scans revealed that he already had liver involvement. He went to Memorial Sloan Kettering but refused surgery, which would have meant a permanent colostomy. Enduring radiation treatment, he succumbed not long after at the age of 48. Jack's unique insights, global views and out-of-the box thinking in conjunction with support from the Bratton team has made a paradigm shift in policing across the country.

Bratton left after only two years; Howard Safir replaced him. He was an outsider to the NYPD. His previous career was with the U.S. Marshall Service, and he had recently been the Fire Commissioner under Giuliani. I had my first interaction with him when he was Fire Commissioner. I had heard that he was working on a solution to the problem of fire officers with limitations who couldn't pass the yearly physicals and were facing restricted duty or termination.

The NYPD had only one yearly requirement, namely firearms proficiency. There was an ongoing problem with officers who couldn't or didn't qualify with firearms. Some clever officers who wanted disability or didn't really like patrol would go to the range and fail to qualify with a 65% accuracy at target practice. Some officers had received hand injuries and failed to qualify. Others had no discernible injuries or minimal injuries but also failed to qualify. Some officers were motivated by the desire to obtain disability pensions related to hand problems and therefore wouldn't cooperate to qualify. If you still failed to qualify, you'd be required to surrender your guns. That automatically placed you indoors on restricted duty. You can't shoot, or won't try to, but nothing is wrong with you. Now what?

Safir, as fire commissioner, had firefighters who couldn't pass or didn't want to pass the agility test but also didn't qualify or get approved for disability by the Medical Board. Safir found a regulation allowing him to eventually furlough without pay those who fit into that category. If after a reasonable time on furlough, you couldn't qualify, you could be terminated. Maybe we could fire the hand cases. Never happened. If you can't shoot or don't want to, you can stay on the job until you get the disability pension you're hoping for, decide to try to qualify or until you turn 63.

During the early days of Commissioner Safir's term, numerous cops were assaulted, shot, and killed. I responded to most of these events and spent countless hours with Giuliani and Safir. Commissioner Safir also had a few medical problems, knew of my reputation and sought me out for referrals to physicians I knew. I must admit that having a personal relationship with the Police Commissioner of New York City had endless advantages.

You get to go places and do things that most others don't have the opportunity to do. Yet you don't have to suffer the public criticism and invasion of your private life that major public figures have to endure.

Police shootings increased in the early years of Safir's tenure, one of which included the shooting of Francis Latimer, shot at point blank range in the head in August 1996. He was taken to Columbia Presbyterian Hospital where superb medical care saved his life, although he was blinded by the injury. The bullet pierced the frontal lobe of his brain, causing major personality changes. At times, he would "see things," unable to recognize or realize that he was actually blind.

In May 1996, police officer Vincent Guidice suffered a major laceration to his femoral artery while responding to a domestic dispute. An out-of-control husband hurled a mirror at him, which smashed and cut him. I was out of town at the time. Taken to the nearest hospital, he underwent hours of surgery, but eventually succumbed to his injury. Dr. T., Supervising Chief Surgeon, responded to the event and had apparently been told by the operating surgeon and hospital administrator that the officer should be o.k. He simply related that news to those in attendance. Soon that information would prove false. The officer died in less than eight hours after surgery.

Commissioner Safir asked me to look into the events. It was my impression that more aggressive resuscitation during the intraoperative events might have made the outcome different. It's easy to be a Monday morning quarterback, and since I wasn't present at the event, I could only rely on the information I was provided by reviewing the hospital chart. I don't think, in 1996 that exsanguination is an acceptable outcome after hours in surgery. Dr. T.'s optimistic reports that the officer would be o.k. placed him in an untenable situation. As the messenger, however, he lost future credibility. Far better judgment would have had him let the operating surgeon give the report.

Brian Jones was a Housing Authority Officer shot in October 1996. Housing had merged with the NYPD under Bratton but they continued to have their own medical officers. I still responded at that time to Brookdale Hospital, as did Commissioner Safir. He approached me at Brookdale and suggested that I be promoted to a two-star chief position. He felt that I would have a more independent position and actually deserved more recognition for all I had done. Although I was complimented by the thought, there was a problem for me. A two-star chief in the NYPD is actually designated an Assistant Chief. Frankly, in my mind that would make me the assistant to Dr. T., who although not an unpleasant fellow, I felt that I couldn't really tolerate that association.

First, he told me that the promotion might have to wait until the next budget since there was no part-time medical two-star position in the NYPD. Then he told me that the paperwork would take even longer to establish the title under the usual bureaucratic setup if I wanted more money to accompany the position. I told him I didn't want the position called "assistant chief" and that I didn't care if I got a raise.

Richard Sheirer, Safir's Chief of Staff came up with the solution. Richie had begun as a fire dispatcher, became part of Safir's staff first in the Fire Department, and moved with him to the NYPD. He was a terrific guy with a warm personality, loyal, friendly and someone who was bright enough to know how to handle most situations. He eventually became Commissioner of Emergency Management and one of the major figures responsible for the city after 9/11.

His solution for me was to remain on the books as a one-star (deputy chief) for salary purposes, but be designated a two-star with a newly designated title namely "Executive Chief Surgeon". Perfect. In a quiet swearing-in ceremony in November 1996, I became the only Executive Chief Surgeon with a two-star shield in the NYPD (with a one-star pay scale).

Howard Safir's tenure as PC was tarnished by his loyalty to a long-time friend. He had worked with Marilyn Mode for years in the Marshall Service and brought her along as a spokesperson when he was Fire Commissioner. Naturally, when he transitioned to Police Commissioner, she went with him and became Deputy Commissioner for Public Information. She had a hard act to follow. After all, her predecessor, John Miller, a seasoned reporter and TV personality had helped make Bratton a household name. Marilyn was always around when things were happening. She was at hospitals and every major event. The only trouble was that she was neither very slick nor polished enough to put positive spins on some of the accomplishments of Commissioner Safir or the NYPD.

Every year Commissioner Safir would take a ski vacation in Park City, Utah. Returning after the hiatus, he called me to say that while he had been walking in the high altitude, he noticed pain in his jaw. After a trip to the dentist eliminated the obvious, no dental problems, I encouraged a thorough workup. A stress test revealed that the pain seemed related to heart problems. The next step would require a cardiac catheterization to discover the source and the extent of the problem and the possible need for heart surgery.

Potential cardiac surgery in 1997 was and still is no haircut. I sat with him and suggested that he get his life in order. No, I didn't think he would die, but discussing things in those terms in my opinion helped indicate the potentially seriousness of the situation. Our discussion was on a Monday night in his apartment.

I asked him if he planned to mention the situation to his police brass and he said that he would in due time. I obviously would not divulge any health-related information.

He had a second stress test performed later the same week which confirmed the diagnosis. He then went for cardiac catheterization. One of my medical school colleagues did the catheterization and told me that he had pretty severe disease. They could attempt stenting because he was the Police Commissioner and was in a hurry to get back to work. I simply asked what he would do if it was his father. Bypass surgery. Sometimes doctors forget that VIPs are human and deserve the same care as anyone else.

So after the procedure, his cardiologist, wife, and I all went to his room. Hearing the alternatives, he was gung-ho to get on with the procedure. He was ready, let's do it. Today. And they would. I suggested he call someone at the Police Department because he might be out of commission for a while. Good idea?

Tosano Simonetti was First Deputy Police Commissioner at the time. He had announced that he was retiring from the force in the days ahead, although another commissioner had not been announced as yet. Howard called him to tell him the situation. Simonetti would assemble the executive staff and relay the situation.

Howard also notified the Mayor's office. This was typical of Howard Safir. No doubts. Confident. He was aware of the situation and definitive. Rick Esposito, M.D. was available as the surgeon. The operating room was available. Let's do it. And they did. Five bypasses. Four hours.

Mayor Giuliani arrived early evening to see Safir, who was intubated and in the recovery room (now it's called the PACU...

post anesthesia care unit). Shocked at what he saw, I assured the Mayor that his appearance was actually normal and that he should do well. He was up and talking within a few hours.

Recovery was uneventful, although as I had pointed out, it wasn't a haircut. He had been active and athletic prior to the surgery, which obviously contributed favorably to his recovery. Against my recommendation, he decided that he would appear and march in the St. Patrick's Day parade just 10 days post-op. Not my idea exactly of an appropriate recovery time, I felt he should wait a bit. No sir, he was going to march.

Stubborn, yes. So I sat with the Police Commissioner's people and the plan was to provide a golf cart to transport him up 5th Avenue. The morning was cool but not rainy, so all was in order. He got into the golf cart. It was going nowhere. The battery was dead. No worries. They had brought another one. They transferred him to the backup. Again, the cart went nowhere. Again, a dead battery. So on March 17, 1997, Tom Dingler, head of the detail, accompanying detectives and Greg Fried, Executive Chief Surgeon, pushed Howard Safir, Police Commissioner up 5th Avenue in the golf cart, a float in the St. Patrick's Day Parade. After that, he disappeared for a while to recover.

Two memorable events resonate with me from Safir's years as commissioner. In August 1997, Abner Louima, a Haitian immigrant was arrested in East Flatbush, Brooklyn and taken to the 70th Precinct. While in custody, he was tortured and assaulted rectally with a broomstick causing serious colon and bladder damage. He was brought to Coney Island Hospital where initial surgery was performed. Subsequently, he was transferred to Brooklyn Hospital for further care.

Several days after the event, I was called by the Mayor who had been informed that Mr. Louima was being taken back into surgery. Both he and Commissioner Safir were quite concerned about the unfolding events and for the well-being of the patient. Both were also concerned that the victim might die. Could I find out somehow what the nature of the new surgery might be and if indeed it was life-threatening? A death might lead to a full-blown race riot in Brooklyn.

No, I didn't go to the hospital. I'm neither that brave nor that foolish that I would intrude into the midst of a potentially explosive situation. I did, however, train a lot of younger surgeons and had many contacts in the city. Not needing to know the particulars of the operation, I only wanted to get a general idea of what was going to be done in surgery. After a few phone calls and about 4 degrees of separation later, I was informed that Mr. Louima went back to surgery for an intestinal obstruction, probably related to early adhesions. This news was released publicly by Jean Claude Compas, his surgeon, and in no way was neither privileged information nor a violation of patient confidentiality. The surgery lasted a little more than an hour. It was my impression that he would be okay. He was.

This horrendous assault reverberated throughout the city and the country. Safir was deeply concerned, for he couldn't comprehend the motivation for such brutality from anyone, especially a police officer. Safir visited Louima in the hospital and assured him that definitive action would be taken. He did the best he could in the face of such an extraordinary violation of police behavior by the arresting officers. The police officers were suspended, investigated, and eventually jailed. No cover-up, no obfuscation or attempt to obscure facts ever occurred.

The biggest event during the Safir years was Y2K, the millennium moment when 1999 became 2000. At the time, there were security concerns about a possible terrorist act against the usual crowd that would mob Times Square. There was also the possibility that many computers and systems would fail at midnight, causing people to be trapped in elevators, buildings to cease functioning, electrical grids to crash and countless unforeseen catastrophes that would befall a helpless city. In preparation for the end of civilization as we knew it, task forces assembled for months in advance throughout the city and all over the country.

Never one to be caught short, GM, one of the Lieutenants at Health Services designated himself the person to prepare the NYPD Medical Services for the coming apocalypse. He had previously proven himself as someone who negatively interacted with staff and spent countless amounts of time accomplishing nothing. This would be his shining moment of glory, or so he supposed.

His elaborate plan was to have police surgeons assemble at all of the Health Care facilities throughout the city. They were to be there in case officers were injured or went sick to avoid the different assignments to details or to get New Year's Eve off. The police surgeons were to be ready to take care of malingerers, putting them directly back to work. Emergency rooms throughout the city were advised to bring in extra staff. Unconvinced that the world would truly end that night, I felt the preparations excessive. But I've been wrong before and could only voice an opinion that this was simply overkill. I was convinced that NYPD officers, as on every other occasion, would rise to the occasion and do whatever was necessary to protect the public and make the event memorable.

In any event, I was going to spend New Year's Eve with my wife, Commissioner Safir and his wife Carol, at a black-tie dinner. We would then all assemble on Times Square. Naturally I brought a camera too. Dinner was low key but delightful. After dessert, we all went outside to lower Broadway to join the festivities. The weather was freezing, so we would hide in the Police Substation on Times Square to thaw out. This had often been the case on other New Year's Eves that I spent on Times Square.

Walking between the pens and barriers, watching the revelers was hot stuff. Everyone was having a good time. We saw Dick Clark doing his TV stuff, ran into other ranking police and fire officials, greeted the Mayor, and all in all had fun. At midnight, Mohammed Ali pushed the round sphere that started the descent of the ball that ushered in the new millennium. A few elevators got stuck, but the Fire Department crew was prepared to handle this. I guess some computers had problems resetting but in general there was no terror, no terror threats at the time. That was to come in the future.

Fireworks, confetti, kissing, yay...a new century, a new millennium. And the world didn't end.

At 12:20 a.m. January 1, 2000, I requested that Commissioner Safir call off the excessive preparations that one over-thinking Lieutenant GM had made anticipating a surge in injuries and cops going sick. No one abused the system. They just did what they had to and stayed with the detail. I guess it's better to prepare for the worst, but, having the years of experience that I did with the NYPD, I was convinced the preparations were overkill. I guess I was right.

Howard Safir left the NYPD in August 2000. In February 1999, Amadou Diallo, an unarmed, illegal alien was killed in a hail of bullets in an incident at night in the Bronx. The heat was building on the NYPD regarding this inappropriate shooting. Safir found himself also taking heat with other criticisms, including complaints that he had taken a trip to California to be at the Oscars using private transportation. I think he had just had enough. You can only stay for so long until things begin to go from good to tolerable to bad.

Bernard Kerik followed as Police Commissioner. My relationship with Kerik was civil and quite official. I respected both the things he had accomplished since he had been in Corrections for years. He was rough-edged and tough. He treated me with respect and called upon me for occasional medical advice and direction. Once, one of his relatives was having serious substance dependency problems. He reached out to me for help and I reached out to some of my contacts at a detox program. He stood by his family member and saw that appropriate treatment was initiated. I always respected him for that since he was clearly concerned and involved with his relative and was unconcerned that perhaps he or his relative might be associated with the detox situation. He wanted the best for that person. He was definitely a stand-up guy. I was recently informed by Commissioner Kerik that after another intervention much more recently, his relative has totally cleaned up and is living a successful and clean life.

I never had a problem reaching him about medical issues that I thought were important regarding the department. We didn't meet often in the hospitals, however, since things were quiet until 9/11/2001, after which I was out of commission. He reached out to me several times after I was injured and was partially responsible for submitting my name for departmental recognition for my actions on 9/11.

The real person who submitted me for the Medal for Valor was the First Deputy Police Commissioner, Joe Dunne. I had known Joe since I first became a police surgeon. He had worked at Health

Services as a Lieutenant, moving on to bigger things in his career at the NYPD over the years. We had remained in touch as he rose in his career. He commanded Brooklyn North, worked in the Housing Police and eventually on 9/11 was the First Deputy Commissioner. He had ruptured his Achilles tendon in July 2001 and called me while I was in Tralee, Ireland for assistance. He was still on crutches on 9/11.

Joe is a good friend. By many accounts, he should have been made Police Commissioner, but apparently some doubters in City Hall felt it necessary to tell Giuliani that Joe's loyalty was closer to the NYPD than to the Mayor. At the end of the Mayor's term in City Hall, he had asked me to come by and speak to him, just one on one. As we looked back at events we had shared, I simply asked him why he had failed to make Joe the Police Commissioner. Giuliani smiled and told me that he had promised Kerik, his former driver when he was a Federal Prosecutor, that if he ever became Mayor, he'd make Kerik the Police Commissioner.

"That's bull," I challenged the Mayor and told him to tell me the real reason. The first was that indeed he had made the promise, but more importantly, he realized that Joe was committed and totally loyal to the NYPD. The Mayor told me, that he knew if he appointed Kerik, he'd actually get both of them. Joe would never turn his back on the department and would be there to support Kerik and the NYPD at all costs.

The role of Police Commissioner of the New York Police Department can be one of the most difficult positions in government. The decisions that come from that office reverberate with the eight million people who live in the city, but have much further implications for policing across the country. The Commissioner must balance decisions that impact public safety and crime prevention with protection of citizens' civil rights. It has been one of the more fascinating aspects of my job with the NYPD to interact closely and personally with the varied commissioners.

My position was unique since most careers in the NYPD start at the bottom and progress slowly upward with promotions. After Commissioner Ben Ward promoted me quite early in my career, I always remained near the top brass, seeing them and getting to know them as they came and went.

CHAPTER 13

ABSENT!

When an officer is killed in the line of duty, the Police Department Honor Legion memorializes them at their meetings. The Honor Legion president reads the name or names of the deceased to a silent, respectful room and someone says "absent" to recognize and honor them. The Honor Legion represents the group of officers who have been honored with a special commendation or medal. The highest honor, the Medal of Honor, is always granted to the officers killed in the line of duty, but can also be granted to officers who have distinguished themselves with extraordinary and outstanding action usually in the face of extreme danger. I am an actual and not honorary member of the Honor Legion because I was officially awarded the Police Department Medal for Valor after 9/11.

A line-of-duty death at the hands of a criminal is quite different from almost any other mortality event. As a surgeon, I have often dealt with patient mortality from disease and trauma. There is a uniqueness associated however with the murder of a police officer of which most people are unaware. Police officers work a daily job in familiar surroundings and report to work as scheduled. They neither expect to be murdered nor do they particularly plan for it in the course of the average day. If they did, it would be impossible for them to go to work.

Obviously on special assignments, drug busts, criminal arrests, SWAT teams, special operations, officers experience heightened alerts and take appropriate precautions to potential danger. In general, however, in the routine performance of an officer's job, things are generally the same and danger is usually far from their minds. A daily tour is often described as seven and three-quarter hours of boredom and 15 minutes of terror when a threat, real or imagined, appears.

In spite of the hype and the exaggerations, there is no war out there. Cops are not soldiers carrying guns to kill enemies. The majority of officers go an entire career without firing their weapons. They are civil servants whose general motivation is to help people and create a civil environment where the rest of us can function in peace. Yes, there are exceptions, but there are those in every field.

Cops who are shot are shot by strangers. The perp is firing at a symbol that represents civil society in general and to the bad guy an impersonal threat of potential arrest and jail. These are uncommon events as opposed to open warfare where shootings and killings are expected. In the worst days of violence in the 1970's and 1980's, fewer than two officers were shot each month and fortunately the numbers actually killed can be counted on one's hands. But it certainly did happen. In the 1990's crime decreased and officer deaths did too but only slightly. After 9/11, one cannot ignore the 24 officers killed at the World Trade Center. Each year, cops are killed in the line of duty. Obviously, everyone is familiar with the new spate of police killings occurring in the last few years.

Cops are generally young. They go to work like everyone else and don't kiss the wife or husband and kids and say see you later unless I'm killed today. All of us are aware of our potential mortality, but we keep it far from our consciousness unless something like cancer or a heart attack brings it forward. Even with the knowledge of a serious disease, most of my patients carried strength and hope with them by keeping a positive outlook, knowing well that something else someday might kill them.

What is it that makes the shooting and death of a cop unique? A cop shot and killed is a very public event. The ritual surrounding it is pretty much standardized unless the cop is murdered on the scene and pronounced dead at the place where he or she was shot. This happened on my watch with Officer Ed Byrne, who was shot dead in an ambush in South Jamaica, Queens. It happened with officers Keith Williams and Richard Guerzon, who were murdered by a criminal who was being transported to jail and managed somehow to conceal a handgun in the patrol car. And it happened to officer Anthony Dwyer, thrown from a roof, among others.

A cop when shot is transported to the nearest hospital. Hopefully this facility is capable of trauma care and appropriate resuscitation. Many times the facility is in a neighborhood with a higher incidence of traumas and crime. This was the case for many of the city hospitals, such as Bellevue, Jacoby, Kings County, Brookdale, Jamaica. Often lifesaving care could be obtained in other facilities, which were not designated as Level One Trauma Centers. Experienced senior officers in various precincts in New York always know which hospital will provide the best care, whether they are designated trauma centers or not. The first responders, those who are transporting the injured officer, whether by police car or ambulance always head to the familiar and known facilities when things are critical.

Suddenly, a tidal wave of blue uniforms, a legion of people, follows the officer into the hospital. The neighborhood shuts down with the invasion of an army of police vehicles, yellow crime scene tape, and investigators. At the hospital, someone from the department notifies Police Operations, someone else calls the Sick Desk, someone notifies the Mayor's office, and the press is notified. Each group notified would dispatch appropriate people to either the hospital or the crime scene. On numerous occasions I would be called by several of these sources.

Obviously, more than one modality of communication was used to notify the police brass, myself, and the rest of the constellation of essential people expected to respond to the situation. Sometimes the news reporters using their police scanners would react to the situation and head for the hospital or the crime scene. I would be notified by the Sick Desk, but the first one who often notified me was Trenchcoat.

Trenchcoat, although working for the police department in his usual free-lance modality, often took it upon himself to notify the Mayor. When Ben Ward was Police Commissioner, Trenchcoat would skip any notification to the Police Commissioner. Because Trenchcoat spent the nights monitoring every communication in the city as he roamed the streets, he knew about the events first. He would notify Mayor Koch's office and ignore Ben Ward's. The outcome would be that the Mayor would arrive at the hospital before the Commissioner.

This would consistently make Ben's blood boil. He was an active Commissioner and arriving after the Mayor made it appear that he was less involved. He would take his own people aside and complain loudly and threateningly about Trenchcoat. It was both embarrassing to Ben Ward that the Mayor would sometimes arrive at the hospital and be waiting for the arrival of the Police Commissioner. Naturally this would not endear Trenchcoat to the Commissioner's detail.

When David Dinkins became Mayor, he appointed Lee Brown ("out of town Brown") who never seemed to care much who arrived first or who was notified first. Still a major player in the Dinkins administration, Trenchcoat would hover around the Mayor's entourage giving orders and directions.

Trenchcoat made a serious political mistake when Dinkins was running for a second term, once again against Giuliani. Attending a police funeral, Candidate Giuliani had assembled in the front line with police brass and other public officials. As a candidate for mayor and a former Federal Prosecutor, this was appropriate. Trenchcoat, doing his usual strutting and directing, felt it necessary to reposition Giuliani towards the back of the assembled dignitaries, seating him apart from them when the entourage entered the Church.

Clearly this was a poor decision, as Giuliani handily won the election. Although I don't know if the new Mayor Giuliani remembered the incident, I don't think this behavior endeared Trenchcoat to the new Mayor or his staff. Seeing that his glory days were waning, Trenchcoat kept a much lower profile during the Giuliani days.

If the injury to the officer was non-lethal, it was my job to obtain as many reliable facts as I could so that when the press conference was held, the Mayor and Police Commissioner could give the public appropriate descriptions of the injury and facts regarding the critical incident. Occasionally I would proceed to go to the operating room to assess the situation. I always attempted to stress the severity of the situation. I honestly believe getting shot, regardless of the extent of the injury, is major. If I wasn't able to make a reasonable prediction about the expected outcome, I would say so.

I consider anyone getting shot a very serious injury regardless of the location of the bullets and regardless of the initial assessments. I followed enough gunshot victims in my career to know that the repercussions of getting shot in the civilian setting were numerous both physical and psychological for the victim and the fact that someone survives is not the equivalent of "doing fine."

If the officer dies, the situation is totally different. Every member of the Police Department feels it very personally and becomes an extended family in a show of unity around the officer. The massive numbers of officers assemble to remind the immediate family that they are all affected by this loss. This, however, may also interfere with the actual family and loved ones and can a huge wedge between a young, devoted, but now newly widowed spouse and the newly lost officer who left home that morning to perform his routine tour.

The press releases the information that an officer was shot. The location of where the incident occurred is released, although the name of the officer is not released until the family is notified. Picture the horror for a family or relative or even a friend hearing about the death of a loved one over the news. Everyone whose loved one works in or near that area and who hears about that event is now placed on edge and alert.

The "10 card" is the card the officer fills out in the precinct where he or she works and provides the information about the next-of-kin notification. Often the information may be obsolete if an officer has remarried or had other changes in his life. The best information is gathered from the precinct, his or her fellow officers or from police operations. Someone is dispatched from Employee Relations to go to the house or find the next of kin. Usually a chaplain is sent if the religion is not clear because until recently the majority of officers are Christian.

When Joe Galapo was killed in Brooklyn, the assumption was that because of the "o" at the end of his name that he was Italian. It turned out he was Sephardic Jewish with Egyptian roots and the family was Jewish. But a priest was still dispatched. In the pandemonium that can follow a shooting, best intentions can lead to erroneous decisions.

Many of the shootings and killings I was involved with occurred in the evening or at night and therefore often the families were at home. Arriving at the homes, after the radio or TV announced the fact that a cop was shot, the Employee Relations people are harbingers of the worst news regardless of what they say: "Your husband was shot and was taken to blank hospital...We're here to take you to see him or her...No we aren't aware of his condition." The next of kin fears the worst until it's proven otherwise.

Appropriate family members are transported in highway-patrol cars to the hospital. If there are babies or young children at home, someone is designated to stay there and babysit. Rushed to the hospital by siren, the entourage at the hospital awaits the arrival of the family. The press outside awaits their arrival to catch the photo of the petrified family entering the hospital not knowing if their loved one is alive or dead.

One night two cops, Chris Hoban and Michael Buczek, were killed in totally unrelated incidents. Michael's wife lived in Rockland County. The Employee Relations people and Father Mychal Judge were transported to his home by helicopter because of the distance. They decided to tell Michael's wife of only a few months of his death without transporting her back. Christine Buczek was convinced to relinquish the privacy of a funeral to a double funeral in Brooklyn at the Cathedral with dual coffins ascending the stairs into the chapel. Impressive, but she felt that not only was Michael taken from her but so was his funeral and her ability to actively participate in his final farewell. The department took him away twice.

When Joe Galapo was shot in the head, he was taken to Lutheran Medical Center in Brooklyn. But they were at the time incapable of performing neurosurgery. He was then transported to Bellevue for an attempt at neurosurgery. He was pronounced dead at Bellevue, but his family was transported from Brooklyn. Because he was shot in the head, his facial features swelled and became grotesquely distorted. Thinking they were sparing the wife the agony of seeing her loved one in that state, the powers that be, including Trenchcoat, felt it best to deny her access to viewing his body and talked her out of seeing him. Weeks later, learning that I was present when he died, but not having met her immediately upon his death, she reached out to me. She told me of her pain and turmoil at not having seen him. She would repeatedly ask me questions about his death, which I always answered honestly.

She taught me a tremendous amount through her grief about what should belong to the family and where the department should draw the line. Unfortunately, the knowledge I gained from her grief was used far too many times in the future when officers were killed and I attended the situation. She also taught me about the realities of what happened to the families.

Joe's funeral was near his home in Brooklyn. His family plot, however, was in Staten Island. It turns out that the union, the PBA, upon the death of the officer issued an advanced check immediately to the surviving spouse because they were expected to pay for the funeral. After the funeral, the family followed the hearse as it wended its way from Brooklyn to the cemetery in Staten Island. Dozens of cars and motorcycles in the cortege followed the hearse over the Verrazano Bridge. Several weeks later, not only was Joe's widow expected to pay for the funeral, but she received a bill from the Port Authority for all the cars and motorcycles that accompanied them to Staten Island.

This situation was beyond my belief. The widows had lost their husbands. Everyone who spoke at the funerals regaled them with heroic, dedicated speeches. Applause filled the overcrowded church or hall. Now they got the bill? I related this story to my friend Peter Johnson, an attorney who was one of Governor Mario Cuomo's lawyers. Peter obviously saw the injustice here and asked me to meet with the governor.

Taking full advantage of this opportunity, I brought several young widows with me to the meeting. I introduced them to the governor, who was a warm and courteous family man. No one could help but be impressed by the three young police widows. I told him about the funeral, the costs, and the bills. I also pointed out that these young women, whose lives had been devastated by the heroic sacrifices of their husbands would lose their husbands' pensions if they married again. Yes, if they remarried, the pensions would be taken away. Hard to believe? It had actually happened to some of the victims' families in the past.

The governor introduced COPS (concern for our police survivor) legislation that numerous other states had in place already. This legislation had New York State assume the responsibility for payment for the funerals. There would no longer be the first check cut the day after the line-of-duty death to pay the funeral home, but rather the New York State Crime Victims Board would provide funds to assist in paying for the funerals. In addition, the women could remarry and keep their pensions. Their children would be allowed and encouraged to attend New York State colleges without tuition costs. Governor Mario Cuomo proudly announced the passing of the legislation at a formal ceremony in his office.

In 1988 Susan McCormack, Mary Beth O'Neill and Kathleen Sullivan, all police widows, formed the Survivors of the Shield support group to provide for social, economic, and emotional needs of survivors and families of slain police officers. They were instrumental in the passage of the COPS legislation. These dedicated survivors and those who have come after them speak directly to the families. No one can offer more accurate and appropriate counseling to the bereaved or tell them what to expect in the short and long-term journey than these unique and brave widows could.

Police funerals are well-coordinated, scripted displays, designed to remind the public of the universality of the tragedy that has befallen the city. Thousands of cops in uniform stand at full attention as the motorcycles precede the hearse. All are silent as six white-gloved officers carry the casket on their shoulders into the place of worship. Eulogies are given sometimes by loved ones, the Police Commissioner, the Mayor, the local clergy, the departmental chaplain. "The cop was a hero...He gave his life so others may be safe...We are all your family...We will never forget what he did...Giuliani began the practice of asking for a round of applause to thank the officer. Back into the hearse, six helicopters flying in missing-man formation above. Travel to the cemetery. Burial.

Wife and kids go home. The large entourage over the subsequent weeks begins to dissipate. Only friends of the officer visit. We remember the officer and his children at Christmas, on Medal Day when he is awarded the Medal of Honor posthumously, and on other police memorial occasions. His name is placed on the Wall of Honor in Police Headquarters. Life does go on. We do forget. They name a street or a park after him. Honor Legion roll call. "ABSENT!"

CHAPTER 14

FIVE COPS, ONE NIGHT AND AN EVENING IN HELL

With my new promotion to Deputy Chief Surgeon and the trust and authority granted to me by Chief Koehler and Commissioner Ward, I began responding routinely to hospitals where seriously injured officers were taken. This was actually a new role for the Police Surgeon but one with which I was comfortable. Indeed, I was a board-certified surgeon, with extensive trauma experience obtained at Bellevue. If I could provide assistance to the officers, become a liaison to the doctors in the hospitals or help decide the appropriate facilities to which officers should be evacuated, I would.

It didn't take very long. I was home watching television when the call came from Police Operations. That was the switchboard, the coordinating center located at Police Headquarters where all the information about what is happening across the city is would be managed.

Serious injuries, unusual events city wide, and anything that needed wider communication beyond the precinct level would be sent to Operations. Any medical problems would be called into the Sick Desk. It was located at Lefrak City, in an apartment complex in Queens, where Health Services was located. Usually attended by a sergeant, the Sick Desk would be the central area where officers who were going out sick and not reporting to work would call and report their illnesses. The Sick Desk supervisors would determine when to reach out to the surgeons and when the officers would be expected to report to the surgeon as well as other administrative actions including line-of-duty reports and exposures by officers to dangerous chemicals or infectious diseases such as by needle sticks or exposure to blood.

I was now notified by both Police Operations and the Sick Desk regarding injured officers and very often would get the first call from Trenchcoat. The call came almost simultaneously on my home phone and beeper. Cops shot in the Bronx. I would call in to find out what hospital would be the designated receiving facility. By this time, I was pretty good at getting to one or another Emergency Department across the city in my "non-descript" dark blue Chevy with flashing lights and siren.

Injured cops were being brought to Bronx Lebanon Hospital, Fulton Street Division. I'd never heard of the place. I hadn't a clue where it was but I did have a police radio and as I drove north on the Bronx River Parkway, they sent a Highway Patrol car to meet me at the exit and lead me to the hospital. Arriving at the South Bronx facility, I pulled up to the flashing lights in front of the Emergency Room to be greeted by Chief Dennis Ryan, Borough Commander of the Bronx. He was a big guy, a protective Irish cop with a pleasant disposition and someone I had met on numerous occasions before. Looking disturbed, he immediately took off his bullet-resistant flack vest and threw it around me. "The scene's not secured yet. I think they're still firing shots." I was in the Emergency Department parking lot.

It turns out that a situation had occurred directly across the street from the hospital. Larry Davis, a small, young man with outstanding warrants had been tracked down to his sister's house across the street. Special Operations and a Detective Bureau were trying to coordinate in arresting him. As the group entered, they discovered that there were children present in the apartment where Davis was hiding. Davis had opened fire on the officers, supposedly using a small child as a shield or at least knowing that with children present, the officers would be quite reluctant to return fire. The cops had hesitated, with apparently five of them getting shot. Larry Davis, in the pandemonium that ensued and the need to get the officers to safety, had somehow escaped.

As I walked into the Emergency Room, a poorly equipped non-trauma facility, it was clear that this was not the place for injured officers or probably anyone else with more than a cut finger. I was told that one officer had been shot in the neck and was rushed to the operating room as soon as he was brought in. Apparently there was an available surgeon in the hospital who immediately started the surgery. Introducing myself to the administrator and asking permission to go to the operating room, I was accompanied by the administrator upstairs. Going to the operating room, I looked through the window and could see a surgeon throwing sutures into the bloody neck of Officer TM. Since he was in surgery and was being taken care of, I returned to the ER where two other cops were brought.

I always made it a point to introduce myself when I was at a hospital, identified that I was a board-certified practicing general surgeon and would simply like to observe. I attempted not to step on too many toes or take too many liberties. I usually stepped on numerous toes, but never scrubbed or operated on shot cops, because I didn't have privileges at the numerous hospitals, and wouldn't be following them as patients, but was granted temporary privileges to observe and round on them. I actually was, granted official privileges in multiple hospitals across the city and had maintained my privileges at Bellevue. This was before the days of HIPPA (The Health Insurance Portability and Accountability Act of 1996) and before increased governmental oversight and regulatory standards. In those days hospital administrators relied on intuition to allow folks into their facilities and I also had a police shield (i.e. a badge) and appropriate identification. I was also accompanied by many cops who referred to me as sir or doc. (My involvement often seemed to be to the benefit of everyone involved since I was a practicing surgeon and integrated into the officialdom of the police department).

Obviously, whenever a shooting occurs, all of the major police brass, press, and the Mayor's office are notified of the situation. Sirens screaming, traffic control outside the hospital, reporters all over the place trying to capture all the sordid details for the next news release are par for the course. As I looked around the ER, everyone was wearing tuxedos. It turns out that this was the night of the Police Foundation gala held those days at Police Headquarters where large donors to the Police Foundation mingle with Police Brass.

Three cops it turns out were walked or carried into Bronx Lebanon Hospital only because it was across the street from the crime scene. Unfortunately, the Fulton Street Division of Bronx Lebanon hospital was essentially a Band-Aid-and-lollipop facility incapable of providing the advanced care I always demanded for injured officers. I had to make the best of the situation.

The next officer to come to the Emergency Room, after the one already in surgery was an ESU (Emergency Service Unit) cop. John was wearing a thick flack vest at the time but was shot with a shotgun, and the pellets sprayed into his face. An X-ray showed multiple small pellets under his skin, but one under his eye near the area of the optic nerve. A physician from the hospital with a thick accent told me that he would have to remove that eye because of something about blindness in one eye caused by injury can cause blindness in the other eye. I'm far from an expert in ophthalmology, basically knowing that there are two eyes, one on either side of your nose. Before I would consider allowing anything to proceed, I'd need an expert. John was stable with a good blood pressure and was awake. He could make out shapes from the injured eye. I immediately got on the phone to the Bellevue Emergency Department and told the attending what the situation was and that I planned to transfer at least one patient, possibly three. I'd need an ophthalmologist when we arrived. John agreed to move to Bellevue as long as I went along.

As always, Trenchcoat was present and ready to do whatever was necessary. I explained to him that before I'd let anyone touch the cops, I'd want expert opinions. I'd plan to accompany in the ambulance any officer that I needed to transfer. Trenchcoat as always was 100% reliable, causing the FDR drive to be temporarily closed in sections with police cars to accompany us on our journey. The highway cops do it for the president, so it's certainly appropriate to do it for seriously injured cops. It's usually late at night when the transfers occur, so there's not much disruption, although it's been done at rush hour. Highway cops also do it for civilians when necessary.

I told the ESU cops present to surround John's gurney and be sure no one did anything until we moved to Bellevue. I would always copy whatever records were available, and usually carried copies of any X-rays taken whenever I was involved in a transfer. Then I moved into another room where Mary, another ESU cop who had been shot was being attended to. She had been shot in the face, and her most serious injuries had been to her mouth and teeth. Her tongue was beginning to swell and she had bleeding from her mouth. Her vital signs were stable.

Deciding that John was stable to move, I had him transferred into a city ambulance, got in myself and we took the five-mile ride from the Bronx to Bellevue. Since I had full privileges at Bellevue, I became the receiving physician, although when we arrived, he was placed in the care of the Trauma Service. This was the usual situation. As we rode downtown John said, "There goes my career in aviation." He explained that he had been accepted into the aviation unit and had been studying to become a helicopter pilot. Now that he might be blinded in one eye, he didn't think he could possibly function in that role. I told him that it was most important that we get him stabilized, do whatever was necessary for his acute situation, and see what they said at Bellevue. John got to Bellevue and the ophthalmologist was on his way.

I also promised him that I would do whatever could be done to see that every effort would be made to allow him to join the aviation unit. Some communication with the FAA and the Aviation unit as John recovered revealed that a pilot with one functioning eye is acceptable as long as he flies with a qualified co-pilot. It turns out that after months of recovery John eventually wound up in aviation. No one ever (except for one doctor in the Bronx) considered removing his eye.

I took the ambulance back to Bronx Lebanon to be sure that the other two officers were doing satisfactorily. Mary developed serious swelling around the mouth and tongue but was breathing successfully through her mouth and nose. She was awake, alert and stable. I felt she'd do better at Bellevue. I explained to her what I considered the appropriate facility to offer further treatment. I held her hand while I explained that because she had been breathing on her own without intubation for the last hours and that I felt her airway wasn't compromised, we'd transport her with an endotracheal tube and a tracheostomy set on standby in case there was a problem. I examined her neck and saw that an emergency cricothyroidectomy (an emergency opening in her windpipe in case her airway became compromised) would be straightforward. Yes, I was nervous, although I had performed many of them in emergency situations before. Weighing the risks and benefits of the transfer, she and I agreed it was the right decision. She was incredibly brave considering what had happened and how seriously she was injured.

As we drove downtown, slowly and carefully, I could see the fear, worry and concern in her eyes. Attempting to lighten the situation, using my usual dark sense of humor carefully, in critical situations, I looked at her and said, "I heard you weren't much to look at before. With new teeth, you'll probably be gorgeous." I got a big smile from Mary, her tongue hanging out of her mouth. No need for intubation or a tracheostomy. Mary arrived and remained intact. Long afterward, Mary told me how much she appreciated my comment.

Third trip back to Bronx Lebanon found Tom out of surgery. Entering the Recovery Room, he was basically alone, intubated, with one nurse who was not near the bedside. He had been out of surgery for an hour, but only one vital sign was recorded. The only ones around were cops and Trenchcoat. Are we going to move him? Finding an appropriate Emergency Service Cop with paramedic training, we took all the necessary equipment to make the ambulance into a mobile recovery room. Tom, the third cop, post op neck exploration was successfully transported to Bellevue. In the interim, during the three trips downtown, someone drove my car to Bellevue so I could drive myself home.

Whenever there are serious events and traumatic injuries, there are press conferences. These are usually done by the Police Commissioner who narrates the events surrounding the attack, followed by the Mayor who tells of the police heroics, reminds the public of the hazards of the job, and gives a general update on the police officer's condition, sometimes a medical report from myself or more often by the attending physician at the hospital.

I got enough publicity and would avoid the press conference, allowing the dedicated physicians at the specific hospitals to be in the limelight and explain the treatment rendered. This publicity and 15 minutes of fame appropriately acknowledged those who would be working directly on the cops and thanked them on behalf of the department.

LP, M.D., was at that time Chief of the Trauma Service at Bellevue. He and I had trained together at Bellevue and I knew him for years. It was certainly appropriate that he do the press conference. I'm afraid he may have gotten a bit carried away with the publicity. "Mary stopped a .45 with her teeth," said Leon. Not quite, but I guess it sounded good to him. The shotgun had knocked out her front teeth and caused her tongue to swell. I explained later in private to Leon that if there were no .45 present, they'd use this to cause doubt in the prosecution of the case. Mary had actually been hit with pellets from the shotgun. More importantly, this description of Mary as supergirl had caused her quite a bit of embarrassment and made her uncomfortable. Reporters and cameras sometimes bring out peculiar behavior in people.

Whenever I was called on to do an interview, I tried to stress the extreme nature of being shot. I followed the officers after the incidents and knew the difficulties in adjusting to the peculiar situations in which they found themselves. Mary, for example, had a young daughter who would ask her mother why they shot her. In my opinion and experience, getting shot is totally out of the ordinary and the victim of the shooting, no matter how minor the injury, faces a struggle readjusting to life.

The other two injured officers were not as serious as these three. I didn't get to the hospitals to which they were evacuated and all the attention was directed at these three. Tom, in spite of the less than ideal exposure and aggressive surgery survived without a neurological deficit and in spite of the numerous sutures I had observed being thrown into his neck to stop the bleeding from his carotid artery.

John, after joining the Aviation Unit had several plastic surgery procedures and would occasional have a pellet spontaneously extrude from his face. Mary had the hardest post injury course. She underwent months of reconstructive mouth and jaw surgery requiring bone grafting. Eventually she recovered, and rather than taking a retirement pension, she became part of the SWAT team sniper force. She was truly a special lady.

Prior to Mary's recovery, she had to report to her district surgeon for authorization and further treatment. HR, MD, the hard-boiled, loudmouth former military man who knew everything there was to know about everything—just ask him—was her district surgeon. Mary during her recovery was expected to report to him for authorizations for the extensive surgery she was facing. He supposedly was double boarded in medicine and emergency medicine, was in one of the military reserves as a colonel and had his district in the Bronx where Mary lived. He fancied himself as tough as nails and never saw an injured or sick officer that wasn't fit for full duty.

Mary was in HR's district. After she got out of the hospital and was on the road to recovery, she reported to HR in the Bronx Clinic. HR was a heavy smoker and never hesitated to smoke around officers in the clinic. When Mary saw HR for the first time, he began trying to regale her with stories about his own bravery and strength. "Getting shot in the face was like getting hit in the face with a stick," according to HR. Fortunately Mary, who was devastated by his cavalier attitude, called me.

I became Mary's personal district surgeon. FL, DDS, was our in-house dentist and I brought Mary to our office in Lefrak where Dr. FL saw cops and asked for his opinion. Sure enough, major reconstruction loomed in her future and Dr. FL would keep an eye on her. She would never have to see HR again. I personally authorized thousands of dollars for the reconstruction of Mary's demolished upper jaw. HR and I would meet in the future.

Dr. R., M.D., was another Deputy Chief Surgeon. He was there before I got there and long after I retired and is still there even to this very day. He almost never responded to night emergencies or other critical situations. He had designated his role as the scrooge of the department, overseeing all medical authorizations for treatment based on cost. He was a supposed vascular surgeon with an office at NYU but, although I had trained there, I never encountered him performing surgery.

In my opinion, he was a small man with a narrow mind who felt that either the cops or the treating physicians were focused on scamming the city out of money for excessive and unnecessary treatments at exorbitant costs. He may have been right on occasion, but was often over critical, denying payment or services and putting the officers in the middle between the doctor and the department. None of that made a difference to him. He kept a written, running tally of the amount of money he was saving the city by denying what he considered unnecessary and overpriced treatment. He was the person who failed to authorize treatment or payment for Officer Stephen McDonald when he was transferred to Craig Institute in Colorado.

It was far from unique for me to disagree with his denial of services to an injured officer and assume responsibility for authorizing and referring officers to various specialists. Sometimes it was necessary for me to assert my authority over what I considered bad decisions by the district surgeons; other times it was necessary to be the focal point for authorizing major expenses that were far beyond the ordinary. I always felt that cops injured in the line of duty were entitled to the best possible medical care available in New York City. I also felt that they were entitled to choose the physician, location, and nature of treatment within acceptable medical guidelines. Rather than spar with Dr. TR when he would deny someone treatment, I simply took the responsibility myself to authorize what I considered reasonable or necessary treatments.

Meanwhile, the manhunt continued for Larry Davis. The usual "Cop Shot" truck with the $10,000 reward was sent through the neighborhoods. Larry realized and feared that because he had become a hunted desperado and that it was open season on Larry Davis. None of the posters said "Dead or Alive" but I guess he was scared so he decided to surrender. Davis was spotted entering a housing project in the Bronx. The building was surround and Davis forced his way into an apartment taking 6 hostages. After several hours of phone contact, police negotiators convinced Davis to surrender without harming anyone else. Chief Robert J. Johnston would accept his surrender.

Bob Johnston was a large man with the reputation of being a tough SOB, an old-fashioned cop's cop. He was smart, street-wise and made some major contributions to police tactics that are still in effect. Bob wore his big fat blue combat helmet that day emblazoned with four glorious gold stars. Marching behind Larry Davis, who was shorter and smaller, he looked like a caricature of the big cop, little man. He later told me that he felt it appropriate to wear the helmet as an example for the other cops who were expected to do the same in possibly dangerous situations. Unfortunately, he resembled General Patton leading the troops into France and became known from then on as Patton among the rank and file. Although he avoided discussing the newest impression of his behavior, I think he secretly enjoyed the comparison to Patton.

Larry Davis was afforded a defense by William Kunstler, a well-known radical attorney who took on radical causes. Kunstler's fictional defense strategy was that the cops were coming to kill Larry because he supposedly knew they were dirty. The legal defense against the charges of attempted murder of cops was essentially self-defense. I was actually called to testify by the Bronx D.A. simply to say that although no officer was killed, getting shot was attempted murder, not simply just assault or, as in Dr. HR's opinion, like getting hit in the face with a stick.

The Bronx Courthouse was characterized correctly in Tom Wolfe's novel, *Bonfire of the Vanities*. It had large dark-paneled courtrooms with high ceilings. Sitting in the witness chair, I saw the jury of Larry Davis's peers. One sat knitting; another dozed; others simply stared into space. "Yes," I said "I've had extensive experience with gunshot wounds during my days at Bellevue. Yes, I work for the police department. Yes, I consider any gunshot wound a potentially life-ending event since no one ever aims a gun with the plan to simply injure someone." The verdict? Not guilty on attempted murder. Amazing to all of us who were involved with the events. Guilty on gun possession. A year. Eventually Larry Davis met his maker while doing time in prison for another crime. He was murdered by another inmate, stabbed to death with a shiv. No loss. No surprise.

If all this sounds matter of fact or routine or without emotion, it isn't. Traveling from one hospital to another, sitting in an ambulance with an officer who had that afternoon gone to work and now experienced a life-threatening and life-changing event definitely takes its toll. It's not always easy to block the horrendous events one experiences, although years of surgical training and experience teach one to keep emotions under control and tragedies at arms length. Life and death decision-making as a physician requires objectivity. Fortunately, in most of the events I was involved with, the decisions were obvious. Weighing the risks and benefits, the scale clearly tipped towards one choice or another. I'm sure, however, as we rode from the Bronx to Bellevue, the officers pondered, "Why me, why now, what could I have done differently?" Time, however, only goes in one direction. Suck it up and move on.

CHAPTER 15

TALES FROM THE OPERATING ROOM

The major portion of my life during the years of active practice was taken up with performing surgery. General Surgery has become a subdivided specialty over time, but when I was practicing the scope was much wider so we saw more and varied patients. I worked in Manhattan where there are probably more doctors per square foot than in many parts of the country. Being a trained general surgeon in Manhattan dictated a narrower scope of practice than would be appropriate somewhere else in the U.S. I eliminated vascular, pediatric, chest, cardiac, neuro, urologic, plastic and orthopedic surgery. That still left most major general surgery. I did breast, hernia, gallbladder, stomach, colon, pancreatic, rectal and numerous office procedures including minor excisions, lumps and bumps, cysts and other operations of varied types.

In the face of all my police department activities, I still maintained an active surgical practice. I would see patients in the HIP office at least three days a week for more than 15 hours during the week. HIP was unique because the office visits were free to the patients, although several years later they added nominal copayments. Supposedly, appointments were by referral since surgery was a specialty, but self-referral was a frequent route by which patients saw me. HIP patients, however, were middle-class working people who really didn't want to be sick and certainly weren't big fans of having surgery.

The most common consultations I had were for breast problems. Surgeons at that time had the most familiarity with breast diseases, treatment and diagnosis. Gynecologists probably performed the most breast examinations but don't perform any of the surgery. Whenever a mammogram was suspicious, whenever someone complained of feeling a lump or when the gynecologist or internist thought they discovered something suspicious, they would send the patients to me. I doubt if there is a more anxiety producing situation for a woman than to be told after she has been examined by her physician or gynecologist, "I think you should go see the surgeon."

I would accommodate as many patients as I could as quickly as I could fit them in. HIP pioneered the early studies on the effectiveness of mammograms to diagnose early cancers of the breast. It has universally been thought by the public that early diagnosis leads to higher survival, but I'm not convinced that it's that simple. In general, there's an advantage to early treatment, but it's not universal that the earlier treatment leads to better outcomes. Different cancers and pre-cancers multiply and spread at different rates in different people.

I would see a new case of breast cancer at least every other week. Many breast cancers were easily palpable and could essentially be diagnosed by the feel. Others were far more subtle and presented as small microcalcifications, dots in small clusters on mammograms, requiring far more follow-up and diagnostic procedures prior to definitive diagnosis.

During my residency, if a patient were seen with a lump in the breast, or following a suspicious mammogram, she would be admitted to the surgical service the night before. Consent would be obtained for biopsy, frozen section, possible mastectomy. This meant that the next morning she'd be put to sleep, the lump excised and sent to the pathology lab where it would be frozen, embedded in wax, stained, and examined microscopically. If positive for cancer, the breast, the underlying chest muscles including the pectoralis major and minor, and 30 or more lymph nodes in the armpit would be removed.

The operation was massive and deforming. The technique and protocol was actually developed by William Halstead, M.D. at Johns Hopkins in 1882. Halstead, a surgical pioneer was renowned for his surgical prowess, study of surgical disease and surgical skills. He was also a known cocaine and subsequent heroin addict, which was used to free him from cocaine. He developed the mastectomy after performing dissections on women who had succumbed to breast cancer. He noted that there was tumor involving the chest muscles and lymph nodes and therefore reasoned that a radical removal of these structures would assist survival.

The consequences of this surgery were numerous. The women would be severely deformed with only ribs showing under the skin. The removal of multiple lymph nodes would often lead to a swollen, edematous, heavy arm, easily prone to severe infections from simple nicks or cuts. To save some chest contour, occasional surgeons who thought themselves advanced would perform the "modified" radical mastectomy, namely leaving the pectoralis minor muscle in place. This didn't really make much of a difference in appearance to the ladies. To the eyes of the surgeons who did this, they decided it did. Why bother to ask the patient?

My mother developed a lump in her breast in the early 1980's. Women who lived on Long Island had a statistically higher incidence of breast cancer. She had me examine just the lump, which I felt through her clothing. There was no doubt in my mind that it was breast cancer. I sent her to one of the older, more staid surgeons at Beth Israel who performed a modified radical mastectomy, all done at the same time as I described before. She was admitted the night before surgery, signed consent for biopsy and mastectomy and awoke to find her breast gone. The surgery also involved the removal of 44 lymph nodes. I was not present in the operating room, nor was I involved in the decision-making process during the surgery. Years after the surgery she bumped that arm and developed massive swelling from lymphedema which persisted for the rest of her life. She, however, survived the breast cancer and passed away in her 90's from natural causes.

Nothing changed from 1882 until the early 1970s when Bernard Fisher, M.D., dared to question the necessity to mutilate women to effect a cure. Facing all sorts of criticism, skepticism and aggressive investigation, he defended his position that lumpectomy, just a wide removal of the tumor with limited removal of surrounding tissue, was a sufficient treatment in many patients. As with any surgical advancement, like the concept of microbes, anesthesia, sterility and other major advances, change came slowly, with numerous dissenting opinions. I was present at an early American College of Surgeons Convention where Dr. Fisher presented his findings to an extremely doubtful, very vocal and critical audience.

In spite of attempts to discredit the findings, after numerous studies, it became apparent that the most radical surgery wasn't necessarily the best surgery. The general public has come to understand that it wasn't necessary to take off every breast which has cancer present in it to effect cure. The debate still rages, with public opinion swinging from very conservative surgery such as lumpectomy to radical surgery such as the removal of both breasts, usually followed by reconstruction. Genomics, BRCA testing, awareness of familial factors, and treatments chosen by public figures have further complicated decision-making regarding treatment. Someday, an appropriate medical therapy may make the arguments obsolete.

Being in general surgery, I had hundreds of patients over the years who faced breast cancer. Obviously, I don't remember them all, but some of them remain fixed in my memory. My most vivid memory was that of Katherine.

Katherine came to see me after a suspicious mammogram revealed microcalcifications, tiny dots of calcium in small clusters scattered throughout the breast. This can be indicative of early breast cancer. Surgical biopsy was really the only reliable way to determine whether or not this was an early cancer. An excision of this area revealed DCIS, that is, a ductal carcinoma in situ, an early change that had a high potential to become full-blown invasive cancer but is considered a pre-cancerous condition.

Since there were other areas in her breast that contained the same findings, the only rational approach indicated at the time was mastectomy, removal of the breast. There was no guarantee that this would become cancer, although I stressed that it would be very appropriate for her to have the procedure. Rather than undergo any definitive surgery or consider more biopsies, Katherine elected to wait, have repeat mammograms, and return every few months. I stressed for her the need for close follow-up and my own insecurity of her personal choice to simply follow with X-rays.

Katherine was a very talented lady. She lived in Greenwich Village and Paris. She was a professional photographer, so naturally I looked forward to her visits, as I had always been an amateur photographer and enjoyed hearing about her latest exploits and trips. She would come to see me either before or right after spending months photographing in New York or Paris.

Over time, her mammogram became more suspicious with increasing numbers of microcalcifications. In spite of the growing possibility of cancer, she refused further biopsies and wished only to be watched with serial mammograms. One afternoon she called me in the office. She was in Paris but had developed a lump that she showed to a surgeon in Paris. He did a biopsy of the lump. She had breast cancer. She was going to fly back to New York and wanted me to see her as soon as she arrived. I asked her to bring her pathology report and the slides with her so that we could obtain another opinion although I knew the diagnosis was correct.

Sure enough, what had been precancerous had evolved but the latest mammogram revealed diffuse involvement of the entire breast. The only appropriate treatment would be mastectomy. She agreed and the following week I removed her breast and biopsied some of the adjacent lymph nodes. There were 10 positive nodes and cancer throughout the breast. She was immediately referred for chemotherapy but obviously with such extensive cancer her prognosis was at best poor.

The chemotherapy that she got was quite aggressive. She lost her hair. She took pictures of herself holding an egg over her bald head, since she and the Parisians saw her as the proverbial "egghead". Seeing me before she left for Paris, she asked what she should bring back for me. I suggested the Eiffel Tower. To this day I still have the small brass two-inch replica souvenir she brought me.

She went back to Paris after the chemo. The egghead pictures were extremely popular and she became a major spokesperson for breast cancer awareness in Paris exhibiting the photos in major shows. When she returned, she requested that the other breast be removed after mammograms showed the same problem beginning there.

Several months after the second mastectomy, she came and requested reconstruction, but only wanted one breast done. Although a quite unusual request and I never really understood why only one, I proceeded to request the procedure be covered by her HIP insurance. Although at first the HIP bureaucracy hesitated, with sufficient cajoling by me they bought the idea that she wanted one done at a time. She eventually obtained approval and had the procedure performed by a plastic surgeon.

Time went by and she would visit every three to four months. We were both aware that she had a guarded prognosis and that the cancer could reappear at any time. Her hair grew back. Meanwhile she lived an active life, becoming a spokesperson for breast cancer awareness. She moved in with her female partner and travelled back and forth to Paris.

I had not seen or heard from her for about six months when her live-in partner appeared in the office. "Have you heard about Katherine?" she asked. Expecting the bad news that she had succumbed to the cancer we had all expected to eventually take her, she told me that Katherine had indeed died. She was riding her bike in Greenwich Village and was hit by a bus.

Maybe she was too preoccupied with worrying about dying from her cancer to pay attention to the bus but I sincerely doubt it. It was much more likely that she was zipping around on her bike thinking about her next trip to Paris or thinking about her next photographic project than to be paying attention to what was happening around her.

With Katherine as an example, I always deferred in making predictions for patients of their statistical chances of survival. Often asked by patients what their chances are for a five or 10 year survival, I would point out that in a single person statistics have little meaning and that they will either be alive or dead in five years. No one survives 50% or 28%.

I also point out that if there's any chance of survival, which there pretty much always is, then they should look positively since the negative really is useless. I stress the reality and changes that the cancer diagnosis has made in their lives, that they should take care of business, but that they should plan to live and enjoy each day. Having nearly died several times myself, that's the way I live.

The distance of time and retirement has obviously dulled the memories I have of the large numbers of my patients. Many of them I'm sure are still around and remember probably more vividly than I do the fact that I operated on them. Clearly, major surgery can be one of the more significant events that are remembered in a person's life. There are quite a few surgeries that I performed that provided me with life lessons.

Marcia was 39. She was strikingly pretty, smart and had a major job in finance. She was in the Bahamas taking a shower when she felt a large, golf-ball lump in her right breast. She was back in New York on Sunday and was in my office on Monday morning. No question in my mind what her diagnosis was, but I did a needle biopsy of this mass to be sure. It was a large breast cancer. The following Monday, she underwent mastectomy with removal of sufficient numbers of lymph nodes to document spread. Bone scan and CT scan performed the week prior to surgery were both negative.

She was obviously crushed. She went for multiple opinions and ended up with an aggressive oncologist who offered high dose, massive chemo. The protocol was marginal and aggressive, but as was often the case, she agreed that the most was best. Returning to me for follow up after the surgery, she was bald, shriveled, and beaten. Her white blood cell count was so low that the oncologist wouldn't give further chemo until she rebounded. She never did. I found that she had developed sepsis and died within 2 weeks of her last visit to me. The chemo had done what the breast cancer might have done.

Looking back, it's probably easier to remember those cases that turned out bad or surprised me with their results rather than remember the "routine" surgeries I performed that turned out well. Hundreds of gallbladders, thousands of hernias over the long span that I performed surgery were done successfully and the patients sent home without further sequelae.

As a surgeon, you have an unwritten bond and contract with your patient. The patient literally trusts you with his or her life. Surgery, even the simplest and most routine operation can go wrong. Hernia repairs can get infected, bleed post operatively or recur. Patients can receive too much anesthesia or have an unanticipated and serious reaction to the simplest sedation or other drug. In spite of any lengthy preoperative explanations or written "informed" consents, most patients and surgeons are quite optimistic about the expected outcomes and don't dwell on the possible negatives.

Hernias have been a problem and a mystery since ancient Egypt and Roman times. A hernia is a bulge (hernios is Greek for bud or out-pouching) which most often presents itself in the groin (that's an inguinal hernia). The problem with a hernia is it may entrap a loop of bowel (incarcerate) and the bowel may swell, may not be able to return to its normal location and actually compromise blood supply causing it to die (strangulate). So attempts to repair hernias date back probably as far as the beginning of civilization.

In ancient Rome, hernias were treated with cauterization, burning to the skin to attempt to cause the sac to scar and close. I guess it worked sometimes because they kept doing it and many people had hernias. In the Old West, a strangulated hernia would present itself with a painful, often red lump in the groin. Over time it became clear that left untreated, the patient would die, so these lumps were incised. Cutting into the strangulated hernia was actually cutting into the bowel and gas and some fluid would be extruded depending on how long the hernia was left untreated. This was affectionately known as a "wind abscess." Sometimes these patients survived too.

The techniques for repairing hernias evolved even from the time I began doing surgery and continue to evolve today. One of my surgical mentors, John Ranson, M.D. used to admonish that if there were many ways to do things, none of them were best. Hernia surgery is the surgery most performed by general surgeons.

When I was a resident, the (Bassini) hernia repair was basically done by cutting into the groin under general anesthesia and sewing "good stuff" to good stuff." By "good stuff" the surgeon meant strong fascia or membrane that seemed to hold stitches. Muscles when sewed seem to shred. This approach often worked. Usually a small slip of the peritoneum (the sac that contains the bowel) would intrude into the hernia bulge and often along with it came the bowel usually inside it. This was the hernia sac and the key at that time was tying the sac (without tying the bowel into it) as high as you could and letting it go back. Sometimes over time these hernias came back.

The next hernia repair that became popular was the Shouldice, originating in Canada at the Shouldice Clinic, and the attraction here was a very short stay. You would fly up to Ontario, spend the night in the hotel next to the hospital, get your hernia fixed the next day and spend another day or two there before going home. The repair sewing "good stuff," a specific fascial layer was done with thin wire and was accomplished under mostly local anesthesia.

I didn't particularly want to journey to Ontario to learn the technique but lots of local surgeons did. The wire, an unforgiving suture material, was hard to use. Tying wire would cut your fingers like a paper cut; it was abandoned and replaced with a synthetic material, a sort of a plastic wire, known as prolene. It, however, wouldn't hold as well as wire and often slipped.

The next phase of hernia repairs involved the use of materials applied over the hernia as a patch. This was designed to reinforce the natural fascia and muscle and be a sort of over-lay to cause the space in the tissues to be closed without putting tension on the repair. This was like using shingles to fix a hole in your roof by putting something on top of the hole. Metal screens were some of the earliest materials used. These didn't last long and weren't durable.

Next, a more porous synthetic material was tried, a Gor-Tex® like the material used in waterproof vests. The problem with Gor-Tex® was that it wasn't porous enough to become integrated into the normal tissues and would simply sit there like a patch. Occasionally the area would get infected and the Gor-Tex® would be removed totally intact affording no benefit.

Then hernias began being repaired with a synthetic mesh, called Marlex®. This would integrate into normal body tissues but, being a non-natural substance, could cause inflammatory reactions. It was also learned that ligating the sac caused more pain than not ligating it and things would work just as well if you didn't ligate it.

The technique of putting the material on top of the hernia evolved to the "plug and patch" which involved pushing a lump of synthetic material into the hernia and sewing a patch on top. For the last 10 or 12 years, the question of laparoscopic repair, namely, entering the abdominal cavity, where the intestines sit, would make sense.

This exchanged the pain of the cut for a plunge into the cavity containing the bowels and a different chance of injury for the avoidance of a cut. It seems like more risk of injury than it's worth. It's the old risk versus benefits decision. The risk of intestinal injury seems to outweigh the benefit of a bit less pain.

I can only personally reflect on four hernias. Two of them are mine. I still have them quite successfully avoiding any surgery. They occasionally pop out, and occasionally hurt, but usually related to coughing after a cold, or allergy season. Recent studies have weighed the benefits of surgery against the bother of repair and right now great doubt is being placed on the absolute necessity of repairing any hernias. I guess if I were planning to climb Mt. Everest or going to Antarctica for an extended period, I might consider having them repaired but at present neither has become a major consideration.

The third and fourth hernias I might mention is one that my son and one that my father had. My son showed me this giant hernia that was protruding and interfering with his ability to do half marathons. He had it repaired successfully and without much discomfort. The surgeon who repaired it used the plug and patch method.

Years ago, my father, then 84, complained of some pain in his groin. After examining it, I discovered a small and what I considered an insignificant hernia. Not wanting to be his diagnostician or even his doctor, I sent him to Dr. Slattery at NYU whose white hair and tall, dignified manner convinced my father that he knew what he was doing. He advised opting against repair and my father died with his small hernia untouched.

One of the more common surgeries I performed in training was a gastrectomy, a removal of part of the stomach, to treat chronic ulcer disease. The classic teaching was that ulcer disease was related to the excess production of hydrochloric acid by the stomach, mediated by the vagus nerve. So if one removed the acid producing cells of the stomach and cut the vagus nerve, the ulcer was supposedly cured but the sequelae were sometimes worse than the disease. The surgery was often quite difficult. Tomes in the literature discussed ulcer surgery.

The removal of a stomach for ulcer disease became a career in itself. During my residency, I must have scrubbed on or performed hundreds of these ulcer curative operations. As time went on, it became apparent that removing part of the stomach for ulcers traded one disease for a possible constellation of others, some even far more serious. (The risk of the surgery is always real.) Further, antibiotics could cure the ulcer faster and more effectively than surgery. In a major scientific breakthrough, it was discovered that many ulcers were caused by infection, a bacterium, H. pylori, rather than stress so antibiotics and pills that would decrease acid production became the first line of treatment, supplanting surgery. I doubt if there exists a surgeon under age 50 who has ever seen a gastrectomy, a removal of a part of the stomach performed for chronic ulcer disease. That's a good thing.

The operating room is a legendary location, one of mystique, folklore, and legend. Movies, cartoons, and fables have followed the surgeons in and out of the operating room. Hushed whispers, tense beeping monitors documenting the patient's heartbeat are some of the images of the operating rooms that fill the popular imagination. Television and movies have created an image of the operating room which includes tension, life and death decision-making, nurses wiping the brows of sweating surgeons, time passing. Blood transfusions, mysterious chemical intravenous infusions, beeping, whispered conversations, and nervous looks among the O.R. participants are always accompanied by ominous music.

OK. Some of that is definitely true. Most of which happens in the operating room is routine and quite controlled. That's really the way it should be. The lights are hot and intense. They'd better be because they have to illuminate things. That's changed considerably with the advent of laparoscopic, minimally invasive surgery. Now the television monitor is in the primary position, sometimes even requiring two monitors depending on the complexity of the surgery. Three dimensional views of the open body have been replaced with two-dimensional television views. The surgeon no longer reaches in with two hands and large metal retractors. He peeks in with a small camera and manipulates tissues with increasingly perfected mini grasper instruments and scissors, or a robot, inserted through tiny holes in the patient's abdomen.

There are several important folks who must keep the surgeon honest. There's the scrub nurse or scrub technician and the unsung hero who doesn't scrub but is the "circulator." The circulator, usually a registered nurse, is the "go-for" who brings in the equipment necessary for the case, counts the instruments and sponges with the scrub nurse to make sure that nothing that doesn't belong in the patient is left inside.

Everyone has heard about the flagrant errors of scissors and clamps, and rags (known as surgical sponges) that have been inadvertently left inside. It's the circulator who has to keep track of what was given to the table and what's left outside, the count obviously supposed to match except for things like hips and valves and arterial grafts that must necessarily be left inside.

Not unexpectedly over my 30-year practice I encountered folks who became known for unfortunate and regrettable events. Egregious surgical mishaps have always been alarming and newsworthy, often contributing to major changes in the ways things are done.

Dr. AZ was a obstetrician/gynecologist with whom I had trained at Bellevue. He had become one of the more prominent abortion-performing physicians at an abortion clinic. Needless to say, performing endless abortions on a regular basis might have played havoc with Dr. Z's head. He was working in a group practice associated with Beth Israel when he became quite friendly with a pregnant lady. Z was performing a Caesarian delivery on the patient, who was also a physician when she jokingly requested that he take extra care with her scar when closing her skin.

Always a bit off base, Z went with the suggestion, saying he so admired the appearance of her scar that he would be initialing her surgery. He carved a notable "AZ" above the scar on her abdomen. Needless to say, Z surrendered his license to practice and was fined by New York State. In addition, Beth Israel was sued for negligence. Running into Z several months after the incident, he could only express his own wonderment as to "what came over me." He was a decent physician, a talented gynecologist, but became "Dr. Z" forever.

Another talented surgeon was a resident with whom I had worked at Bellevue. He was chief of trauma surgery at a hospital in the Bronx and had operated on and saved the lives of some of our injured police officers. He relocated in Florida. Entering the operating room with a patient already on the table for an amputation, he performed the amputation on the leg that had already been prepped and draped. Unfortunately, it was the wrong leg. The publicity surrounding this event reinforced the need for surgeons to document and mark the proper site for the anticipated procedure.

I was always a bit paranoid about hernia patients, since it's difficult to expect to remember which hernia needed to be repaired. I would tell the patients in my office that on the day of surgery I will ask them which side needed to be fixed. I would tell them that they might laugh at the question, but I was serious since I could never rely on my recollections to perform surgery. I would examine them anyway preoperatively, but would make a note in their preadmission chart clearly documented the anticipated side. Because of errors in deciding which site was appropriate, surgeons came to drawing an "X" to indicate where to cut. "X" marked the spot. Sometimes patients would come with their own "X" in place.

A young surgeon I knew who had recently finished his training had admitted his first patient with appendicitis. The appendix is almost always on the lower right side of the abdomen. That's where the pain is. Residents in training are usually allowed to perform appendectomies and he had done so throughout his residency, assuming a position on the right side of the table. That night, as the attending, he assumed the position of the assistant on the left side of the table. Deciding he would perform the surgery, he then asked for the scalpel. The nurse, the resident, and even the anesthesiologist attempted to interrupt him prior to the cut but he insisted on no conversation. Quickly he made a cut on the left side. It was quite problematic the next day explaining to the patient why she had two incisions.

Surgeons are clearly subject to the same stresses and influences that everyone else faces. One morning, on my way to perform gallbladder surgery, a car skidded on an icy patch of road and smashed into my car as I drove to the hospital. I wasn't injured, but clearly was shaken. I sat with my patient, explained what had happened, and why I was going to cancel the surgery. All she could do was yell at me because she had taken days off from work and had planned for the recovery. I apologized and tried to explain that I was in no condition to perform her surgery. I guessed a little heat from an unhappy patient was preferable to a serious error that I could have made while preoccupied with my car accident.

In the operating room, the head of the patient is behind a small drapery tent, administered to and observed and protected by the ever-present anesthesiologist or nurse anesthetist. He or she monitors vital signs and inserts, and must watch all kinds of tubes, devices, temperature probes, plastic tab monitors, and other invasive instruments. The patient's life is in the hands of that person. The surgeon is busy doing his thing, generally counting on anesthesia to keep the person alive or to share the possibility that things may be going amiss.

The O.R. team approach, empowering everyone to a degree in the room has had a positive effect on decreasing errors. More surgeons are coming to realize that everyone in the room is a colleague and all are there for the benefit of the patient. Regulatory agencies formally investigate the "team" after the fact when an unintentional mishap has occurred. We all know how well bureaucracies run things, however. In spite of that, surgical errors have diminished.

The surgeon usually has one or more assistants. In a "teaching" hospital, the assistants are usually residents. If there's a surgical residency program, the residents all want to perform the surgery, but the attending, standing on the other side of the table, will decide who does what and how much the resident will perform. If the hospital is a smaller place, the assistant may be another attending or a hired assistant. It is in these places where the surgery can actually be performed more efficiently and often faster.

As the surgeon, I would think about the case, plan the attack, and think about what I had to do before I took the major step, namely, cutting. In the old days, it was a major slice, often down the middle from here to there so that I could adequately see whatever I needed to see and deal with. No it doesn't keep bleeding. A little pressure with the surgical pads (called lap pads) makes it stop. I know, if you cut your finger, it bleeds for hours, but it really doesn't. Same thing at surgery, a little pressure during the case stops it. That is unless the patient has a bleeding disorder or took aspirin or some other drug that interferes with clotting. Then it bleeds, as we say, "like stink".

The scrub nurse or scrub tech gives the doctor the instruments. Most of the time, he or she gets the ones asked for. Sometimes, the experienced nurse gives the doc the ones he needs, not simply the ones he asks for. Instruments are named after long-forgotten surgeons, probably some of whom either designed the instruments or owned part of the company that manufactured them. The Kelly clamp, deBakey forceps (forceps is the surgical term for tweezers), Kocher clamps, fionchietto (rib spreader), lebsche knife (used to open the chest as previously discussed), mosquito clamp (don't ask me why, but it's a tiny clamp so I guess it's a tiny reference).

Many procedures also have names attached to them and locations on the body do also: McBurney's point is usually the location of the appendix. Murphy's sign is wincing when pressure is applied to the right side of the abdomen during a gall bladder attack. Fowler's position is head up at 90 degrees, while semi-fowler's is 30 degrees. Then there's the Whipple operation, the Gramm patch, the Puestow operation for pancreatitis, the Ripstein procedure, and the Rokitansky incision done at each autopsy, and so on. Some of these names persist today, commemorating either the inventor of the instrument or the person who perfected the operation.

Usually surgery went as planned, smoothly and without problems. Sometimes it didn't. Tension obviously builds in the operating room as time passes and the surgeon, the anesthesiologist or the nurses encounter unanticipated problems. The biggest problem one might encounter is the fact that there are no do-overs. Damage to vital structures, unanticipated bleeding, unexpected findings like cancers and internal scars that obliterate the anatomy can ruin the surgeon's day. Bad assistants can make for obscured vision and contribute to increased gray hairs on the surgeon's head.

Yes, some surgeons threw instruments and had temper tantrums. I never did. I would get stern and demand quiet, but the tenser things would become, the more in control I would be, although I always was in control. I always tried to maintain an informal atmosphere allowing open communication with everyone in the room. I think the discipline that I maintained in the operating room, the conditioning I became used to when events were tense, kept me calm when I saw the World Trade Center falling.

Usually, however, I would play the radio and evolved to bringing my own CD's to inspire me and my assistants. I think of surgery as a well-played symphony, with an opening, a melodious progression of events eventually reaching a critical point or points and then a rapid decrescendo. Not a classical music buff, I played the Rolling Stones or up-tempo rock and roll. If I were displeased with the residents, I would play country songs. That would inspire them to move along.

Surgery was exciting and challenging. I was on the crux of the revolution and movement towards minimally invasive surgery when I was injured on 9/11 and had to retire. Things have changed dramatically in the time since I left the operating room. As with everything else, the technology had to catch up to the imagination of what could be done. It has. The world of the video game has made the younger surgeons skilled with robotic and minimally invasive techniques that have changed the world of surgery. That's a good thing. I still would know what's inside, but I'd have a much harder time getting there if I were to enter an operating room today.

CHAPTER 16

WE JUST DISAGREE

> "There ain't no good guys,
> There ain't no bad guys"
> —Dave Mason, 1977

Meanwhile, back at the house, my wife and I were growing more distant. I had two nice kids. I was enjoying my jobs; I was staying busy and very active. My marriage was dissolving and I knew it. Here's where all the clichés come in, all the lyrics to all of those separation songs. Linda and I hardly related. Those who tell you that kids don't keep your marriage together are right but they are also wrong.

Kids allow you to remain apart from your partner. You can talk to your kids and never to your spouse. You can hold the kids' hands and never bother to touch your spouse. They are a perfect buffer to the need to have a real relationship and also provide an excuse to stay together even though you know it's not working. You can always try to convince yourself that you're staying together "for the kids." This, however, is pure fiction.

I'm convinced life is far too short to remain miserable. Obviously it wasn't that clear to me in those days. After my life-threatening hepatitis, Linda and I became more distant. During the time I was in the hospital, she had separated herself from the situation, sitting at my bedside, doing crossword puzzles. She even began writing a list of people she would call if indeed I had died. She picked me up when I was discharged from the hospital, only to disappear within hours, playing scrabble with neighbors who lived across the street. When you're in the midst of a situation, it is sometimes difficult to see the obvious.

I drifted. I made new contacts at the hospital and surrounded myself with friends. I was delighted to be alive. She wanted a child. She gave birth to Sandra. As I said, now there was a reason to remain together, a new project. There was someone to allow us to keep our distance from each other, but also be a common cause. In spite of the increasing coolness and separation, we'd go our separate ways but reunited over Sandra. We got together enough so that Eric came along several years later. By the time Eric arrived, there was little contact in a relationship that was actually long over.

Feeling depressed, Linda finally decided to see someone to talk to. I agreed that it was a good idea. I asked her for one favor, namely, process the health claim forms so that we could get reimbursed. Coming home one evening several months after she had begun her therapy, I noticed a haphazardly stacked pile of papers. Claim forms. Upset that she hadn't bothered to do what she had promised, we entered one of our fight events. "What do you care, you've got plenty of money." The sentence changed my life. Like in the cartoons, a bell rang in my head. "Get yourself a lawyer, and tell me what it's gonna cost to get this over with." It's going to be all about the money. When the love has gone, all that's left is the money, and each of you get half of it in New York.

One of the characteristics of a surgeon is the ability to make decisions. Once it became apparent that life was no longer going to be the same, I moved on quickly. I actually moved out. Contacting my friend in real estate, I rented an apartment a mile away. I insisted on two bedrooms so the kids could stay.

Enter Anne. Anne and I had been friends for years. I had set her up with guys to date. We had worked together and even gone shopping together, but there was no romance. We really were simply good friends. I knew her family. But it became apparent that we felt more for each other than either of us really wanted to acknowledge. I was married forever. She respected that. But when my marriage ended that night, it became clear to both of us. We started spending more time together. It came easy to both of us.

Linda left for Florida for a week to personally tell her parents about the separation and divorce. She was bizarre in that she absolutely never communicated with them on the phone, but would keep things a big secret until she finally decided to talk. Encouraging her to leave, I also took this opportunity to spend time with Anne. Another major decision came easy. I'm moving out and I want you to move in with me. I'm getting a divorce.

This came as a bit of a surprise, but not a shock. We both had become closer over the months before the bell rang with the final comment about my money. Neither of us really expected things to come to a head so quickly, as Anne had just moved out of her rented apartment and bought a coop in Queens. She had used some of her pension money for the down payment. She would close several months later, in the spring.

My kids always knew Anne. She and I had dinner together the night Eric was born. She was a dear friend. I knew her father before he died, and knew her mother and her sisters. We were always good together. When you're Jewish and 24, and you have a fairly pushy Jewish family, you look towards Jewish girls. The first time you sort of fall into the mold. When you grow up and look further, you have a wider choice. Life teaches you things and when you're 45 and have had two kids and a big career and a bank account, you have more choices. My choice was clear.

So Linda and I started divorce negotiations. Linda got a local attorney. I got a referral from a friend in Manhattan to "New York's premier matrimonial law firm." I actually kept hearing Linda's comments about how much money I had and saw this opportunity as a financial way to end my unhappiness. Sometimes it's not so terrible to pay for things to become better.

As the title of this chapter says, there ain't no good guys, there ain't no bad guys. We just disagreed. I wasn't about proving that Linda was a terrible person or that I deserved a divorce. That's not what it's about in my opinion. We would have to remain civil. We had two kids. There was no longer a need to yell and scream at each other. We just needed to go our separate ways. I didn't need or want her to admit fault or guilt or anything else. I just wanted us to be apart. We knew we would see each other on many occasions in the future.

I had a pension fund and a doctor's house, an old mansion. It was an oversized Tudor with a circular driveway in a fancy neighborhood on Long Island. She could keep the house minus a small amount, and I would keep my pension. When the house sold, I would take money for a deposit on a new house and she could keep all the rest and certainly have enough to buy another house. Unfortunately, I knew Linda quite well. I knew that over time she'd let the house deteriorate and lose more and more money on the sale. I wanted the price to be established quickly. It was. I kept my pension. She had the remainder of the price for which the house would sell.

One day, driving home, I realized that there was sufficient money in the bank to cover the mortgage. Calling the lawyer, I suggested we wipe out the savings so there'd be only the house to split, and Linda would be getting the money anyway. No mortgage but also no money to split was the situation, so the pressure was on to sell the house. I wanted a small portion of the sales to cover a down payment on a house of my own. The rest was hers.

It was difficult to keep a large house in good shape so the house showed poorly. Linda was angry, and seemed to take it out on at first the house and then on the realtors. She wouldn't allow them access. She denied them the ability to stage it. She didn't straighten the place when it was going to be sold. It languished for months. Finally a dentist who was leaving his wife and lived around the corner bought it. I took my portion and my pensions. She took the rest and bought a smaller house near my apartment so the kids could stay in the school system, the reason we had originally moved to Great Neck 15 years earlier. I bought a house nearby convenient to my kids and their school.

Joint custody without bickering allowed the kids to come and go as they pleased. On the advice of my lawyer, I pretty much agreed to everything with only one condition: namely, that Linda would provide written bills, statements or fill out the forms before she would be reimbursed. She would have summer camp, Blue Cross, life insurance, health benefits, temple membership all paid, and one small pension transferred to her. All were simply dependent on her filling out or providing me the appropriate forms. She never did anything.

She wanted a ghet, a Jewish divorce. I couldn't have cared less, but I didn't mind doing it. Rather than waiting for her to move on the issue, I proceeded to contact the rabbinical group in Brooklyn who ruled on those matters. I filled out the papers, paid the $600 and we both had an appointment to appear before their board somewhere in Brooklyn. We were shown into a conference room with several bearded gentlemen in typical Hasidic garb.

As they were reviewing the paperwork, the head Rabbi looked up and asked, "Fried, do you know me?" "Of course I do, Rabbi Kurzrock. I think it was on Yom Kippur years ago when your father collapsed in temple and was rushed to Beth Israel in shock. I operated on him." "You saved his life." I could never forget this elderly man who had a liver tumor that had ruptured and was bleeding. I resected the tumor and he went home alive and well in a week. He apparently lived another 8 years. With no further fanfare Linda got her ghet.

I had saved money for the kids for their college. I also made enough myself so when it was time for college I paid for it and kept their money separate. I saw the alimony (referred to as "maintenance") as a tax deduction and really never minded the checks. They only lasted 10 years and we were done. The child support was also acceptable and appropriate to me, since I would be paying for them anyway. Linda was working part-time in a small private school and earning almost nothing.

Anne and I planned to get married. She is a practicing Catholic. I think it's fairly evident that, I'm at most an atheist, a heathen. I had no problem with her religion. Just because I don't believe, doesn't mean I'm right. I have no right to deny anyone, especially someone I love, their beliefs or superstitions. So Anne would get one of the priests to marry us. Sitting with the priest, she discovered that, although I had a Jewish ghet, that didn't suffice in the eyes of the Catholic Church. Since my original wedding was performed by a rabbi it was in their eyes considered a valid religious marriage, and I'd have to also get a Catholic annulment.

It didn't bother me, but Anne went a bit ballistic. How is it possible that the Church would require an annulment while I had gotten a Jewish ghet, a divorce? I assured her that I would do what was required. Meanwhile, we had set a date for May. I had neither the final legal divorce decree nor the Catholic annulment. But we had the hall, the photographers, the wedding garb, and the invitations printed. Anne wanted to go through the religious protocols and felt it important for a Jewish ceremony for the wedding as well as a Catholic one. We hired a Cantor and an Anglican Priest. They would do I guess. The divorce lawyer assured me that everything would work out, but we had a backup plan in case I wasn't divorced legally. We would do only the religious stuff and do the civil stuff when the divorce was in hand.

I went to the Archdiocese of Rockville Centre for the paperwork for the annulment. The process was pretty much the same. Pay the $800, fill out paperwork justifying why the marriage was never appropriate, go before the tribunal marriage court, and you'll get the official results in less than a year. On April 16, 1992, the marriage was legally over but the annulment wasn't completed. Anne was concerned that we wouldn't be married in a Catholic ceremony. While waiting for the official religious pronouncement, we attended a wedding where Father Mychal Judge officiated. I had known Fr. Judge for years through the police department and through contacts with Stephen McDonald.

Trotting over to Father Judge, I introduced Anne and explained her concern that she wasn't going to be able to get married in the Church this time. Fr. Judge was as good as everyone said he was and he simply smiled, told us to proceed with the process, and get married a second time after the annulment was granted. He blessed us, saying, "You love him, he loves you and God loves you both." That worked for Anne and she was relieved.

The annulment and tribunal was a bit more complicated than the Rabbis. You needed the basis for the annulment. The universal basis was "lack of due discretion." You needed to write an explanation why the marriage should be annulled in the eyes of the church. I was young, foolish and didn't know exactly what it meant to be committed for life, or even married. The fact that I had two kids didn't seem to matter much.

On May 16, 1992, in the presence of 200 plus family and friends, a Cantor and an Anglican Priest officiated. Anne and I were married. I broke the glass in the Jewish tradition. We said some of the magic words in Hebrew, but basically it was a mixed ceremony that both families approved of.

I went before the tribunal in the Archdiocese. I was young and foolish the first time. I'm older and wiser now. I didn't really know what the commitment was and wasn't smart enough to realize that I was too young to get married. Several months later, the annulment was granted. Anne went to her Church and set up a meeting with the priest so we could schedule the next wedding. We weren't going to be tortured with Pre-Cana, instructions on what marriage should entail. The fact that I had been married for 20 years and we were such long-time friends held some sway with Fr. Kevin so we were exempted from the classes.

He'd only have a few questions for me. If we had children, would I rear them Catholic? "Nope". Anne almost fell off her chair. Smiling, I said that she would. I assured him that, although I was a non-believer, I had no objection to her faith or her beliefs. Next question: "Well, you surely believe in God?" Nope. How can there be a God when kids die of illness, people murder each other for no reason, and so many people died in concentration camps. "That's why I do believe," he explained. There must be something better and a reason for all this. I gave no argument.

On May 16, 1993, our first anniversary, Anne and I got married on the altar of St. Mary's Church in Manhasset. We didn't have a Mass. My father was uncomfortable about going into churches, although I assured him that it was unlikely that he'd be attacked. In any event, we all went back to our house for a celebration in the backyard with family and friends. My father was fine with that.

The best decision I ever made in life was marrying Anne. If you plan to be sick, it makes sense to marry a nurse. Anne is smart, caring, thoughtful, devoted, and loyal. She saw me through numerous crises. We have been there for each other in sickness and in health. Life with her has so far been more than I could have ever expected. It's probably a good thing to marry your best friend. The worst crisis, however, was yet to come...

CHAPTER 17

THE DOCTOR BUSINESS

> I don't care too much for money
> 'Cause money can't buy me love
> —John Lennon & Paul McCartney
> Money don't get everything, it's true
> But what it don't get, I can't use
> I need money (that's what I want)
> That's what I want
> —Strong-Gordy

Sometimes the songs tell it all. You go into medicine to help people but you also need to make a living. I became a surgeon. Surgeons need patients to operate on in order to get paid. I was ensconced in the New York Police Department, part-time, and was receiving a salary. I was also working for HIP, the group practice in New York City and receiving a paycheck.

Beyond the clinical and surgical concerns of the patients, there are the day-to-day realities of surgical practice and the troubles encountered outside of the world of patients. In medical school, there was no course called "Business Skills for Doctors."

In surgery, the skilled surgeon always has a backup plan in the event an untoward complication is encountered or a situation arises that requires one to abandon the original operation that was planned. These problems include unexpected bleeding, untoward reactions to anesthesia, discovery of unanticipated tumors or cancer while doing a routine operation like an appendectomy or removing a gallbladder. Sometimes in the doctor business world, the complications can be personal and at least as serious. Bad choices can jeopardize your livelihood, your future and destroy all you worked for.

It is extremely expensive to operate a solo or small group practice. "Mom and Pop" surgery in small offices with minimal staff was dying when I was practicing. In the New York Metropolitan area, it was nearly impossible to exist as a solo or small-practice surgeon. Malpractice insurance in New York State for surgeons exceeded $60K a year. Offices for surgeons require personal such as nurses, medical assistants and other professionals, who must also function as chaperones. They need office space, office furniture and equipment, phones and answering services, waiting rooms, bandages and suture material, and hazardous material disposals just to name a few expenses. It was clear to me that this was not going to work for me in the long run, although at one time I had a private practice and private office. Those realities were some of the reasons that I joined HIP, a group practice in New York City.

My first office was provided by my first job at Cabrini Hospital. I was given space in their office building and shared the space with a urologist. My first secretary was Susan Callaghan, R.N. who was working as a nurse in the Emergency Department at Bellevue. She would come when needed, because I saw few patients in the early days of practice. Fortunately, Cabrini gave me the space rent-free. I still had to pay Susan, keep the books, get New York State unemployment and disability insurance for her, and pay the appropriate taxes for her wages. Like any other enterprise, solo practice was a business.

There are realities in surgery as in everything else. In the 1960's surgical practices evolved via hospital referrals from medical internists and family doctors. Patterns of referrals were established and persisted so that the younger surgeons struggled on the periphery to break into the system. Young surgeons would cover other practices hoping to gain their own reputations or they would work for the hospital. The busiest surgeons, (usually the old guys in the hospital) would have the biggest reputations, got the most referrals, and controlled the operating room schedule. They ruled because they brought the most income to the hospital. They could actually occasionally turn down patients, although few ever did.

There is a real conundrum in surgery. Surgeons get paid to operate. When a patient is sent to the surgeon, the expectation is that the surgeon will operate and perform the appropriate procedure. He will also use the referring doctor as a consultant to examine and follow the patient in the hospital. This reciprocity is economically driven and doesn't consider the real necessity of the surgery or the quality of the referring physician. In plain words, if an old guy with a hernia is sent for surgery, you'd better fix his hernia even if you don't think he needs it fixed and you'd better use the referring doctor to see him before and after the procedure or you won't get any more patients from that referring doctor.

HIP, the Health Insurance Plan, was created after World War II in New York City for the benefit of union and city employees. The original model was one of "managed care" where the member and their family would have comprehensive health care with the cost shared by the employer and employee as a deduction from their wages. HIP offered free visits at their health centers for members. HIP members were municipal workers and union members, cops, firefighters, teachers and other civil employees.

HIP was different. The patients essentially belonged to the insurance company, namely, HIP, which contracted with groups of physicians, internists, surgeons, gynecologists, cardiologists, and radiologists to render the appropriate care. HIP paid the group a capitation, that is, a fee per month for every patient who was a member of the group. This was the model of "managed care." In other words, the patient belonged to the group and had to use group physicians and use hospitals affiliated with that particular group.

Emergency care would be paid out of group if the patient went "out of network" or used a non-group physician. Out of that money, the group created a complicated formula to determine the actual salary of each physician. If the patient went outside the group and failed to notify the group and the situation was considered non-emergent, then the patient would be responsible for all the bills. Naturally this created multiple conflicts and problems, but generally the patient complied with the requirements since no cost was better than paying. HIP also owned its own insurance company, Group Council Mutual, which provided malpractice coverage for Group physicians.

Despite these advantages, there were disadvantages to belonging to HIP. HIP doctors were generally looked down upon by the rest of the medical community. More than half were foreign trained. We made less money. We had internists who couldn't function independently or in private practice. We were practicing socialized, although it was called "capitated" medicine since there were no individual patient fees or fees for services.

In my mind, however, the advantages to HIP outweighed the disadvantages for my surgical practice. You had a turnkey office with no out-of-pocket expenses. You had medical assistants, a phone and answering service, a location, a way of disposing of medical waste, an x-ray facility, and expenses spread over a much larger base. HIP paid your malpractice. I was also permitted to keep my police salary separately without giving any part of it back to the group. You had fixed vacation time, although when you left, no additional surgeons would be hired to fill in. Other HIP surgeons would only cover the patients you had in the hospital. This meant when you returned, all the patients you might have seen during your absence would be added to your appointment schedule.

I could also answer the surgical conundrum. If I felt surgery was necessary, I would schedule it. If I didn't think it was indicated, I'd tell the patient. This, of course, led to disputes with patients who felt that surgery was absolutely necessary because their Uncle Harry at age 86 had his hernia fixed by a "good" surgeon. I also had an endless source of patients, giving me leverage and the ability to fill operating rooms in the affiliated hospitals without having to court every internist to send me cases.

Being part of HIP worked for me. Office hours were full of self-referring patients with the bulk of the practice being breast concerns. There was and is a considerable incidence of breast cancer in the Metropolitan area. HIP published a pioneer study in the 1960's by Phil Strax, M.D., who had lost a young wife to breast cancer. The study using more than 60,000 women seemed to indicate that mammograms helped in the early diagnosis of breast cancer and seemed to help save lives. The final decision regarding screening mammograms is still controversial even today, more than 50 years later.

There were numerous HIP groups, privately contracted groups of physicians, in Brooklyn, the Bronx, Manhattan, Queens and Staten Island. They formed independent affiliations with various hospitals in the New York area. The groups seldom interacted and when a HIP patient from one group ended up in a hospital and cared for by a different group, the groups would bill each other. This certainly made no sense economically and, more importantly, negatively impacted the quality of patient care.

With numerous independent micro-groups in the five boroughs, it became apparent to Robert Biblow, CEO of HIP in the 1980's, that consolidation rather than reduplication of services was appropriate. To accomplish this in Manhattan, he appointed Martin Gold, M.D. who had previous successes with groups in Queens. He thought he was so good that he named a HIP center in Queens after himself, the Martin Gold Center. And he wasn't even dead.

Using a carrot and stick approach, he convinced the separate Manhattan groups—the New York Medical Group on 23rd Street, the Central Manhattan Group on 55th Street, the Yorkville Group on 86 Street, the Upper Manhattan group on 188 Street— that one large entity would be more secure than many little ones and thus he got the various groups to agree to consolidation. Thus the Manhattan Medical Group was created. I was designated the chief of surgery. My job consisted of making the on-call schedule for surgery, accommodating vacations, and numerous and sundry miniscule tasks.

Therefore things were functioning with a larger group. A big center opened on the Upper West Side of Manhattan, an area known for liberal inclinations and populated by some of the more leftist-leaning union types. This was a perfect area for a "managed care" system, providing decent medical care at no out of pocket to the patient.

Martin Gold, M.D. was an aggressive and visionary leader. He decided that further expansion into New Jersey would benefit the group or at least his son, who had come to New York after completing an oncology fellowship. He would become director in New Jersey. As the expansion into New Jersey progressed, two separate geographic locations, one north near Paramus and the other 90 miles south near Cherry Hill and Philadelphia at the other end of the New Jersey Turnpike, became affiliates.

Dr. Gold would hold monthly meetings in the Manhattan Group optimistically touting the expansion plans and paving the future with profits. Slowly, however, it became apparent that to support the Jersey group and his son, the Director in New Jersey, Manhattan would have to be the banker. Funding and cash flow became more difficult since New Jersey was a money loser. We were paid monthly. One month my check bounced. I had a fit.

There are certain rules that I live by. Keep your hands off my wife, my kids, my dinner, and my paycheck. Although Marty Gold and I had a professional relationship, I went to see him and threw the bouncer on his desk. Originally he smiled and said he was embarrassed. He said, as everyone does when they bounce a check, that it was a bank error. However, it was becoming clear to me that he was playing fast and loose with group money. This straw broke my back. I copied the check and sent a copy to every group member. It turns out that I wasn't the only one who received a bouncing check.

Manhattan Medical Group was heading for bankruptcy. Bouncing checks were a sign things were not good. Cash flow was balancing salaries, expenses, and monies being sent to New Jersey. The CEO of HIP at the time realized it was time for Martin Gold, M.D. to be replaced. Under pressure, he resigned. The Martin Gold loyalists blamed me.

A New Director, Dr. ML, a physician who had previously merged the Bronx Groups, was appointed to run Manhattan and also merge the Manhattan Groups with the Bronx group. The Bronx group was strong, profitable, and larger. Dr. ML, as we shall call him, was an aggressive, headstrong director who took no prisoners and heard only one or two voices, mostly his own. Manhattan was a wasteland, a bankrupt group and would be swallowed by the Bronx. They had a well-funded pension plan and Manhattan was weighted down by New Jersey. Dr. ML, forced the issue, merging Manhattan group with the Bronx. Manhattan had no leverage and would pretty much do as told in order to survive at all. HIP would infuse the necessary capital to make the merger work, separate and totally break financially from the New Jersey group, and negotiate with other hospitals.

Negotiations and machinations that were never discussed with the physicians in Manhattan continued for months. HIP obviously threw money into the mix. Dr. ML, held meetings with his Bronx physicians and then met with the Manhattan doctors to tell them how it was going to be. The groups merged and kept certain finances, especially the pension funds, separate. Manhattan Medical Group was now called the New York Medical Group. I remained chief of surgery. I still did the schedule and other mundane chores.

Anthony Watson took over as CEO and president of HIP in 1990. Tony Watson was the epitome of what a strong, determined leader should be. An African-American, six foot, five inches tall or more, he was a member of the U.S. Olympic Team in 1960. By 1993 HIP, the insurance plan had close to one million members, employing over 980 doctors, with revenue greater than $1 billion a year. I had great respect for all he had accomplished and knew he was no one to mess with.

A visionary in health care, Watson had constructed a huge HIP center on 95th Street in Manhattan, Manhattan East Center.

Employing a large number of HIP physicians, 95th Street became a showplace of what HIP care could be. Staff included internists, cardiologists, radiologists, orthopedics, urologists, gastroenterologists, surgeons, gynecologists, social services. I was elected Medical Director of the center giving me the day-to-day responsibility of handling local problems, patient complaints, and communicating to the physicians in the group information that would be obtained at larger meetings in Manhattan.

Previously HIP and Manhattan doctors were affiliated with secondary hospitals in New York City. Our original hospital had been Cabrini and then had become Beth Israel. No major medical center would accept a HIP physician on staff as an independent practitioner. HIP would negotiate hospital affiliations and send groups of physicians to affiliated hospitals. Many HIP physicians were foreign-trained and not board certified. Major teaching hospitals had no interest in these physicians.

This was soon to change. HIP patients were unique. They were limited by the plan as to which hospitals they could use and were limited as to which internists and surgeons they could use. These patients represented a unique source of patients to the affiliated hospitals since they were outside the general public and could represent a steady source of patients and income to the affiliated hospitals. If the hospital had a contract with HIP, the hospital would get paid.

One day Tony Watson called me asking if I would like to work at New York Hospital, Cornell Medical, one of New York's premier facilities. He used me as one of his selling points to the Director of Surgery, Tom Shires, since I had come from Dr. Spencer's residency at NYU and had credentials that would not make getting privileges problematic. So HIP was now affiliating with *THE* New York Hospital (emphasis on the "*THE*").

New York Hospital, Cornell Medical, considered itself a mecca. If you were lucky enough to get privileges there, you'd be allowed to have the name recognition imply to patients that you were one of the best in your field. HIP cared. I didn't. At my *pro forma* interview with the chief of the operating room, I was told that I would be notified by 7p.m. what time I was going to begin my surgeries the next day. Obviously if cases before mine ran longer than anticipated, I might be delayed. I would be expected to notify my patients as to the anticipated time and, if they were to be admitted the day of surgery, tell them when to report. I would clearly have to be flexible in order to perform any surgery at New York Hospital. Yeah, sure.

My world was quite different. This couldn't work for me. So since the patients were mine anyway, I just said no. I couldn't function that way. Realizing that I offered a new source of previously untapped patients, I was called the next day and asked what my needs were. I got block-operating time, meaning a regular scheduled O.R. time every Thursday. There were not a lot of happy faces in the old timers when they heard this new guy was on board and given his own operating room every Thursday. Worse, he was a HIP doctor.

First cases, hernias. Then gallbladders, then mastectomies . I was faster at surgery than most of the older surgeons working at New York Hospital. I was young, fresh, and energetic. I knew what I was doing. The residents liked to scrub with me. When you first come to a new place, it's appropriate to start slow. Avoid complications and controversy for a while.

Things were going smoothly until I brought in my first colon resection. I asked for the GIA stapler used to resect and reattach the bowel. I might as well have asked for a bar of gold or a chainsaw. We don't use the staplers at Cornell came a chorus from the residents and the scrub nurses. "They let us use the staplers at Memorial, (Sloan Kettering where Cornell surgery residents rotated for further training) but they insist we sew everything by hand."

What year are we in? No staplers?? Yes, it was important for residents to learn how to sew, but skills with staplers were just as important and they saved time in the operating room, were totally reliable in well-trained hands and were standard of care in most operating rooms. I wasn't the only voice advocating for staplers. Within a month, the surgical administration ordered a full set of staplers. Although I was given admitting privileges to work at New York Hospital, most of my colleagues, internal medicine doctors working for our HIP group could not get privileges to work at New York Hospital. I was essentially working there alone. Since we were a group, there was no point in my continuing there. I eventually left New York Hospital and went back to Beth Israel.

Meanwhile, Dr. ML, would hold monthly meetings bragging about how successful the merger had been and how physicians' salaries would be increasing. The only problem was that membership was stagnant and slowly contracting. Salaries to the group depended on yearly meetings between Dr. ML and Tony Watson to negotiate a per patient, per month payment.

The problem with becoming too important and powerful is that you actually believe your own propaganda. Dr. ML began selling the doctors in the group the idea that HIP would be non-existent without the doctors. HIP, however, was an insurance company, first and last. The doctor part, the centers, was an addition and Tony Watson had been toying with the idea of separating from direct involvement with the groups. As a Medical Insurance company which served unions and city workers, it became apparent that dealing with so many discordant groups of physicians was a growing problem.

The HIP model was changing. Originally HIP would pay the hospitals and pay the groups who would in turn pay the physicians. It might be easier to simply allow physicians to participate in the insurance plan and bill the insurance company for their services, rather than paying the groups who would pay the doctors.

Dr. ML went to Watson to ask for a raise. No dice. Falling enrollment, increasing rents and expenses, and stagnant income for HIP was not the way to convince anyone to give you a raise. Dr. ML reported that Watson was adamant and obstinate. Dr. ML said that if he didn't get what he wanted, he would dissociate the groups from HIP and the doctors would go out on their own, believing that the patients would remain loyal and also leave HIP.

The plan had only a few small glitches. HIP owned all the leases to the centers. HIP only paid for care rendered by physicians affiliated with HIP. HIP owned the malpractice company that insured the doctors. Many doctors were granted privileges at hospitals contingent on the affiliation with HIP. New York City had sufficient doctors willing to be replacements.

I called Tony Watson to find out what was happening. He told me of the impasse and warned that Dr. ML was proceeding dangerously, jeopardizing everyone in the group. Iceberg dead ahead. He suggested that I leave before the Titanic leaves on its voyage. Watson had all the marbles; Dr. ML, in my opinion had none. I held meetings as the director of my center warning of the collision that was about to occur and the danger that the doctors were facing in the course that Dr. ML was touting.

Several of us realized what was happening and could envision the future. In our minds, it was a crazy plan being offered by Dr. ML. As I said at the beginning, medical school offers no "Business Skills for Doctors" courses. Dr. ML stirred the group and then confronted me. He accused me of being a traitor and fired me as medical director of my group, a move directly taken from the "Richard Nixon playbook." He threatened to end my career. I announced at a general meeting that each doctor should consider his position and future. I resigned from the group. I went to Beth Israel, where I had performed surgery for years, and with Watson's blessing and a phone call or two became a member of the surgical staff of the hospital. Whew. Dr. ML was rid of me. He was happy. So was I.

A few months went by with apparent negotiations ongoing between Dr. ML and Watson. They went nowhere. Finally, with the general support of the misguided group, Dr. ML pulled the trigger and notified HIP that the doctor groups were leaving. That killed things. Watson did exactly what he said he would do. HIP became an insurance carrier in Manhattan. All the physicians were fired. It was August 5, 1981 when then President Reagan fired the group of striking air traffic controllers. I guess most of the physicians who threatened their own strike forgot the outcome of that event, an event that had happened years before.

To make matters worse, in the malpractice company agreement that each physician signed in order to be insured was a clause that said the carrier Group Council, could demand a single year's payment from each insured physician to support the company. I was already insured by Beth Israel. A group of more than a hundred unemployed physicians were obligated to come up with thousands of dollars for the malpractice company.

Dr. ML had the Manhattan group declare bankruptcy as an attempt at revenge. This tied up any pension money for years. Some of the doctors retired. Some opened offices. Some joined hospital staffs. Hospitals near the former, now empty HIP centers received offers to run the centers and did so, replacing the fired doctors with their own staffs. The fired doctors survived but faced years of uncertainty; they now became hospital employees with far lower salaries.

Surgical discipline demands that one attempt to always have a fall back plan if the worst happens. During surgery, before burning bridges and committing to a particular course of action, it is important to know if indeed there is another alternative to what is contemplated. I saw that remaining with the group, what with Dr. ML's aggressive, egotistical and less than professional behavior, would end in the worst possible outcome. The members of the group, like lemmings jumping off cliffs, followed the leader to their own detriment.

It's hard to win at marbles when the other guy has all the marbles. Some leaders have insight into the possible negative outcome of a poor negotiating posture. Others can't seem to see that an inflexible position with a far superior adversary would only lead to disaster. Dr. ML was responsible for the loss of income of many of the physicians who listened to him and followed his ill-conceived plan. Those who don't learn from history are forced to repeat it. Maybe it's time that medical school teaches "Business Skills for Doctors."

I stayed with Beth Israel until a day in September 2001 changed the world forever for everyone.

CHAPTER 18

SEPTEMBER 11, 2001

The attack at the World Trade Center on 9/11 killed more than 2,600 people. At least 6,000 more were injured. Approximately 400 people who escaped from the rubble were hospitalized for more than two days. I was one of them. This is my story.

On Monday afternoon, September 10, 2001 I had performed surgery on two patients, removing their gall bladders. Because the surgery went late into the day, both patients remained overnight at Beth Israel. I would see them in the morning to see if they were ready to be discharged.

Tuesday morning, September 11, was bright, sunny, and warm with clear blue skies. Anne had dropped her car off for routine servicing and I drove her to work. After the usual good-bye-and-see-you-later kiss, I headed into Manhattan. Crawling along the Long Island Expressway during the morning rush hour, I passed Lefrak City in Queens, where the Police Medical Division offices were located. I usually spent afternoons in my office there after making rounds or seeing patients in Manhattan. I would be back later. Or so I thought.

Suddenly, a message came over the police radio that a plane had crashed into the North Tower of the World Trade Center. The time was 8:46 a.m. Chatter and communication franticly filled the police airwaves. I turned on a news station on my commercial radio to hear the preliminary reports. News folks struggled to make sense of the bizarre event unfolding. From the Long Island Expressway, I could see in the distance that the North Tower was on fire.

Initial reports had said that a small plane had crashed into the Tower. It became quite clear, quite quickly what had really happened. Air traffic controllers at the Logan Airport reported that a commercial flight heading from Boston to Los Angeles had been hijacked. No report ever fully documented that the air traffic controllers ever notified NORAD (North American Air Defense Command) about what was happening, but flight attendants on the flight told American Airlines about the hijacking via telephone until the plane hit the North Tower.

The dispatcher over the police radio called for a general mobilization with units to report to the World Trade Center. Having responded to the first terrorist attack at the World Trade Center in 1993, I knew there would be horrific injuries and deaths. Multiple units attempted to communicate with the dispatcher but, because individual calls on different frequencies overlapped each other, most of the talking was unintelligible. I used my cell phone to call Anne at work. A plane had hit the World Trade Center. I'm going. "Be careful," she said. I always kid her by saying that if she had said don't go, I wouldn't have responded. Yeah, sure. She knew better than to waste her breath saying that.

Very quickly, the situation mushroomed. This was a commercial airliner, not a small private plane, and it was no accident. The Long Island Expressway stopped moving. Turning on a siren and flashing lights in my unmarked police car, I edged my way first into the express bus lane on the other side of the highway. It was blocked with a mile of buses and was totally stopped. I edged over further on the highway into oncoming traffic, which fortunately was light. Blasting my air horn, flashers and siren, I succeeded in approaching the Queens Midtown Tunnel, actually leading a caravan of Emergency Service Vehicles also responding with lights and sirens.

Entering Manhattan, I headed south on the FDR Drive towards the World Trade Center. Police roadblocks were already beginning to be in place causing immense traffic jams but allowing emergency vehicles access to the highway. Knowing that the last place to put a car was near the emergency, I took Broadway further south and parked in front of the famous Charging Bull statue on lower Broadway about a half mile from the burning World Trade Center. I made it a point to locate where I had parked because after any major event, it's important to remember where the car was, although I had often wandered around sort of aimlessly many minutes after police funerals, shootings and other events that preoccupy your attention.

Exiting the car, I put on my police jacket with Executive Chief Surgeon emblazoned on the back. On the street, there was debris that resembled the engine of the jet. I'd see it again many months later at the Staten Island landfill. At 9:03 a.m., a second plane crashed into the South Tower. All I could think about was the number of people in the Towers, the potential numbers of dead and injured and the overwhelming catastrophe that was unfolding. Nothing that was happening made any sense.

As I walked towards the Trade Center, a small Emergency Service police van picked me up. "Doc, you better wear a helmet." They gave me one from the van. Until that morning, I had never felt the need to wear protection at a trauma scene. As we drove on the West Side Highway, a woman who had fallen or jumped from a high floor crashed down to her death. Before she hit the ground, she was still moving and it was clear that she was awake for the time it took hit the ground. Paper, smoke, debris filled the air. Silence ruled the van. We turned left at Liberty Street, directly in line with South Tower. As we turned and stopped, I and exited the van. Charles Hirsch, M.D., a long –time colleague and the New York City Medical Examiner was already on West Street. We exchanged a brief greeting. We both knew what would be happening. But neither of us ever could imagine the magnitude of the unfolding events.

As I exited, I encountered Theresa Tobin, at the time a Police Lieutenant and a long-time acquaintance, who was walking along Liberty Street. "Where are we setting up?" I asked. I needed to know where we planned to establish a temporary headquarters to provide a central location for assistance to the injured. She said it would be the same staging area that had been used in 1993 during the first attack: West and Liberty Street. It was outside and made access to the highways easy so that victims could be sent north towards St. Vincent's Hospital or South along the FDR to Beekman Hospital. Both facilities had been inundated with patients suffering smoke inhalation and minor injuries from the bombing in 1993. Some patients had been delivered by ambulance but the bulk had walked to the hospitals for help. Terry would be right back. She was going to her car to change from her uniform shoes to sneakers. It was going to be a long day.

I walked west on Liberty Street. Paper flew everywhere but so did glass, metal, smoke and debris. Smoke from the burning towers filled the air and made it difficult to breathe. People were falling or jumping from the high floors of the inferno. The thought of healthy young people who had gone to work an hour before who were now crashing to the pavement to their death, gripped me. What could go through your mind in the 15 seconds as you plummeted to your death, escaping a death by fire? What went through the minds of the passengers on the hijacked planes as they saw New York City appear ahead of them as the hijackers headed the plane directly into the World Trade Center? The horror of the events unfolding before our eyes was incomprehensible.

As I approached the temporary evacuation location, there was in front of me, lying on the ground in a pool of blood, a rescuer in a brown jumpsuit who appeared to be a firefighter. He was hardly moving. All around us, shards of broken glass, metal and bits of building fragments hissed by and crashed to the ground. I was quite thankful for the helmet. Bending over, identifying myself as a doctor, I quickly tried to assess the source of bleeding. Blood was pouring from his upper chest staining his clothes, his blood eventually getting on my lower pants. Clearly he had been hit by something sharp and penetrating. My plan at the time was to put pressure on the source of the bleeding and to get him evacuated by the van that had transported me to the site. As I bent down, someone from a distance shouted, "The building is going down!"

A huge low rumble told me I was in big trouble. Looking up, all I saw was debris blotting out the sky. It was far too close for me to even think of running. I was out on the street, located between two bridges that connected buildings on Liberty Street. The South Tower was crashing down on top of me. Out in the open, near the curb, there was nowhere to run and no time to do it.

Suddenly, I remembered the old duck-and-cover drill practiced in high school. I rolled into a ball, grabbed the back of my neck and waited to see what was next. I was a doctor. This wasn't supposed to be happening. In the minutes that the building took to come crashing down, I thought I would be killed. How can you survive the collapse of a thousand foot building only a few hundred yards away? No, I didn't pray. I figured if there were a god, he or she would know I really didn't want to die. So why bother?

I vaguely remember what happened. My face got hot and I felt a burning in the back of my throat. Then it got cold. I was told afterward that the first was residual fire and jet fuel and the second was air conditioner coolant, but I really have no idea except that explanation seems to make sense. The heat significantly burned the back of my throat and nose leading to future complications. Then it got dark. It was so dark that I actually thought I'd gone blind. Removing my glasses, I couldn't see shapes or anything. I felt a searing pain in my right chest and my right back and numbness down my right leg. I heard ringing in my ears and muffled sounds. But I wasn't dead.

It got very quiet but it was so dark that I couldn't see my hand in front of my face. From a distance, I could hear weak voices shouting for help. I thought I was a blind surgeon but again nothing made sense. It had been just another sunny day, but now the air and the ground was filled with smoke and debris and everything was black. Sitting in the blackness, I began to wonder why I had been blinded. There was no flash of light, just brightness from the building. Maybe the back of my head had been struck so I felt for the helmet. It was missing, and all that remained was the liner of the helmet, just the rim. The force of the collapse had probably ripped it apart.

Staring up at the sky, contemplating what to do next, a band of light streaked across the sky from the Hudson River. Slowly light began to come back. The area was now inundated with gray, ashen, foul-smelling dust. It permeated my hair, face, nose, mouth and clothes. It was a ghost world; you could barely make out any shapes. It was the dust cloud that had blotted out the light. I wasn't blind. Buried to my shoulders in debris, I realized that if I was going to survive, I had to dig myself out and get out of there. The firefighter I had bent over several minutes before was gone. (My police friend Lieutenant Gene Whyte who worked the morgue detail identified him by the location I described and from the firefighter's DNA sample taken from my pants legs). They recovered his body that night about a half of a block away from where I described. I didn't learn about him until weeks afterward.

The area where I had been hit was later designated the "kill zone." This was a wide circumference around the South Tower where a predominance of bodies had been recovered. I really never knew what hit me, but I think it must have been part of the aluminum façade that had covered the World Trade Center. If it had been concrete or steel, I would have been crushed and wouldn't be writing this book. If I hadn't had the helmet, I know the head trauma would have been horrendous. Now it was time to gather my thoughts and get help.

My right leg tingled from my butt to my heel. It still does. I diagnosed my symptoms as a spinal cord injury causing a neuropathy. But I could move everything in spite of the tingling and the pain. This was not so bad considering. Breathing was a chore. I coughed continuously. My right chest hurt when I took a deep breath or coughed. I realized that the right side of my butt was swelling quickly and causing considerable pain. I figured I was bleeding internally because I took the brunt of the crush on my back. My forehead was wet with a small amount of blood coming from my head.

Digging myself out, it was clear that if the South Tower had gone down, it would not be long before the North Tower followed. I decided I had better get away. The only direction was west, towards the Hudson since rubble and debris and the shell of the building was just down the block on Liberty Street. The ghostly landscape, the thick gray dust, the massive debris, made the situation more surreal.

Sometime earlier I acquired a water bottle. Good old Poland spring came in very handy as I soaked my handkerchief (my mother taught me to always carry one) and breathed through it. It seemed to help a little. I sort of wandered west intuitively, realizing that was the only direction to go. Knowing I was somehow bleeding from my back, I pulled my belt down over the area and made it as tight as I could, hoping to compress and contain the bleeding. I was thirsty, dizzy, disoriented—signs that I was going into shock. Only a very few people were around, all totally dazed.

As I looked back, I could see the destroyed façade of South Tower, impaled on the concrete, an image that was photographed for weeks showing how devastating the destruction had been. It reminded me of the final scene from *The Planet of the Apes* where Charlton Heston sees in the distance the ruins of the Statue of Liberty on the beach. This, however, was real.

There is a seawall at the shore of the Hudson on the west side of Manhattan capped by a fence. I headed there as I wandered through the fog created by the pulverized concrete that surrounded me. Having been nearly crushed by the collapse of the South Tower, I instinctively headed west to escape. Somewhere near the seawall I encountered Sean Crowley, a police captain who was in charge of Commissioner Bernie Kerik's security detail. Both of us had been completely engulfed in the wave of dust from the collapse; we were gray from head to toe. Sean told me how awful I looked and told me that I had to get out of there. At first, I said that there would be so many who needed help. He told me I really needed help myself. He told me the harbor boats were responding and he'd help me get evacuated. I knew I was still bleeding internally. I got dizzier and thirstier. I could feel my lower back expanding. I didn't disagree and accepted the idea of getting away. He told me that Police Harbor Launches and Police boats were responding from the Hudson River.

The sea wall has a wrought iron fence on top of a concrete wall. The harbor launch pulled up against the wall, about 15 feet below. I couldn't figure out how I was getting aboard until James Cowan, a sergeant in charge of the launch extended a ladder hooking it onto the fence. I had ridden with the harbor launch many times and knew Sgt. Cowan. On previous trips we have talked about his aunt, another Bronx native, having gone to high school with my mother-in-law.

Somehow I made it down the ladder and lay on the side of the deck. I stretched out on my back hoping to stop whatever was bleeding. The launch was not very full, although it was small. I could make out someone running and standing at the sea wall. Impatient to wait for the ladder, he jumped onto the deck, smashed his leg and began screaming. He kept me awake all the way to New Jersey.

The launch began to move. The sergeant told me that he knew how urgent it was to get me to a hospital. My glasses fell into the Hudson but they were useless anyway, having been scratched and destroyed by the blast of the building debris. I was now on my way to somewhere in Jersey, still bleeding internally from the injury I had sustained to my lower back. I remained barely conscious, very dizzy and increasingly thirsty. I used to teach residents that thirst is a clinical sign often diagnostic of decreasing blood volume and shock.

Staring at the blurry sky (with my blurry vision with my glasses in the Hudson), I saw the light become a narrowing circle. This was certainly similar to the famous "tunnel" of light that people with near-death experiences describe and think it might be an otherworldly experience. I thought that it was the arteries to my retina constricting and decreasing the blood supply. I think both theories are probably wrong, but they make a good story.

I'd been in these situations before, but always from the other side. I'd taken care of trauma patients suffering from stabbings and gunshot wounds or victims of serious car accidents who were bleeding. The difference was that when I was with them I could transfuse them, give them intravenous fluids, and resuscitation. I knew what was happening, but I was here on the Hudson on a harbor launch. If I got to a reasonable medical facility soon, I should live. If not...

Arriving at the Liberty Pier, it was time to exit. I felt the painful area in my lower back continuing to expand. Trying to roll onto the dock, I heard Captain Crowley who had ridden with me to Jersey, shouting, "not that way, doc!" He later told me if I had continued to roll, I would have ended up in the Hudson. Somehow, the group evacuating me lifted me onto the dock. A large group of medics and EMTs had assembled preparing for the evacuations. Unable to feel my own pulse, I felt guys poking at my arms trying to start IV's and failing. Still somewhat awake, I advised them that I was Executive Chief Surgeon for NYPD, a real surgeon and was probably bleeding from my lower back. "If I'm not in a hospital soon, I'll die," I said. Taking the hint, the EMT's put me into an ambulance and rushed me to Jersey City Medical Center.

I've ridden in ambulances before. I've also been evacuated in them. It's a bizarre sensation. One rides staring at a ceiling with no orientation as to where you're going or how long it's taking to get you there. You sort of hang on watching IV's and blood pressure cuffs and breathing assistance (ambu) bags rock back and forth next to and above you. It takes endless time, sirens blasting away. When you arrive, again you're looking straight up as you are wheeled on a stretcher into the hospital. With no glasses, in shock, the experience is surreal and almost a hallucination. It's certainly a bad dream.

Jersey City Medical Center was an older facility but they were ready for the onslaught. They immediately cut off my Chief Surgeon's jacket. An Emergency Department. attending came over, identified himself and told me to give him my valuables which he would safeguard. I handed him my Rolex and my NYPD Chief's Shield, telling him that he could give them to my wife if I died, but I'd prefer getting them back. Someone inserted a subclavian catheter (an intravenous line that invades the large vein beneath the collar bone). Everything hurt. My back hurt, my butt, my chest, my nose, my head. My blood pressure was very low and it was apparent that I was still probably bleeding, so they began immediately transfusing O negative blood, the universal donor blood type.

A nurse introduced himself to me saying he'd stay with me until I was stable. He asked if anyone had checked my neck? Not that I was aware of, so he improvised a cervical collar to stabilize it in case the head trauma had broken my neck. He would give me something for the pain as soon as the second blood transfusion was in and my blood pressure was higher (or could at least be obtained). As the morphine went into the subclavian line the pain began to ease but, as a side effect of morphine, I became very nauseous. Unable to turn my head, the nurse was abruptly subjected to my breakfast. I pointed out that I had passed the test of a non-broken neck because I had no collar on me from the time of my evacuation until the time he attached it and because I turned my head frequently with no neck pain. He agreed to release me from the collar.

So here I was: the doctor, patient, trauma victim all in one. I was totally aware of the events, the treatment and what should be done. When I had hepatitis during my residency, there was little I knew about the disease and very little in terms of experience that I or anyone else had with it. Now it was totally different. I had taken care of so many trauma patients that I could envision myself standing over someone just like me. With the blood transfusions, I became more awake. With my glasses gone, however, I couldn't see much.

From the time in Queens, when the first plane hit, my cell phone was useless. I still needed to contact Anne and tell her that I was alive, where I ended up, and discover from her what was happening in the rest of the world. A firefighter was in the space next to me and had a companion in attendance who had a working cell phone. I borrowed his and actually got through to Anne. One of the emergency attendings in Jersey had called her and told her that I was in Jersey City Medical Center. He had told her that they didn't know the extent of my injuries simply stating that I might have a kidney injury or other serious injuries. By the time I spoke to her I was able to reassure her that I had been crushed but didn't need surgery. I asked her to call the Sick Desk at Lefrak and tell them where I was and see if they'll transport her here. And try not to forget to bring me a spare pair of glasses.

Apparently, as I found out later, Mayor Giuliani, in the face of everything happening had been told that I was missing and might have been killed. Later I learned that he had been trapped himself and was also covered in dirt but was uninjured. At some point the harbor crew notified Police Operations of the fact that they had transported me to Jersey and that I was not dead.

As the afternoon dragged on, a young man who identified himself as an ENT specialist said he needed to look down into my airway to determine if I had damage there. He inserted a thin endoscope down my nose, made me cough and then, pulling it out proceeded to tell me that I had to be intubated because I had sustained a pulmonary burn. No way. A pulmonary burn is accompanied by coughing up soot, hoarseness, singeing of nasal hairs among other findings. The good news is that I was a surgeon and knew exactly what characterized a pulmonary burn. What he was seeing was simply the nasopharyngeal burn I had gotten. Definitely not. I refused to allow him to intubate me which I told him in a clear, non-hoarse voice.

He disappeared for a moment, returning with a tracheostomy set, which he abruptly plopped onto my bedside table. Admonishing me, he promised that if I became unconscious and was unable to be intubated, he would have to perform a tracheostomy. I simply said that if I indeed passed out, he was free to do whatever he wanted, but for the time being, I would continue to refuse intubation. I never developed respiratory problems severe enough to even remotely require intubation but realized that inhaling the pulverized particles of the South Tower might be a bad thing. I knew that if I were intubated, I'd be there far too long and end up sedated for days until everyone decided I had recovered. Sometimes it's a good thing to be a doctor and a patient at the same time.

From somewhere in the blurriness and the noise, I was told that Anna Van Tuyl, who was one of my surgical residents at Beth Israel at the time, was calling to check on my status. Since I was in intensive care, I couldn't really talk to her, but those around me told me they assured her that I was still alive. She told me afterward that somehow she found out that I was there and had to find out what was happening to me. Hearing her name from the din of the ICU somehow reconnected me with the real world.

Time dragged on. Darkness fell but the televisions that were on kept reporting more about the attacks. Between the morphine relieving the pain and the blood transfusions, I became somewhat more alert. Suddenly, standing next to my bed was Father Robert Romano, police department chaplain. "What are you doing here?" he said. Smiling, I told him that I guess I wasn't going to die because they don't send a priest to say last rites to a Jewish person. He had heard through Police Operations where I had ended up and came over specifically to see me. We had spent many a night together at hospitals when cops were shot or killed. Subsequent to the terrible events of that day, Fr. Romano held Mass daily for the responders working at Ground Zero. Each year he holds a memorial Mass around the anniversary at his church in Brooklyn. I don't know where the Police Department Rabbi was, but I never saw or heard from him.

Sgt. Andra Copeland, working at the Medical Division, was actually assigned to pick up Anne in Great Neck and transport her to New Jersey. Whenever police officers were injured or killed, someone from their command would be assigned to drive the families to the appropriate locations. Anne reached out to Ed Weiss, my doctor, who had taken care of me during my hepatitis siege. He was also a neighbor in Great Neck but had remained in his office in Manhattan in the event he was needed to respond to his hospital to assist survivors. He agreed to be picked up and ride with Anne and to see what had happened to me.

New York City was in a panic. No one understood what was happening or why. Roadblocks by NYPD, New York State Troopers and some military were all in place. Most access roads, bridges and tunnels were closed. The most direct route to New Jersey, the Lincoln Tunnel, was closed to all vehicles. Detoured, Anne, Sgt. Copeland and Dr. Weiss were forced to head north in Manhattan and crossed the George Washington Bridge after negotiating with the officers at the roadblock. They finally made it to my bedside around 8 p.m.. Anne had a spare pair of my glasses in hand. I could see again.

Clearly it wouldn't be convenient for me to remain in Jersey as I lived in Great Neck. I'd stay the night but asked Anne to find a place closer. After Dr. Weiss consulted with Anne, they both felt it preferable that I be transferred to NYU Medical Center, where I had trained and Dr. Weiss was an attending physician. The next morning, I got in touch with Police Operations who patched me through to John Odermatt, liaison to the Office of Emergency Management for the NYPD. He dispatched an ambulance and early on the morning of September 12th I was taken to NYU. It was so early, that Anne, who was headed to Jersey in a police car, missed me and had to turn around to see me at NYU.

NYU is one of the outstanding hospitals in New York City. The City of New York, however, was under siege. The unimaginable events of the day before impacted everyone in the medical community. All available staff was called in to await the possible influx of large numbers of survivors. The air was filled with smoke. Volunteering physicians, nurses, and staff headed down town to provide medical assistance to first-responder rescuers. Eyes were red because of the toxic dust that permeated the air and volunteers were there with eyewash. Rescuers were experiencing uncontrollable coughing and shortness of breath. An indescribable malaise overtook the city. Fear and dread were everywhere. No one really knew what was happening or going to happen. Repeated images of the attacks were replayed day and night on television.

I was the only victim of the attacks hospitalized at NYU. Being a cardiologist, Dr. Weiss transferred me to the Cardiac Care Unit to keep an eye on me, although the only evidence of a heart abnormailty was a pulse that persisted at 120. I had some elevated blood enzyme changes, characteristic of muscle trauma, but no cardiac damage. Being in shock for a considerable length of time can put a significant strain on your heart. The fact that I hadn't had a heart attack was a testament to the fact that somehow my heart was ok.

Since I did my surgical training at NYU, it was a familiar place. The rest of the city, however, had become strange and hostile. Rescuers headed downtown continuously, accompanied by wailing sirens. Smoke permeated the outside air, blowing over the city from the burning towers. I was actually the first survivor of the attack admitted, but the medical community expected a deluge to begin at any moment. People would stick their heads in my cubicle (the CCU was open without separate rooms) and give me a hello and tell me they'd be back to see me. Fortunately, there wasn't much that they needed to do. They all wanted to help, to feel that in some small way they could contribute their medical skills to this tragedy.

A plan was put in place that all survivors would be triaged and examined at the West Side steamship pier, a huge building that would be equipped with medical supplies and volunteers. The staff at NYU was planning to go to the "pier" to attend to the injured that were supposedly being evacuated there. Except, there were no patients evacuated. Every survivor had been pulled out pretty much within a day and the estimated numbers of the injured didn't exist. Only about 20 people had been pulled from the rubble alive in the first 24 hours after the attack.

The other problem reported by those who stopped by for more than a wave was that the NYU computers were somehow tied into the Trade Center and weren't working. Until things were fixed, no CT scan could be done. The CCU was extremely noisy. The televisions were constantly on in the background reporting over and over again about what had happened and what was now happening. These were absolutely the worst of times. It is truly a testament to the rescuers and medical staff that they could focus at all. I by contrast had the luxury of lying in bed and being attended to.

I had a policewoman assigned to "watch" me. I really hadn't planned on going anywhere. Suddenly after a day of lying around listening to the continuous din of the CCU, one of the folks bringing a new patient up from somewhere dropped an oxygen tank. Blamo! I jumped out of bed. Less than two days before a skyscraper fell on me and now...Blamo! I totally freaked out. All I remember thinking is that I've got to get away from this noise.

Attempting to calm me, the police "watcher" tried to talk me down but to no avail. Then a resident in medicine gave me an injection in my exposed butt (not the swollen one). I asked what he gave me. He said it was Haldol and that before it kicked in I should go back to bed. I complied, feeling dizzy. I slept a good night's sleep and woke up the next morning, less panicked and less frenzied. They also turned down the background noises.

By Friday morning, when it was apparent that nothing more than routine X-rays could be done, Anne and I realized that I wasn't going to die and that I could go home. We both realized that we absolutely had to get out of the city. So we left. On discharge I still needed an MRI of my spine and chest to determine the extent of the damage. Her friends, physicians at Pro-Health, a major outpatient facility located near our house, accommodated all of my needs. The staff was amazed that they were caring for a seriously injured survivor. There weren't many of us.

I had multiple broken ribs, although none had affected my lung except to limit my ability to take a deep breath, three herniated discs, three fractured bones in my spine, a large blood clot in my right butt, (I eventually turned purple from my right nipple to my knees), and a nasopharyngeal burn in the back of my nose into my left sinus. Commenting to me about the CT scan, the radiologist said he was "impressed" with the extent of my injuries. Things hurt but there appeared to be no immediate need for any surgery.

Home was the best place for me. I had the best nursing care anyone could have asked for: private duty from my recovery room nurse, Anne. I couldn't have asked for more. On my return home, we discovered that our telephone message taker had become filled to capacity with well-wishers. Sometimes, it's encouraging to know that so many people care about you. Sometimes, when you're in really bad shape, it's difficult to know. To anyone who called during those days, thank you. I simply erased all the messages. Food baskets, flowers and visitors started pouring into our house

CHAPTER 19

AFTER 9/11

I was different. My injuries were severe enough, although I didn't know it at the time, to change my life. New York City was different. Everything changed. Security, military patrols, and defense posture became a recognizable presence in the city that had not been aware of previously unseen danger. The city would recover, although it would take time. So would I.

My back hurt. My lower back was swollen and misshapen. I coughed. I found it hard to take a deep breath. I survived. I still thought I could resume practice and return to the Police Department. I just didn't know how long it would take me to recover or what the sequelae would be. I was just glad to be alive. Since the trauma didn't kill me, it would make me stronger. Or so Nietzsche would have thought.

Getting home after a major hospitalization has always required a readjustment. Hospitalization is almost a time warp for me where my normal daily activities have been suspended and time has stopped. Financial obligations don't. Our answering machine continued to fill up each day. I still couldn't listen to all the greetings and would erase them. I knew I would need a lot of time both physically and psychologically.

Although the world had been greatly changed by the events of 9/11, life moved on. So would I. For years I cared for patients, some of who underwent life-changing surgery. I cared for police officers who had sustained serious life-altering injuries. Now I was in the same situation in which they had been. The advantage for me was that all of New York City and even the U.S. were aware of what happened. My situation was a unique and major public event. All I had to tell people was that I was injured and hospitalized on 9/11 and doors would open. Being a doctor always opened special doors for me, being with the Police Department opened even more doors, but being a survivor of 9/11 put me in a most unique position.

On Monday September 17, 2001, I got a desperate call from Police Operations. Some doctor, according to them, had set himself up at 75 Barclay Street to "monitor" any respiratory problems for rescue workers. The Emergency Service Unit occupied this location. It was where the cadaver dogs would be stationed and where the rescue-and-recovery units would report. According to the ESU, this medical monitoring was getting in the way and was unauthorized. They claimed that the Supervising Chief Surgeon, had approved of them but he had neither contacted ESU or anyone in the command nor had he been seen down there.

They would send a car for me. Since I was barely recovered, but also a survivor, I called the Medical Division to tell them that I wanted a specific officer who was working at the Medical Division to be my driver. Eileen had been a special friend for many years. She had lost her husband, a Sergeant in the NYPD, to a brain tumor years before. After his death, she had also lost her long-time psychologist and at one point thought I would be the third close person in her life that she was losing. Not me! She had transferred to the Medical Division and was available for this assignment. She would be of major assistance to me. I felt I could count on her to keep me safe. She also understood how much physical and emotional pain I had. Naturally, I was partially out of it mentally, requiring fairly strong pain medications to get me through the day. I was also curious and eager to return to the scene where I had almost died to see what it looked like almost a week later. With Eileen driving me and Anne accompanying me I hoped I'd be ok. Off we went.

Helped from the car, I could barely catch my breath. The air was filled with unnamed contaminants making it impossible for me to take a deep breath, so I headed indoors where I found I could breathe better. Getting there took us through a landscape that has been vividly described so many times: Bombed out, devastated, war zone, ground zero, etc. Rubble and destroyed buildings were everywhere. Smoke and fire poured out of the rubble. Dust still filled the air. It was reminiscent of a war zone like Beirut. But this was lower Manhattan, not Beirut. For those who experienced 9/11 first hand as I did, the images of that tragic day still sear our souls.

Inside the temporary headquarters was the Emergency Service Unit, the elite group of police officers who were still engaged with possible rescue, but now evolving more toward recovery work. They had been there for nearly five days. Maps, blue prints, hazmat equipment, respirators, Hurst tools used for extrication, flags and multiple telephones filled the spaces.

The makeshift monitoring area that was taking up unnecessary real estate was the work of a former football player who in his next life had become a thoracic surgeon. Apparently, having heard about the destruction, he had packed his bags and gear in New Jersey and headed for the site to provide "medical screening." Upon arriving, he had spoken to someone at Police Operations and in turn was transferred to Dr. T., the Supervising Chief Surgeon. Dr. T. gave him some kind of consent to set up his monitoring station without ascertaining need, crowding, or location. Indeed, he had not even visited the site himself. Emergency Services needed the doctor from New Jersey to leave. That is why they had called me.

The doctor originally protested and said he was there to be sure that the cops underwent pulmonary testing. However, he was clearly in the way. So I at first suggested he leave, then told him he'd be moving elsewhere. Seeking a compromise, we contacted Chief Eddie Delatorre who at that time was in charge of the Police Academy several miles north and far from Ground Zero. He agreed to house the doctor and his New Jersey entourage and allow officers after working the "pit"—the area that became known as Ground Zero, where the major wreckage was concentrated—to go for pulmonary and medical testing.

Apparently, a significant number of officers went for testing. However, none of the results obtained were ever sent back. Although he reportedly stayed for quite a number of weeks, no significant publications or medical information seems to have been generated from his "testing." At least he was out of the way of the recovery team. I went home after dispossessing him. I had my own obvious difficulties to deal with.

Days later, while sitting at home and watching the news, it became apparent to me that my lower back and right buttock were becoming more swollen. Standing and swaying, I could actually hear splashing from inside. This occurred about 10 days after the initial injury. Calling my wife at work, she came home armed with an Emergency Department physician who agreed with my assessment. He examined me briefly and then he turned pale. He remarked that he had never seen anything similar to what I was showing him. He was amazed that I had survived the events and was already home.

At 10 to 14 days, blood clots liquefy. I had been transfused six units of blood on 9/11. Most of the bleeding now sequestered in my lower back. Now it was time for the blood to try to reabsorb or dissolve. Realizing that I had an industrial-size hematoma in my back, I called my radiologist friend Dr. Al Messina. He had a large radiology practice in Manhattan. I told him I needed to have a CT scan to determine exactly what was going on. Being a doctor, especially a surgeon, sometimes helps, and saves considerable time.

Eileen, my police driver delivered me to Manhattan. CT confirmed several quarts of non- clotting blood, so Al used a harpoon-sized needle to aspirate the available bloody liquid. Relieved, I went back home. Within two days, however, the fluid reappeared and there I was splashing again. Back to Al, another harpoon, several quarts of fluid removed and my shape was normal again. This time the fluid was not unclotted blood but yellow serum. Back at home, fluid re-accumulated again within two days. It was time to get more information. I called surgeon friends. I was reassured that it would reabsorb by itself and to leave it alone. I doubted that it would ever resorb, so I consulted with a plastic-surgeon friend, Dr. Dennis Barek. Conveniently, he had an office in his house and lived a mile away.

Plastic surgeons deal with extensive seromas, that is, accumulations of fluids that may occur after face lifts or liposuction. Dennis was impressed with my splashing butt and agreed that if it wasn't drained continuously, it would never reabsorb. Quite used to being poked, prodded and stabbed, I had no problem lying down and letting him put a medium-sized silicone drain into the large space that was in my right butt. He ran the drain externally down my back along my side. It had a squeeze bulb attached and was made of silicone so I could empty it when necessary. He advised me not to shower since the area was potentially a great spot for an infection.

Yeah, sure, don't shower. No way. The drain worked as expected, and I recorded the output daily. The first week, it put out over a pint a day, but there was no way I wasn't going to shower. I was uncomfortable enough and knew that I could manage showering. So with care, I would protect the drain, first with plastic and by not getting it wet. Silicone is quite a forgiving material and doesn't take too much effort to keep clean.

It took a long time for the pain to become tolerable. Sitting, walking, travelling was a challenge. Painkillers and anti-inflammatories helped. Sometimes I would take hours to fall asleep and would wake whenever I turned. It was peculiar because as I drifted off to sleep, I was sort of aware that some of the pain would abate. One Friday evening, I was sitting on the couch finally drifting off to sleep when another of the innumerable phone calls was intercepted by Anne. It was Bo Wagner. Someone needed to speak to me. Protecting me, as she had been doing since I had gotten home, she simply said that I was finally dozing. Could this call wait?

Bo was the personal bodyguard for Mayor Giuliani. He and the Mayor were at Yankee Stadium but the Mayor had been thinking about me. He had wanted to wait for me to have some time to recover. Bo told Anne that he thought I'd want to take this call: the Mayor really wanted to talk to me. Anne whispered that someone wanted to talk with me.

Enthusiastic and very animated, the Mayor wanted to know how I was doing and if there was anything I might need. He told me that he'd heard all about me and was following my recovery from information he'd gotten from his police people. He described how he had been trapped and how Commissioner Kerik and he had escaped from a building through a window that needed to be smashed. He was glad that I was a survivor. He told me that when

I felt up to it, I should come and visit him at the Pier on the West Side, where a temporary headquarters had been established.

The following week, Eileen, still my personal driver, drove Anne and me to the pier. As I entered one of the policy meetings attended by all the city officials involved with the recovery. Mayor Giuliani looked up to see me coming. Stopping everything, he introduced me to the rest of the group, many of whom knew me quite well. I was a bit shaken by a round of applause and a standing ovation by people who were spending days and nights trying to restore a semblance of decorum and order to a city still numb from such a terrible crime.

As I resumed my normal activities and travelled more, I would tuck the squeeze bulb of the drain under my shirt. When it got full, I'd simply detach it and squirt it into a sink or toilet. After a month, the drainage decreased to a trickle. Consulting with my plastic surgeon, we both agreed it was in long enough. Reaching back to cut the sutures, I pulled it out. To this day, one side of my butt is bigger than the other, but at least it doesn't splash.

These were strange days, recovering after 9/11, trying to get back to some sort of rhythm of life and still contemplating resuming my previous activities. I went for medical and in particular neurologic exams because of my persistent and often debilitating back and leg pain. I would occasionally report to the Medical Division attempting to resume some sort of work activity, only to find myself quickly exhausted.

Being seriously injured in the line of duty allowed me, as it does for all seriously injured cops, to have a police officer to drive me around when necessary. I needed numerous trips to medical facilities and had an interview with the media, but I was pretty well set on the road to recovery. Being as stubborn as I am, I planned to return to work. My secretary at Beth Israel would call me once a week to ask when I was returning, but the time seemed to move slowly and recovery was still limited. I was impatient and disappointed that recovery was taking so long, and really didn't fancy not working.

I was sent locally for physical therapy. The first goal of the physical therapy was originally designed for pain relief. I had obtained copies of the most important X-rays from my radiologist, and would transport a heavy shopping bag full of them to each physician I saw. The physiatrist reassured me by commenting that he'd never treated anyone with such a massive injury. He, as was most of my treating physicians, a bit intimidated by the fact that I had been crushed by the South Tower. Ultrasound, massage, limited exercise, however, all added to my pain. So the therapist and I agreed it was probably wiser to stop. I would live on painkillers for quite a while.

I also had the good fortune of knowing Nancy a special friend who was a practicing psychologist. Nancy reached out as soon as she heard what had happened and offered to be available for me. I asked her if the fact that she knew me so well would interfere with her helping me. She assured me that she would address my problems as objectively as she could, but that if she detected any growing problems she would refer me to a colleague who could then treat me more objectively. That never happened. I would call her or meet her and describe things that were happening in my head. She'd usually reassure me that they were normal.

One of the ongoing problems that I would ask her about was the fact that I didn't seem to be depressed or overwhelmed by what I had experienced. Was it normal *not* to have flashbacks, nightmares, or to be depressed after all I had gone through? My life, as everyone else's had changed dramatically. I experienced extensive physical pain and disability, but it seemed that I was quite adaptable and was coping. We both sort of agreed that being a surgeon for so many years, experiencing so many life changing events in other people had allowed me to distance myself from my own events and begin to both accept the reality of my new situation and not allow them to overwhelm me. I guess that after all those years of diagnosing cancer, seeing trauma deaths and the seriously injured, I had no survivor guilt. I was glad I wasn't dead. I focused on recovery and the future.

I had persistent gnawing back pain running down my right side and right leg. I knew this was the result of the fractures to my spine. Essentially some of the aches and pains have diminished but the numbness has remained the same since the day of being crushed. I wasn't about to run around to physicians and expect to fully recover. I knew I could live with it. I did. I discovered that the pains increased significantly whenever I stood or sat for more than an hour. Not wanting to plan to do surgery with serious back pain, I reluctantly put my surgical practice on hold, waiting to see how I felt over time.

Sometime in the middle of October 2001, while I was still trying to recover, I was contacted by Police Operations that some of the ESU officers had responded to Dan Rather's CBS office for a letter containing a suspicious white powder. Testing the employees, the diagnosis was anthrax and one of the employees got sick. One of the ESU officers had also had contact with the area, but hadn't been fully diagnosed. The tests were pending.

It was a Friday afternoon and I contacted the CDC. Obviously I knew nothing about anthrax, its diagnosis or treatment. A return call from Atlanta told me to wait until a formal diagnosis was made. Formal confirmation would probably wait until Monday. Checking with the medical literature, calling infectious disease physicians

I knew, I discovered that the treatment, however, required high doses of Cipro ®, a fairly benign commonly used antibiotic.

I had no intention of waiting, however, and immediately prescribed the medication to anyone suspected of contact with any suspicious material. I could see no reason not to begin treatment if there was a remote chance that someone had been exposed to anthrax. These were extraordinary times which I felt required extraordinary action. Sure enough, one of the officers contracted anthrax eventually causing significant changes in his chest X-ray. Fortunately, he had started taking the antibiotics before confirming the diagnosis or it's possible the delay might have killed him.

Months passed and I was still undecided as to whether I would or could return to work. I pretty much realized that I would never be resuming my surgical career. So rather than get crazy over it, I just decided I'd consider all my options. I had disability insurance. I was financially sound. I also knew that I couldn't successfully stand for long periods in the operating room with increasing back pain and concentrate on performing surgery. I was still working at the NYPD. Leaving surgery just meant moving on to something else.

Meanwhile, realizing that some of us who were injured as well as those who died should be recognized, the Police Department asked for submissions for those who should be honored for outstanding service. Not really thinking about it, I didn't expect anything and didn't plan to submit anything about myself. The First Deputy Police Commissioner, Joe Dunne, however, felt that I deserved recognition. He went ahead and contacted the Medical Division to submit information on my behalf.

Because of 9/11, Medal Day was divided into two ceremonies. Medal Day is traditionally a day when officers injured or killed in the line of duty as well as those who have performed what the department considers outstanding actions above and beyond the call of duty are given recognition. The Medal of Honor is the highest award bestowed upon such men and women. Twenty-three NYPD officers had died on 9/11. On December 4, 2001, the Medal of Honor was awarded in a solemn ceremony to the families of those who died.

The second Medal Day ceremony occurred on January 17, 2003. I was awarded the NYPD Medal for Valor. Although I never considered myself a hero, I responded to a situation far more dangerous than I had ever anticipated. I did what I felt had to do. I'm very proud that I'm the only police surgeon ever awarded the Medal for Valor.

I did, however, plan to fully resume my career with the NYPD. But this intention came to an end in March 2003. I was called at home in Great Neck: Two cops had been shot in Staten Island and were being transported to St. Vincent's Hospital in Staten Island. I dragged myself to my reissued and cleaned unmarked police car, which had been covered with the dust cloud on 9/11. Turning on the lights and siren, I realized that this was the first hospital response I had made since before 9/11.

From Great Neck to St. Vincent's in Staten Island is a long trip, more than an hour with minimal traffic. I arrived and headed for the Emergency Room, as I always had done so many times before. Upon opening the car door, however, I realized that I couldn't get out. As I struggled to get on my feet, I experienced severe back pain and really couldn't walk. Two cops saw me struggling and helped me out.

It turned out that two cops who were murdered during an undercover operation had been rushed to St. Vincent's Hospital in Staten Island. Unfortunately, my back pain, cough, and general fatigue severely hampered my ability to run around and respond as I usually did in the past. The decision was clear. I approached Commissioner Ray Kelly, who had been reappointed commissioner when Bloomberg became Mayor. I had known him for years and he was aware of what had happened to me. He asked me how I was feeling and I told him that it looks like I was done. It was clear to me that I really couldn't continue doing what I used to do. My physical stamina just wasn't there.

So the following week I returned to the Medical Division to put in my papers. The standard for approval for disability was and remains whether or not one is capable of performing the duties of a full-duty police officer or, in my case, a Police Surgeon. Unfortunately, I could no longer perform my basic functions as Executive Chief Surgeon.

My final day with the NYPD was August 31, 2003. Although I am not particularly sentimental, I looked back fondly on what I considered a notable career. But my life certainly wasn't going to end with my leaving the NYPD. I was grateful for the opportunities that I had and was just as happy to move on. Tradition in the NYPD in those days required large retirement parties at posh NYC hotels filled with thousands of your closest friends giving tedious speeches and serving rubber chicken. Attendees were expected to spend more than $100 for a ceremony recalling all the magnificent accomplishments of the honoree. I should know. I had gone to plenty of them. Rule of thumb for most police affairs is if they're called for 7:00 o'clock, almost every uniformed member of the service who planned to be there usually has arrived no later than 7:30 p.m. Right after the speeches 1/3 of them leave. The rest are gone by 9. Anyway, I truly didn't want or need one of these big deals. I remembered the police adage, "when you're in, you're the best; when you're out, you're a pest." So I didn't much care whether I had a big shindig or not to tell me that I once mattered.

Eileen, my driver after 9/11, insisted that she do something to commemorate the occasion of my retirement. So on November 14, 2003, she organized a party at a local gin mill exclusively attended by a small special group of female cops. It was terrific. Anne, of course, knew all of them and attended. There I was surrounded by a very special group of female officers. Nothing too fancy. Beer and burgers. Just the kind of retirement party I wanted. These ladies had worked closely with me and obviously appreciated the times we had spent working together.

I did have many friends on the job. My friend Joe Dunne, the First Deputy Police Commissioner, insisted that I attend a small going-away celebration. He and Maureen Casey, a former Police Research administrator, a Deputy Commissioner, organized an affair to be held at the South Street Seaport in Manhattan. I didn't want it to cost everyone very much and I certainly didn't need more testimonials.

When Mayor Giuliani heard a party was being planned for me, he insisted on setting the date. It was held on January 27, 2004. It so happens Giuliani was going to be in Arizona that day but would be back in town in time to make the party. And he did. In spite of a predicted snowstorm, the affair was packed. Six former Police Commissioners actually attended: Bob McGuire, Dick Condon, Bill Bratton, Howard Safir, Ray Kelly, and Bernie Kerik. (Ben Ward had died in June of 2002 and Lee Brown had gone back to Houston to become Mayor.) With that guest list, I think I achieved unique status.

That night it snowed heavily. My mother-in-law Alice and sister-in-law Michelle made the party and trudged home in near blizzard conditions. I must admit I was quite proud and happy to see so many friends in attendance. Some of the doctors from Beth Israel came. The Police Department Ceremonial Unit turned out in full force. Not to be outdone, the Medical Division gave me a farewell luncheon at a local restaurant on January 30, 2004. So, despite not wanting a party to celebrate my career, I had three.

Retirement has been a fulfilling time for me. I look back at my career and the demands of my profession and wonder how I ever could have done all that night call, being out at least two nights a week and staying up all night on countless occasions. After leaving surgery, I became a consultant, which was almost a vacation compared to the previous demands that I faced. I wasn't completely ready psychologically to totally separate from surgery. But there was no night call. I could actually sleep through the night, although sleeping was sometimes quite a challenge.

CHAPTER 20

EPILOGUE

My journey obviously didn't end with my leaving surgery. To quote Bob Dylan, "I was so much older then, I'm younger than that now..." In those early days, I was more regimented, more driven, more goal oriented. I was far more preoccupied with what I needed to do and had to do in order to accomplish those goals. Retired, I am now more able to enjoy many leisure activities that are simply fun, that interest me or that sat on the back burner until I had the time. I had always tried to get off the treadmill of my active life and look around. Today, I can really do all the things I've wanted to do. Still, we all know that life presents us with challenges and never goes completely smoothly, even if you're retired.

It took me over six months to recover from my injuries to resume some everyday activities. I was fortunate enough to have made acquaintances throughout the medical community and was offered numerous positions that could utilize my experience as a surgeon and as the Executive Chief Surgeon for the NYPD. I accepted a position as surgical consultant at St. Barnabas Hospital in the South Bronx, a hospital serving a large Hispanic and otherwise underserved community. The area was one where street violence was commonplace.

Years before I had met Ron Gade, M.D. when a cop shot in the heart, was brought to St. Barnabas Hospital and somehow miraculously survived. Dr. Gade was president and chief medical officer of St. Barnabas. He reached out to me to provide surgical guidance so that St. Barnabas could achieve certification as a Level I Trauma Center to provide high-quality care to the community. I rounded with the Trauma Team, examined patients and provided my expertise in bringing new surgical talent. With some effort St. Barnabas was approved.

Although it became clear that I would no longer be performing surgery, I remained affiliated with Beth Israel, again becoming a consultant. I was linked with the business development network that performed outreach to organized groups and unions to use the hospital and the full-time physicians.

My consulting activities were finally terminated after I was hospitalized multiple times with complications of the sinus burn I experienced on 9/11. After five sinus surgeries complicated with multiple bleeding episodes, I finally got past another major life-threatening complication directly related to 9/11. I was glad to be alive but had a year of neurological complications following the surgeries. I stopped working after that.

Dizziness, double vision and hearing loss were some of my neurological complications. Rather than give into this, I sought expert rehabilitation and recovery Double vision was ameliorated with prismatic lenses in my glasses, bringing the two images back to one. Hearing loss was treated with hearing aids, the most modern and up-to-date devices available. They actually connect automatically to my "smart phone" so I can hear conversations on the phone inside my ears.

In 2005, Anne underwent a 64-slice CT scan, offered for the first time at her hospital. Since her father had died prematurely of heart disease, she felt it appropriate to check her for potential heart disease. Her coronary arteries were normal, but as an incidental finding, a myxoma, a potentially deadly tumor of the heart, was discovered. It was a coincidental finding, but one that would be life saving because myxomas are typically diagnosed when fragments of the non-malignant tumor break off and end up in vital areas of the body, causing strokes, blindness and even death. Anne, a former cardiac nurse, chose Dr. Stephen Colvin for the surgery at NYU. He and I had trained together years ago. He had vast experience with the disease and had successfully treated hundreds of patients.

I became her nurse for her recovery. Our roles were now reversed. Open-heart surgery always takes months until the patient returns to a semblance of normal. After several months, Anne got better and slowly returned to work. She remarked that it was like she had been in a dreamlike state until she felt better. She also credited my excellent nursing care to speeding her recovery. Or at least I told her it was my nursing care that pulled her through.

After a six-month leave of absence, Anne resumed her work towards her doctorate. When she finished, we both drove to Cleveland for the hooding ceremony and the awarding of her degree. This was a terrific accomplishment especially since we had both gone through so much.

Now there are two doctors in our house, one a DNP (Doctor of Nursing Practice) and another a retired surgeon. She worked hard at her thesis, never complained about the outside forces that interfered with her smooth progress, and is now a faculty member in a new nursing school for graduate nurses. She is a dedicated teacher, inspiring excitement and interest in her students. She truly believes that nursing is one of the noblest professions. I totally agree as I credit her and the nurses who took care of me on my multiple trips to the hospital with saving my life.

The best decision I ever made in life was marrying Anne. Anne is smart, caring, thoughtful, devoted and funny. She saw me through numerous crises. Her attempt at a doctorate was interrupted several times including the death of her mother, my father and my second attempt to bleed to death. She was right by me through all my hospitalizations, watching out that nothing bad that could be prevented would happen. I tried to reciprocate as best I could when her open-heart surgery interrupted her life.

Alice, Anne's mother with whom we had traveled to Ireland, had smoked from the time she was 16. Emphysema slowly sapped her strength and she became oxygen dependent. Yet she was still spunky enough to drive her car with the oxygen tank attached. She eventually got pneumonia, as do most folks with end-stage emphysema and finally succumbed in August 2006. Awake until near the end, refusing a tracheostomy and respiratory dependency, she passed away at almost age 80 with the family at her bedside. Anne was well enough by then to give the eulogy.

As time passed, so did the generation of my parents. Years ago, my father decided that he wanted to close his business. The new tenant agreed to clean out the years of accumulated contents, used furniture, discarded souvenirs, possessions taken from liquidated homes containing memories of people who had passed on, various and sundry unorganized masses of junk. Twenty-eight dumpsters allowed my father to realize that his business was actually over. Alarmed that he could actually "see the back of his store," a business that defined his life, he called to tell me that "without his store, he might as well die." Within two months of the store being emptied, he died at age 91. His work defined his life. Neither Anne nor I were shocked by his passing, but it was also clear that our work or various jobs would never define either of us.

My mother spent several years in assisted living after losing her husband of over 68 years. She functioned day-to-day with little short-term memory but fully alert and oriented. One day, she "took to her bed" refusing to get out to eat. Recognizing a major change in her, the people at assisted living facility notified me and called an ambulance. Meeting her at the hospital, she told me that she decided that she wanted to join my father. Holding her hand, I looked into her eyes and told her that it was ok. At the age of 91, she joined my father that night.

One of the persistent problems I had after my retirement was dizziness. I would occasionally stumble or become unable to focus especially when in a large store. My sister-in-law, a nurse, told me of a specialized treatment center at Northern Westchester Hospital which treated vertigo. Several months of retraining and "reprogramming" my brain has successfully allowed me to function well with only occasional symptoms. While in rehab for the dizziness, I discovered that a recumbent elliptical machine would allow me to exercise without causing undo back pain. I try to exercise and/or walk many days a week and have managed to lose 30 pounds. So now I can drive safely, walk safely, hear and see things the way I should.

Upon the death of my parents, my brother and I inherited several stores in Long Beach, New York, including my father's old store, which now was leased to a gym. My brother wanted no part of any of the stores, complaining that the stores had forced him to pay additional taxes. Without much ado, I became sole owner of the real estate.

When I look around at my fellow colleagues, surgeons and law-enforcement professionals, some of them dread retirement. Often I hear the fear that they might be bored if not punching a clock or working every day. I know of too many people who stayed long after their contributions to their particular job had long expired. Why would someone use an 80-year-old surgeon? Why would a director of a major organization not step aside to allow younger more energetic people to move up to positions of power and influence? How long can one be an effective police officer? How long can one remain in the armed forces? Retirement is the opportunity for another career. I doubt if anyone on their deathbed says they wished they had spent more time working.

Having been through various trials in my own life, full retirement came as a gift. I got past or accommodated to the host of physical impairments that had accompanied my injuries and complications. I wasn't sick. I could get around perfectly well, albeit slower. Retirement for me opened the doors to things I had always wanted to do.

Art history had served me well as a diversion in college. It serves me well today as a wonderful pursuit. I have good friends who own an art gallery in Manhattan. Visiting the gallery, I have had the unique opportunity to meet and interact with many active artists. Nothing is more fascinating in art than to have the opportunity to see an artistic genius at work. Ironically, I had performed major surgery on the gallery owner before 9/11. Discussions of art were a common ground between us, and we remain close friends.

Living close to New York City gives me access to some of the best museums in the world and I'm delighted that I'm able to visit them. Spring and fall lets me drive to the Bronx to photograph the population of the zoo. Digital photography has totally supplanted my darkroom.

My son lives nearby in Queens. He isn't married yet, but continues to look. His passion is music but he has a steady job that pays the rent. My daughter is a lawyer and married with two children in

Raleigh, North Carolina. She has given me grandchildren. I get to see them every few weeks since the flight is only an hour or so. I see them nearly every day using FaceTime®. Who would have ever thought that it would be so easy to communicate or that the world would be so small? In the old days, when grandpa would visit the kiddies, they would hardly know him unless he lived close by. Now, it's like, "Oh, hello, grandpa." That's if their heads aren't buried in their iPads®.

Over the last few years something splendid has happened. Recovering from my physical injuries, I have gotten some of my old energy back and I have found opportunities for sharing my experiences. As an active member of the business community in Long Beach, I serve on local community improvement organizations. Never shy, I managed to network and meet fascinating folks who are non-medical.

One of my associates on one of my committees worked for a technology company that provides video outreach among other services to young students around the country and the world. The lynchpin person who coordinated the video education is Elaine in Sturgis South Dakota. Through her I have brought my first-hand experiences on 9/11 to students in Alaska most of whom have no recollection of 9/11. As a first responder, an injured survivor of 9/11 and a surgeon, I've also been asked to share my experiences with students in Long Beach, Veterans groups and the City of Long Beach..

Looking back at my career, my profession and the opportunities I enjoyed, I have a perspective that many people will never have. Looking ahead, I am optimistic, positive and hopeful that I will continue to enjoy my older age with Anne. I'm neither melancholy nor maudlin about growing older. It certainly beats the alternative. It's been challenging and interesting so far. More to come I hope...

Made in the USA
Monee, IL
25 June 2020